American Constitutionalism, Marriage, and the Family

American Constitutionalism, Marriage, and the Family

Obergefell v. Hodges *and* U.S. v. Windsor *in Context*

Edited by Patrick N. Cain and David Ramsey

LEXINGTON BOOKS
Lanham • Boulder • New York • London

Published by Lexington Books
An imprint of The Rowman & Littlefield Publishing Group, Inc.
4501 Forbes Boulevard, Suite 200, Lanham, Maryland 20706
www.rowman.com

Unit A, Whitacre Mews, 26-34 Stannary Street, London SE11 4AB

British Library Cataloguing in Publication Information Available

Library of Congress Cataloging-in-Publication Data

Library of Congress Cataloging-in-Publication Data Available

ISBN 978-1-4985-2817-7 (cloth : alk. paper)
ISBN 978-1-4985-2818-4 (electronic)

∞™ The paper used in this publication meets the minimum requirements of American National Standard for Information Sciences Permanence of Paper for Printed Library Materials, ANSI/NISO Z39.48-1992.

Printed in the United States of America

Contents

Acknowledgments

This book grew out of a series of panels put together for the annual meetings of the Northeastern Political Science Association, Southern Political Science Association, and Midwest Political Science Association during the summer and fall of 2014. At the time, a divided Court had just handed down a pair of narrowly divided rulings in *U.S. v. Windsor* and *Hollingsworth v. Perry* that suggested an uneasy balance might have been struck, allowing state laws defining marriage as the union of one man and one woman to stand, while striking down the provisions of the federal Defense of Marriage Act applying a similar definition. It was during the annual meeting of the Southern Political Science Association in January 2015 that the Court granted certiorari in the cases that would eventually be consolidated into *Obergefell v. Hodges.* The contributions to this volume were conceived during a period of heightened anticipation and uncertainty in American jurisprudence, and revised shortly after the issue was laid to rest in *Obergefell.* We say this only to explain what might best be described as a sense of urgency in the pages that follow, with authors setting down their immediate reflections on a recently concluded chapter in the annals of American law. Three of these chapters, "Democracy in Justice Kennedy's America: Reading *Obergefell* with Tocqueville," by Susan McWilliams, "Does the Law and the Constitution of the Family Have to Change?" by James R. Stoner, Jr., and "Free and Happy Bonds: *Loving v. Virginia*'s Nineteenth Century Precedent on Marriage and the Pursuit of Happiness," by Adam M. Carrington were first accepted for publication in a mini-symposium in *Perspectives on Political Science* (published by Taylor & Francis LLC, http://www.tandfonline.com). We thank Taylor & Francis, the publisher of *Perspectives*, for granting permission to reprint those articles here.

We owe special thanks to the excellent team at Lexington Books, including Kathryn Tafelski, Carissa Marcelle, and Ashley Bonem, and to our research assistants Meyer Levy, Amanda Gallo, and Ayla Green. And thank you to our students for continuing to bring life to our study of American constitutionalism. David would like to thank his wife Katie and their children, Thomas, Jacob, and Samuel. Patrick would like to thank his wife Courtney and their children, Isaac, Elizabeth, Lucy, Catherine, Madeline, Genevieve, and Samuel. What would know about marriage and family without you? Finally, we acknowledge the great debt owed to our teacher David K. Nichols, who showed us that the study of American constitutionalism affords opportunities for examining anew the important questions of human life. We know of no better way to express our gratitude than to try to be for our students what you were for us.

Introduction

This edited volume in American constitutionalism is among the first to examine the U.S. Supreme Court's rulings in *U.S. v. Windsor* (2013) and *Obergefell v. Hodges* (2015), which struck down federal and state laws defining marriage as the union of one man and one woman, placing these rulings within the context of the Court's understanding of marriage and the family. Leading scholars in the fields of political science, law, and religion examine the theoretical roots and legal implications of the Court's jurisprudence in a number of areas related to marriage and the family including the right to marry, equality and happiness in marriage, the right to privacy, freedom of association, parental power, and reproductive rights. Taken together, these chapters evaluate the extent to which the Court's recent marriage rulings both break with and derive from competing principles within American constitutionalism and western civilization.

In chapter 1, Peter Augustine Lawler provides a theoretical framework for understanding the Court's rulings in *United States v. Windsor* and *Obergefell v. Hodges*. Masterfully uncovering both the philosophical and the theological roots of the modern understanding of marriage, Lawler argues that the Court's recent marriage jurisprudence is a heretical or imperfect reflection of Christian teaching, doing justice to the personal component of marital communion while neglecting its relational character.

Terence J. Kleven, adds further theoretical reflections in chapter 2, contrasting the understanding of the relationship between the household and the city put forward by the classical political philosophers Plato, Aristotle, and Al-Farabi with the Judeo-Christian account. Kleven uses John Witte's history of western jurisprudence as a touchstone to test and make comparisons between these two accounts. He argues that the family acts in its rightful role not as a private institution but rather as one that serves the public realm.

In chapter 3, William C. Duncan gives a broad overview of the Court's marriage jurisprudence, arguing that it contains two distinct accounts of marriage: a nineteenth-century view emphaszing marriage as a social institution, and a modern view that marriage is one manifestation of a more general right to intimate association. According to Duncan, the Court's *Obergefell* ruling completes the replacement of the earlier account with the latter.

In chapter 4, Adam M. Carrington also examines nineteenth-century precedent, drawing from a myriad of both state and federal cases to show how the courts have long used the principles of the *Declaration of Independence* to give content to the meaning of marriage in American society. Carrington suggests that we continue to see evidence of this initial approach to marriage in the Supreme Court's recent rulings, most conspicuously *Obergefell,* which articulates an individual right to marriage directly related to the pursuit of happiness.

David Ramsey's chapter 5 revisits the argument from marriage for the emancipation of slaves presented in Justice Curtis' *Dred Scott v. Sandford* dissent. Ramsey finds in the jurisprudence and judicial temperament of Justice Curtis a useful foil for understanding the approach to law embodied in Justice Kennedy's opinions in *Windsor*, *Obergefell*, and other related cases.

In a similar vein, Martha Rice Martini's contribution in chapter 6 returns to the Court's late-nineteenth-century ruling in *Reynolds v. United States*, which confirmed Congress' power to outlaw polygamy in the Territories. Examining *Obergefell* alongside the arguments advanced by the courts in *Oregon v. Smith*, *Washington v. Glucksburg*, and *Brown v. Buhman*, Martini argues that the Court's recent marriage rulings have dislodged the principles advanced by the Court in its *Reynolds* ruling. In place of these principles, the Court has developed a new understanding of the character of our fundamental liberties whose logic will allow, and perhaps require, a future Court to overturn prohibitions of polyamorous marriage.

Beginning with chapter 7 we turn exclusively to twentieth and twenty-first century conceptions of liberty and the family. Lauren Hall finds in *Buck v. Bell* a vehicle for exploring judicial avenues for the protection of liberty beyond the doctrine of substantive due process. She suggests that the questions raised by *Buck v. Bell* have a direct link to the Court's more recent rulings on reproductive rights and same sex marriage, and that the Court's handling of the questions in these cases would have been aided by a more forthright exposition of the language in the Ninth Amendment, which acknowledges the possibility of additional unenumerated rights.

In chapter 8, Mark Scully looks at how a series of legal decisions have attempted to reconcile freedom with the communal interest in social cohesion, particularly in the realm of education. Contrasting the privacy approach taken in *Meyer v. Nebraska* and *Pierce v. Society of Sisters* with the progressive approach taken in *West Virginia v. Barnette*, Scully shows how these theories play out in subsequent cases such as *Wisconsin v. Yoder* and *Zelman v. Simmons-Harris*.

Stephen A. Block, in chapter 9, critiques liberalism's distinction between the private and the public, arguing that its defense of self-interest cannot provide a sustainable framework for civil society. Block argues that liberalism's success in America was made possible by the contribution of non-liberal entities such as the family, but that in *Griswold v. Connecticut* the Court defined the family in liberal terms. The result, says Block, undermined the family, and therewith, the basis for a lawful and free society.

Chapter 10 also takes up the question of privacy, with Patrick N. Cain tracing out the connection between liberty and privacy rights, beginning with the argument for a right to privacy developed by Samuel Warren and Louis Brandeis. He argues that *Griswold's* adoption of the right to privacy announced a notion of self-ownership and freedom that, while fully separate from governmental interference and public purposes, also requires public and governmental affirmation. *Obergefell v. Hodges*, concludes Cain, employs this theory of privacy to support the freedom to legally marry someone of the same sex.

For Susan McWilliams it is the democratic character of the American regime that drives the historical change in marriage law. In chapter 11, she uses Alexis de Tocqueville's *Democracy in America* to analyze the Court's support of a fundamental right to same-sex marriage. On her account, what is striking about the change in marriage law is not simply the recognition of a new individual right against traditional social and political norms, but also the Court's willingness to submit to the perceived majority.

Scott Yenor, in chapter 12, turns our attention to the link between the legal, biological, and educative responsibilities that parents have for their children. Noting that the Court's ruling diminishes the important link between biology and parenting, Yenor shows how this connection allows families to fulfill their proper function of raising good citizens, arguing that the biologically connected family is better suited for this task than any other conceivable entity.

James R. Stoner, Jr. ends this collection by asking how the law and constitution of the family has to change. Like Yenor, he suggests that the proper legal standard for the family should entail an acknowledgement of the force and significance of biology, giving increased legal recognition and protection to the important biological bond between parent and child. Doing so, he argues, would respond to the natural importance human beings place on their origins, not only for the sake of self-knowledge, but also because these origins unite families. Such a return to nature in law, notes Stoner, would be especially fitting for a natural rights republic.

Chapter One

Defending the Christian Idea of Marriage Today

The Place of the Personal Logos

Peter Augustine Lawler

The Supreme Court has declared that the states are required to perform and recognize same-sex marriages. Its decision was not abrupt or dramatically innovative. It was just continuing working through the implications of understanding marriage, as John Locke does, as a contract between two rights-bearing persons or free individuals. The Court might now go on to deconstruct the very institution of marriage itself as carrying relational baggage not found in the Constitution itself. For now, the threat is to the moral and religious freedom of Americans who hold other, non-Lockean or often sacramental views of what marriage is. The burden seems now to be on them to show that their exclusion of gays from marriage is not merely expression of irrational animosity toward a particular class of Americans. Christians now have to give reasons—rooted in a realistic understanding of who each of us is—to protect the "marriage diversity" on which their place in our country depends.

My purpose here is to use the innovative, or at least challenging, insight of our philosopher-pope emeritus that each of is, as a being made in God's image, a being formed by personal *logos* in order to understand the reasonable distinctiveness of Christian marriage. The understanding of each of us as beings created and animated by personal *logos* is, I think, Ratzinger's (Pope Benedict XVI's) distinctive and fundamental contribution to the recovery of the Christian contribution to the development of philosophy and theology. That understanding of who we are is the result of two key steps taken by the early church: The first was "[t]he decision in favor of philosophy" in articulating who the monotheistic God of the Bible is; the second is "[t]he transformation of the God of the philosophers from impersonal to personal and relational *logos*."[1] According to our philosopher-pope, "*the philosophical God is essentially self-centered*," which means he is so self-centered he's necessarily indifferent to us. But, for the early Christians, God—or "the highest mode of Being—is relational. So God includes the 'involvement' with us that is personal love. The philosophers also erred, quite unrealistically, in understanding God as '*pure thought*.'"[2] But for the early Christians, not only is thought divine but love is as well, because even divine thought needs to be animated by *eros*, which turns out to be more fundamentally personal than, say, Aristotle thought. Christians can say with Aristotle that "Not to act 'with *logos*' is contrary to God's nature,"[3] but, they add, so is not to act with love.

This decision and this transformation were the source of an alternative to the choice between philosophic reason and Biblical revelation, as well as an alternative to choosing between the ancient and the modern philosophers for a *logo*-centric understanding of who we are and what nature is. My intention is less an interpretation of our philosopher-pope's thought than an application of it to the particular question of what marriage is. I will be drawing upon a variety of sources in Christian thought, including Pope John Paul II's "theology of the body."[4] That understanding of who we are aims to avoid every form of dualism—even that found in the classical philosophic distinction between soul and body—but only with the present philosopher-pope's help can we see the road toward an integral vision of who we are and away from natural necessity, especially the modern dualism between personal freedom and impersonal. As our philosopher-pope reminds us, even "the concept of the soul found in Christian tradition is in no sense a simple borrowing from philosophical thought," because it too has been "fused . . . into a new unity" that allows Christianity to speak of the immortality of the soul as meaning the immortality of the whole human being.[5]

LOGOS MUST BE PERSONAL

This understanding of who a person must be is also an understanding of the indispensable conditions of possessing *logos*. The imaginary being we can call pure thought does not possess *logos* because nothing would animate the mind to actually think for itself. Computers, we know, think for others, for us persons. The being we can call pure body—and perhaps it does make sense to call the other animals, or some of them, pure body—also has neither the capacity nor any inclination to think. The world, it has often been said by scientists, is nothing but intelligible material necessity. But if that is so, then it is impossible to explain the existence of beings that are moved to discover and take delight in comprehending that necessity. The necessary connection between understanding and being understood, our philosopher-pope reminds us, is the person, the being that—through both relational love and personal creativity—is more than either a mind or body, or even a mixture of the two. So it is the reality of the person that overcomes our mistake of thinking of *logos* in terms of mere materialism or detached idealism. It is also the reality that overcomes the extremes of universalism and particularism. The universal truth about nature can only be perceived by particular persons—the universal *logos*—the openness to the truth about all things—can only be found in particular persons. It turns out that "truly conscious thinking" cannot be explained by either the materialists or the idealists, because both of those theoretical extremes unrealistically abstract from being personal.[6]

For marriage, it is easier to begin by understanding what *being personal* did to transform the institution of marriage. I will go on to add *logos* as a personal characteristic, to show the deepest ways that being personal is being relational. But the connection of the personal God with *logos* or even relationality turns out to be questionable. That is why the modern efforts to transform by purifying the personal insight are really efforts to free personal—including divine—freedom from *logos* and relationality. Being personal without being relational, of course, includes the attempt to transform marriage by making it a non-intrinsically relational or loving institution. And the separation of person from *logos* transforms marriage from an institution based on a common good mutually discovered and a responsibility shared by two persons to an alliance for one's own—or, as we say, subjective—convenience.

BEING A PERSON

In my view, the idea of the free person actually came into the world with Christianity. We find it, for example, in St. Augustine's denial in *The City of God* that the *natural* and *civil* theologies of the Greeks and Romans could possibly be true. That is because each of us is not merely part of nature or part of some political community or city. Each of us has an irreducible personal identity and is made in the image of the personal and relational God. "The idea of the separation of church and state," as our philosopher-pope observes, "came into the world through Christianity." Before Christianity, "the political constitution and religion were always united."[7] Theology was always *civil theology*—or employing the gods to secure the sacrality of the city. The philosophers, it is true, dissented from civil theology on behalf of *natural theology*, on behalf of the truth about what we are as natural beings. But the philosophers never intended natural theology to displace civil theology because it exploded the communal illusions that hold us together as moral and political beings.

The Christian view of marriage and the family does not negate the merely natural and political purposes of marriage. The dominant Christian view retained the natural idea that marriage is for propagation of the species—a function that we share with the other animals. Marriage is also for perpetuating political order; it has the civil function of producing citizens. But Christians put this natural good and this political good in their proper places by denying that they have a theological foundation. Serving the species and serving one's country are not the highest purposes of marriage, and so marriage, and children, too, cannot be understood to exist for the species or the country. We are not in fact made in the image of the God as merely natural—in the sense of biological—or political beings. True theology, as St. Augustine says, is personal—and not civil or natural. And so, the high or sacramental purpose of marriage is for the uniting of persons for the procreation of persons—beings who can know and love each other, as well as God. The institution that corresponds to our personal purposes is the church. That means, of course, the authority of the state is limited by both the family and the church, and the education of children is of more than being citizens.

Our biological and political existences—our location in a particular body and in a particular place—are, in fact, part of being personal. The person is—but is more than—a part of nature and a part of his country. A liberated woman is not liberated from either the longing for or the responsibility to have children, but she does not understand that personal responsibility the way a Darwinian or a Spartan would. With the coming of Christianity, the city could no longer command men and women to have children to replenish the human cannon fodder that had been lost in the last war, as it apparently even commanded Socrates. And it could no longer be understood to be allowed to treat persons like animals to be bred for improving the species or the city. The objection we have to the eugenics schemes of Socrates in the *Republic* or those of the twentieth-century fascists is decisively personal or Christian.

That is why Christians have dissented from any theology that reduces persons to less than they really are. The early Christians seemed like dangerous atheists to the Romans, and that is why even (or especially) the most philosophic emperors—such as Julian and Marcus Aurelius—were so big on wiping them out before it was too late. As Ratzinger explains, Christians were called to pray for emperors, but not sacrifice to them. They refused to acknowledge or *be* a civic religion, and so they threatened what even philosophic emperors believed to be the indispensable divine authority claimed by the city and its rulers. Christianity "deprived the state of its sacral nature"[8] The Christians denied the very existence of the gods of the city, the divine foundation that secured the political community. Their atheism, in fact, seemed more dangerous than that of the philosophers who exempted only themselves—because of their liberated minds—from the commands of the Laws. For the Christian, every person is liberated *from* the degrading cave that was the ancient city. No person—or not just philosophers—should submit to political domination. We are all liberated by virtue of who each of us most deeply is. That liberation, as our philosopher-pope says, "is a decisive factor for freedom."[9]

The Christians are, in fact, political atheists because they know they are made in the image of the personal God. They are, above all, members of the City of God that transcends every political distinction by encompassing us all—Jew and gentile, Roman and barbarian, man and woman, black and white, smart and not-so-smart, and so forth. So Christian marriage is more personal than the civil marriage of the Greeks and Romans. It's less political or less distorted by arbitrary patriarchal considerations. Every innovation associated with Christian marriage aimed to elevate women to equality with men as free, relational persons, reflecting the truth that we are all equal as sinful persons under God. The prohibition of divorce—a New Testament innovation—was for women because divorce was rarely really available for them. The sanctification of monogamy is all about the uniting of two equal persons for shared responsibilities. Monogamy, together with chastity, was for locating sexual desire in a deeply relational or loving context, and so men could no longer exploit women as mere bodies. Polygamy, found for example in the Old Testament, was more a political than a relational institution, one that necessarily subordinates women to the will of men.[10]

The Greeks and Romans were big on distinguishing between the joys of liberated erotic satisfaction and the civil and reproductive necessities that generated the institution of marriage. That distinction, of course, degraded women in many ways, making them instruments for the satisfaction of male erotic and political desire. It also led, in some cases, to the privileging of homoerotic over heterosexual, or merely reproductive, sex. It was good personal news for women that chastity is a virtue for both men and women equally. It certainly was news to men.

PERSONAL LOGOS

Our philosopher-pope explains that to say God is personal is to say that he, like us, is a being with a name who can name. He's a relational being, whom we can know and with whom we can communicate. "When God names himself . . . he is handing himself over to me"; "he enters into coexistence with them."[11] The possibility of shared communication—living together in the truth—of other beings with names who we can name reminds us that the persons possess *logos*. Through words they joyfully connect naming with being, with the truth about the world in which they can participate and can know in common. So not only the idea of the person but the concept of *logos* can be found at the center of Christian faith in God. God *is* personal *logos*, and so is each of us made in his image. The *logos* who is God is the guarantee—the foundation—of the intelligibility of the world and the intelligibility of each of our personal existences. The world makes sense, and so does each of our lives as a personal destiny of living well in light of what we cannot help but know about particular persons, beginning with ourselves. So, our philosopher-pope explains that the idea of personal *logos* is that he "understands moral values as *responsibility*, as a [personal] response to the Word."[12]

Logos is also relational; no person—not even the monotheistic God—can be or know alone. That means logos is loving and creative. The person who created the world and each of us *is* love and made us and sustains us out of love. So the personal response to the word is not only relational but loving. Intelligence, in this sense, is creative. Universal reason does not negate the significance of particular persons, because the intelligibility of the world is most completely expressed not in terms of mathematics but love. An impersonal or mechanical universe is what we see in the absence of God. But if the personal God works or creates—as do we persons—then we can see evidence for personal logos—loving, creative intelligence—everywhere we look. The discovery of personal logos—or that way of expressing the truth about God and ourselves—was, as our pope explains, the result of the encounter of Biblical revelation with Greek philosophy. It was, he adds, a *decision* to allow Greek philosophy to inform the truth about the person, to make it, as it really is, not only willful or creative but reasonable. The Christians allied theoretically with the philosophers against the arbitrary untruth of religions, ones obviously man-made, because they are clearly weapons to secure the domination of some persons over others. The monotheism of the philosophers and the Bible both show a God who is neither cruel nor arbitrary. Both forms of monotheism point to the liberation of human beings from a world in which the word of God was both a weapon and justified the use of weapons. The logos of God, they both agree, must correspond to what we can know about ourselves and our natures according to our best lights.

Aristotle's god is a wholly unerotic, uncreative, uncaring, and wholly self-sufficient being. He possesses no personal qualities at all. The only real freedom—the only thing genuinely divine about us—is freedom of the mind from delusions about personal significance. Persons come and go, but eternal, impersonal necessity remains. There is no true ground for personal freedom in a wholly necessitarian cosmos. If there were, it would spoil our minds' aspiration to intellectual self-sufficiency through the comprehensive grasp of natural intelligibility. It is through our minds—through learning how to die as particular beings—that we come to see the intellectual good that comes through grasping the insignificance of persons.

The Greek focus is on the eternity of god and the world. The Christian is on the loving creativity of God. The source of our being, for the Christians, has to be someone who cannot be reduced to mind or will or body or even some incoherent mixture of those qualities. God must be a whole, irreducible person, as we are whole, irreducible persons. As far as we can tell, the only place *logos* is found is in persons. There is no such thing as pure mind. If there were, that giant brain would not be erotically moved to actually think. The philosophic or scientific understanding of the world in terms of impersonal necessity cannot account for the real existence of persons. And if time and eternity—human beings and God—really were as distant from one another as Aristotle thought, then we cannot understand why it is that human beings can know god or anything eternal. The Greeks identified with impersonal necessity, which is why the philosopher dies to himself and others as a condition of knowing all that he can. For our philosopher-pope, the *logos* that makes the world intelligible to us comes from a person and is an irreducible characteristic. So *logos* depends not only on *eros* but on personal freedom, and so the *eros* that leads us to understand who we are and what nature is is irreducibly personal *eros*.

For the Christians, the law of nature is love, personal love. Our hardwiring for personal logos, so to speak, extends to the core of being itself, to everything that came into being through the creative logos of the personal, loving, relational Creator. So for Plato and Aristotle, the big questions are about whats—what is God, what is justice, what is philosophy, what is Man, and so forth. For the Christians, the big questions, which can actually be answered, are about whos—who is God and who is man. The whos who we are—the beings with names who can name—are persons made in God's image. The Christian doctrine that expresses the truth about God as personal logos is the Trinity because truth is *logos* (as opposed to arbitrary, whimsical personal will), and true theology must be monotheistic. The Christians agree with the Greeks that all polytheism—including and even especially the gods of the city—is degrading fantasy. The God who is *logos* is one. But it is also true that there are three persons in one God. How that is has an irreducibly mysterious dimension for us. Still, we can see that the personal God must be relational. It is impossible to be personal, to be loving, all by oneself. So not only is our God an awesome God and a rational God, he is a relational God, a God moved by personal love.

The Trinity, as Ratzinger explains, is the articulation of the real discovery of dialogue within God. The idea of being a person—and especially the idea of personal logos or creative intelligence—depends on *relatio* being essential to articulating who God is and who we are. Monotheism cannot mean monologue, because the idea of talking to oneself all by oneself is inconceivable.

Logos is fundamentally dia-logic. For Aristotle, *relatio* is an accident or merely circumstantial; the word does not signify what is deeply real. For our philosopher-pope, God is his own being and can be simply called God. But in being for others, he is also Father, and it is in the act of giving himself, begetting or creating, that God is most deeply himself as a person. There is no real separation of God from the person. So it "becomes clear that the dialogue, the *relatio*, stands beside the substance, as an equally primordial form of being."[13]

The personal God *is* a monotheistic and relational God, and he is both as the condition of being personal logos. So the relational, personal being who is each of us can be deeply distinguished from the self-sufficient individual—the being for himself alone. Nothing else could move the relational God to create but *personal love*. That is why the logos—the oneness of unified wisdom—the *who* that the personal and erotic God is—means love of particular persons. The God who is *logos*, as our philosopher-pope argues against Nietzsche in his encyclical on love, is an erotic God.[14] So our experience of *logos* is the experience of who and what was personally created out of love. That is why Christianity, in truth, is a more erotic religion than the natural religion (say, Unitarianism) of the philosophers. Our philosopher-pope goes so far as to say that the source of sin is not acknowledging what we cannot help but know—that we are both rational and relational persons—and not acting in accordance with that personal truth.[15] We, like God but not like Socrates in his own mind, are relational all the way down, just as we are *logos*—or open to a creative, intelligible truth not of our making—all the way down. Even God who created the world did not make himself three persons.

When Socrates thought most deeply about who he is, other persons disappeared. Even the person Socrates disappeared because a truthful account of *beings*—of what we really can know—has no place for and is no respecter of particular persons. That is why the neo-classical thinker Thomas Pangle is probably right to say that the longing of Socrates culminates truthfully in the wisdom of "transerotic" solitude.[16] But for Christians, *being* itself is somehow personal all the way down. We are, as they say, hardwired for personal, relational freedom, and the cosmos was created as a place for us persons. In that respect, Pascal and Walker Percy are wrong to say we are "lost in the cosmos."[17] That means, of course, that what is most worthy of wonder is not the stars or even the cosmos but us. There is nothing more wonderful than persons, and our longing to know is most deeply the longing to know and love persons. Our personal logos and personal *eros*, like God's, are irreducibly intertwined.

Due to sin—or the invincible limitations and distortions we experience as the result of our embodiment and the miseries of our biological mortality—our desire to know and love other persons does not achieve perfect fulfillment in this world. I long to be transparent—and love just as I am—before other persons whom I love. It turns out that our deepest personal longing is to be transparent before the personal God. The highest human longing, as Thomas Aquinas says, is to know and to love and to be known and loved by God. Next to our longing for God, the deepest human longing is the personal love of man and woman opening themselves to and completing each other through sex, procreation and talking about and getting to know each other through the shared joys and responsibilities of this relationship. A person's experience of erotic union with another person in this world is an image—but not a perfect one—of the love of the personal God for us and our love for him. So the union between husband and wife is about both *eros* and *logos*, about the shared truth discovered through dialogue about shared personal responsibilities. The shared truth of marital dialogue—being so deeply personal—could not possibly be ranked lower than the shared truth of philosophical dialogue. In that respect, the idea of personal logos continues the upgrading and deepening of the friendship between husband and wife that was begun by Aristotle.

The haven we seek from a heartless world, through the family, is never a perfect haven. Even the most intimate of human loves and attachments, St. Augustine observes, are plagued by misunderstandings and even unexpected betrayals because we are never able to really read the whole heart of another person in this world.[18] For us, the mysterious elusiveness of other persons—our inability to fully comprehend and control them—is part of their charm of being lovable. Mystery, of course, infuses even (or especially) our love of God here and now. The idea of personal logos—as we see with the Trinity—does not abolish irreducible personal mystery, at least for us in this world. Because each of us is unique and irreplaceable—a singular creation of infinite value, our experience is that perfect knowing might even be at the expense of personal loving. Perfect personal knowing and perfect personal loving become possible through our redemption, our lives that continue on beyond our sinful experience of this biological life. Our deepest longing does not get fully satisfied here and now, and so our hearts remain somewhat restless even in the best of relational circumstances, while being located in the most loving of marriages and families. In this respect, it seems, the ideas of personal, dia-logic *logos* and irreducible personal identity remain somewhat in tension. This tension is enhanced by sin, but the issues involved in knowing and loving, for us, are not just caused by sin.

BEING PERSONAL WHOLES

We are, as persons, whole beings. There is no true distinction between being a person and being a human being. We free persons have bodies, and our freedom is more shaped than limited by our embodiment. So persons are either men or women. And male and female persons, as we can see from the very makeup of our bodies, are made for union with each other. We relational beings are erotically directed toward the intimate relationship called marriage. As Pope John Paul II explained, in the absence of woman the first man was marked by an existential loneliness.[19] On one level that loneliness could be described by Darwinian evolutionary biology. Man was hardwired by nature to be a pair-bonding and reproductive being. It was not his purpose to be alone, but to be a part of social wholes greater than himself. So existential loneliness, in part, can be understood as simply being detached from any way of satisfying our social desires. But the Darwinians are unable to give an account of how we retain our personal identities as relational beings. We are parts—but not simply parts—because each of us retains our identity as an infinitely valuable and irreplaceable person. Each of us is not merely species fodder or city fodder; each of us is not a means to some impersonal end.

Men and women, that means, are each whole beings, each made, as man or woman, in the image and likeness of a personal God. They are not, as Aristophanes imagined, two halves who somehow merge to recover some lost unity.[20] A man, in a way, is completed by a woman, insofar as it is his true destiny to live in relation to others, beginning with a wife. But he retains his personal identity—his own reason, will, and personal love—as he does even in his relationship with the personal God. To be a person is not to be the merely social animal Darwin describes, and religion and the family are not ways to aid the "individual" to lose himself in the "group."

So existential loneliness, of course, means more than being unable to fulfill your natural purpose as a social animal. Adam quickly realized that by naming the animals he was alone among the animals he named. He had the freedom of the being with a name who can name, and so he could not integrate himself into the rest of creation. "Man," as Pope John Paul II says, is alone because he knows "he is 'different' from the visible world," from "all living beings to which man has given a name."[21] "Self-knowledge" is knowledge of one's difference, one's subjectivity, one's particularity. Adam's loneliness was being without woman, without a person made in God's image who can know and love him just as he is as a whole being—another being with a name who can name. We require loving relationships with other persons, and usually a spouse and children, to be who we really are as relational beings. That need is not merely physiological or biological, although it is that. It is the need of the being made to love and be loved personally. It is through personal knowing and loving that we live in the image of God. We cannot be whole or self-sufficient persons all alone, even as God himself cannot. The remedy for existential loneliness is not the surrender of personal identity—as a Buddhist or Socrates might say—but the loving relationship of one person with another—whole persons shaped by bodies but not determined by bodily necessity the way the other animals are. We need to be loved by a person who complements or completes us, who is not just like us but for us, just as each of us is for that other person. So marriage is, for Christians, the primordial sacrament, the sacrament that is most deeply the visible sign of the presence of God or personal logos in the world. It is through marriage, above all, that man participates in this world in the relational life of the person. In marriage, above all, our logos is most properly directed to personal knowing and loving.

Marriage is like the personal, relational union that is the Trinity. It is not exactly like it: personal identity for us is shaped by our bodies, and so of course our bodily differentiation into men and women. The members of the Trinity are not shaped by bodies, and so God, of course, is more one in being than a husband and wife are. But even in God the three persons do not surrender their personal identities in their relational being. So in understanding the family, Pope John Paul II observed, we deceive ourselves if we do not reconcile ourselves to our personal greatness, the greatness unerotically distorted by Pascal. Human begetting is deeply different from that of the other animals. The human family, unlike, say, the chimp family, is a relational community of persons. There may be nothing more wounding—more existentially lonely—than children who get stuck with coming into this world and growing up with strangers.

For our philosopher-pope, the indissolubility of marriage—the irrevocable commitment—makes sense only "on the basis of God's irrevocable decision, embodied in Christ, in favor of 'marriage' with mankind." Only if love of one person for another is sacramental, in the sense of being an image of the love of the personal God, can marriage be understood to be necessarily permanent. There is no natural or political reason for the union to be ended only with death. The pope does add, however, that sticking with the marital decision is perfectly compatible with what we really know about who we are as persons. The "continual annulment" of relational commitments, after all, depends on "the fiction of eternal youth" and a refusal "to accept the totality of human existence." Personal life cannot be "the circular motion" of the eternal return to the beginning, and so we deceive ourselves if we believe we are free to choose not to be deeply relational beings, if we believe that somehow our choices can be detached from the realities of birth and death.[22]

MARRIAGE AND THE LIFE TO COME

Still, there is no marriage in heaven. That is what Jesus said to the legalistic Sadducees who did not believe in personal immortality and tried to trip him up on the question of which of a woman's seven husbands would be her husband in heaven. We would be in heaven, Jesus said, like angels. That does not mean we would not have bodies—including all of our parts. But our bodies would not have the limitations rooted in the imperatives of our biological existence[23] The natural and civil necessities that shape the institution of marriage would disappear. There would be no need for procreation because no one would ever die. So there would be no need for sexual union. And there would be none of the shared responsibilities that come with raising children. We would no longer need human companionship to counter existential loneliness. Our deepest longing would be satisfied in perfectly knowing and loving the personal God.

We would, it seems, still know our wives (whatever number each of us might have had) and our children for who they are. But we would not love them with any kind of exclusivity or special intimacy. The limited and shaped character of our abilities to know and love would disappear. Each of us will, while retaining his or her personal identity, be one with the whole communion of saints and the personal God himself. So Pope John Paul II concludes that marriage and procreation are only part of "the historical dimension" of having a body and being male and female, and "[t]he resurrection indicates the closure of the historical dimension."[24]

We can also see the limited and temporary good of marriage—even as the primordial sacrament—in the Catholic view of the celibate life. Celibacy is not good for its own sake, but chosen out of love of God. Marriage is not for everyone. Some choose to orient their lives more exclusively around the love of God—to live more directly in anticipation of their heavenly existence—here and now. So religious women often think of themselves as brides of Christ, as choosing, in a way, a more perfect union. The celibate reminds us all, in a way, that we personal beings are not, most deeply, married beings. And we are not most deeply sexual beings. The vow of celibacy is about being a member of a personal community freed up for loving service to others by being freed from the distractions that come from sexual rivalry and the encumbrances of spouse and children.

THOMAS AND AUGUSTINE ON PROCREATION AND THE PERSON

We have to admit that thinking about the perpetuation of personal identity in what should be called the post-biological (while still somehow bodily) life to come makes it tough to know to what extent *persons* are shaped by conjugal love all the way down. It even makes it tough to know to what extent we can say persons *are* sexual beings or are determined by the natural requirement to perpetuate the species. Let me show that both St. Augustine and St. Thomas Aquinas deal with the issue in less than perfectly satisfactory ways.[25]

Thomas Aquinas, of course, is the Christian thinker most attuned to the idea of created nature and so natural persons. For him it is clear "that the rhythm of nature demands that male and female should mate in copulations for parenting."[26] So it is also clear, he agrees with St. Augustine, that Adam and Eve engaged in procreative sex even before the fall. Having sex in the state of innocence occurred in the absence of lust, without losing one's mind in uncontrollable frenzy. Man and woman completing each other through procreative sex has always been part of who we are. It was not the death that was the just punishment for the sin that brought having sex and having babies into being. So human sexual behavior is not to be disrespected as being intrinsically connected with fallenness or as even deeply separating *eros* from *logos*. After rising from the dead, Thomas thought we would continue to be wholly natural beings. The point of the resurrection was to repair the defects of our natures, not to abolish them. That means we will not be lacking anything that was part of our purposeful wholeness as natural beings. That would include, of course, our natural parts with the function of reproduction. My body is an indispensable part of my being a particular being, and so it is an indispensable part of my irreplaceable personhood. In Thomas' understanding, however, we are less a whole than a "compound" of soul and body. He does not abandon the Aristotelian view that to be human is to be a mixed being.

Now Thomas does not think of God as mind (nous), but as person. The personal logos—unlike Aristotle's thought thinking itself—is intrinsically relational. Having said that, part of the mystery of the Trinity is that God is relational and personal without being embodied. And for Thomas, our deepest erotic longing in heaven is satisfied through loving contemplation of who God is. Our relation to the personal God—and other persons—is not sexual or driven by biological desire. Contemplation, of course, seems more passive than creative or active. We persons, unlike God, seem to become intrinsically not only unprocreative but uncreative in heaven. How can we be all that we are without these dimensions of being personal? This question arises most forcefully when we think of being personal as being a soul and not a body.

Thomas says men and women enjoyed procreative sex in innocence. But he does not say that there is any procreation or sexual enjoyment in heaven. To say, of course, that one of the pleasures of heaven would be the endless enjoyment of "safe sex"—sex detached from birth and death—would be to detach the biological act with all its relational or even natural meaning. Nature, so to speak, would no longer need or want babies. And so we would no longer need or want sexual enjoyment. There would be no need for replacements, and so no inducement to the deed required to generate them. And we would not need sex—the way we now seem to need Internet porn—to get our minds off how anxious and boring being personal is these days.

That suggests quite a transformation of who we are as natural beings. Personal identity would no longer depend on the limits and responsibilities of our biological existence as social animals. It would be easy to say that we would morph into a kind of divine self-sufficiency. But Thomas, of course, does not say that. Our relational pleasures no longer depend on the body, but they do not become merely intellectual either. They are self-consciously personal—the love of persons for other persons. Still, we have to say that the sexed body is not the source of our deepest personal longing. There are clear limitations to how sexual difference—and so being married and being a parent—define who each of us is. Our deepest longing is satisfied by loving, relational contemplation of the sexually undifferentiated, personal God.

Thomas's thought tends in the direction of the irreducible particularity of whole persons and, of course, the particular providence of the personal God for persons. But even in thinking about particular persons he does not wholly abandon the classical distinction between body and soul. He says, for example, that "in matters pertaining to the soul the woman does not differ from the man," and the difference between the sexes is insignificant when it comes to our spiritual lives and redemption. But he does not go on to abolish the significance of sexual differences and even male superiority when it comes to political life. We are not most deeply social or political animals, but we are social and political animals. When it comes to our relationship with God, sexual differences are insignificant, but in our personal relationships with each other we are men and women. Our liberation through Christ somehow both is and is not from being a man or a woman. Our liberation both is and is not from being a social (Darwinian, we might say) and political (Aristotelian) being.

For Thomas, the life of celibacy or virginity might be understood to be superior to the vocation of being married with children. It is about freedom to be more "devoted to the divine things," as opposed, we might say, to the merely human things. The liberation, of course, cannot be for everyone, because the species would disappear. Concern for the perpetuation of the species and especially the city is why in "olden" or pre-Christian times everyone was legally required to marry.[27] Contemplative liberation was denied even Socrates for political reasons, and he never denied that his "conscientious objection," displayed in his leisurely life, to being a parent was an offense against biological nature and political justice. The family was not a personal—but a natural and political—institution.

Christianity liberated persons from the universal requirement to procreate by encouraging the choice of the virginal or celibate life by those called to it. That choice, of course, cannot be universal or even common. It depends on a division of labor between those who live primarily as spouses and parents and those who will perform other indispensable human functions—from securing the city through military service to serving God. People, as Christopher Roberts says, are divided "into breeders and nonbreeders," and there's no denying that one choice seems higher or more personally liberating than the other.[28] Those who choose the celibate life are denying themselves one human good for another, for one that is more properly divine, one more in anticipation for the life to come.

This division of persons into breeders and nonbreeders might easily be understood too starkly. Thomas understood Christianity, of course, as transforming the character of marriage itself. The goal is not merely to perpetuate the species but to procreate and cultivate persons. That is why human sexual morality is different from that of the other animals. The personal love of human beings is not shared by the other animals. The sexual exclusivity or lifelong permanence of sacramental marriage is neither merely nor mainly a biological requirement. Marriage—the complementary union of two persons—is not merely for the raising of children. John Locke, for example, says there is no natural reason why a marriage could not be dissolved after the children are raised. If we were merely natural or political in the way the classical philosophers thought, Locke would be right. Still, we return to the thought that marriage is for life—for this world—and not for forever. Each of us can sing to our spouse, with Whitney Houston, that "I will always love you," but not as my husband or wife.

Augustine, for personal reasons, actually denies that, after our redemption, we have any requirement to perpetuate the species. According to Roberts, "Augustine, at least from mid-career onward, believed that with the birth of Christ, the vocation of celibacy opened, in principle, to all."[29] We are not to be understood as divided into breeders and nonbreeders. The future of the species is no longer to be thought to be our responsibility. If everyone were to choose celibacy and the species withered away, it would make no difference for the heavenly city. To be personal, it appears, is to be liberated from the proud presumption that one's preservation is in one's own hands. That is not to say that Augustine denies or disparages sexual difference. Rather, he raises up the family—and loving paternal servant leadership—as the model for all personal relationships. But Augustine gives a different emphasis to the thought that to be personal is and is not to be liberated from the limitations of being biological.

For Augustine, it is not all that Christian to be obsessed with our birth dearth. We should not be concerned at all if most people were choosing against marriage for the vocation of celibate and loving service to God. But we have to acknowledge that there is something perversely semi-Christian—something heretical—about our allegedly liberated women these days choosing against breeding and for their vocations, for being productive and fulfilled through their careers. They are, of course, choosing against both the earthly city—proudly refusing to be reproductive machines for the state—

and against the heavenly city. Maybe that is what it means to be autonomous, to be "one's own person."

All the Protestant oppositions to Thomism have to be with the equivocations that come from his Aristotelianism, his inability to quite give a whole account of the person as *logos*, to quite overcome the classical distinction between body and soul in understanding either this world or the next. He could not quite explain why personal salvation could be of the whole natural being. The sexual, married being—maybe the core of who we are as natural beings in this world—is really perpetuated in heaven. So the Protestants inclined, in an Augustinian way, to say that to be a person is to be free from nature, and so to be free from *logos*. They freed God from *logos* in the name of personal salvation from otherwise inevitable biological fates. If God is somehow defined by *logos*, then how could he be free enough to save us as persons? Luther's concern, of course, was most of all about personal salvation from sin and death. And so he was most of all about showing how the personal God can be free or willful but still relational enough to be able to (and to want to) save each of us.

From this view, the free person—the being with a name who can name—is not open to but creates reality by naming it into being. He is a creator—and so not a describer or contemplator. This "nominalism" frees both God and us from domination by an order not of our own making. For Luther, God's nominalism—his arbitrary willfulness—is what frees us from our deserved fates as natural beings and as citizens. For Protestants—Deists—who became skeptical that such a God would really provide for us, nominalism really means that we, too—through our faculty of naming or "abstraction"—can will a world into being that we were not given. The natural world is not a fit place for free persons, but persons can create a better or more unnatural and more personal one. That world will be a lot less relational, one more like the imaginary world to come in being freed from all of the biological impulses we feel when we are stuck with the degrading necessities of birth and death. The attempt, as they say, to create heaven on earth is to create a world with loving marriage or relational *eros*. So the Lutheran and Deistic (philosophical) forms of Christian heresy were two modes, our philosopher-pope contends, of the "de-Hellenization" of Christian theology, of the separation of the personal God and the human person from *logos*.[30]

UNRELATIONAL PERSONS, CHRISTIAN HERESY, AND THE MODERN TRANSFORMATION OF MARRIAGE

So Protestants in their way degraded marriage by depriving it of sacramental status as a manifestation of the divine personal logos in the world. Marriage became predominately natural but still somewhat Christian. It was not rechained to the paganism of aristocratic patriarchy. For most Protestants, the marriage tie remained relational (or loving) and deeply—if less deeply—binding, and in fact it became expected of everyone—even or especially members of the clergy—as, for one thing, a remedy for the sin of lust.[31] To be personal continued to mean, for most Protestants, to be relational. The status of the Trinity was no longer clearly connected to the requirements of personal logos. But the Trinity remained a mystery that reflected something fundamental about who God is and who those made in his image are. Tocqueville emphasizes that the Puritans were family men and women, and he contrasts them in their civilized religious and communal idealism with the solitary and rather godless adventurers who founded Virginia.[32]

The Protestants—particularly the Lutherans—might be understood, from another view, to have elevated marriage by freeing it from comparison with the alleged superiority of the celibate or virginal or monastic life. By becoming less than a sacrament—or less an anticipation of the world to come—it became what it is in this world. So the jurisdiction over marriage shifted from the church to the state without simply subordinating marriage again to the requirements of the state. Marriage became a contract between free persons authorized and protected by civil law. And so it became a contract that could be—for good, natural reasons—made and unmade. A failure in the loving trust and responsibility required for marital stability could mean a marriage was irretrievably broken. Divorce became possible for adultery and desertion and even the incapacity to procreate. Divorce is typically the sad result of sin, but that is evidence that it can not always be reasonably avoided by sinful beings. And the right to remarriage emerged—there being, after all, no natural obstacle to it. That right might be, for both natural or "sociobiological" and sociological reasons, more effectually exercised by men. But it is surely now understood as a blessing for a woman with children. So in some ways, at least, the "desacralization" of marriage might be understood as progress for free persons. Christian, relational freedom persists, but arguably with a more consistent articulation of the insight that marriage is not part of the more perfect relational world to come. Because everyone is called to live according to the moral and relational virtue required of sinful, biological beings in this world, celibacy—or living too much in anticipation of the world to come—becomes suspect as unnatural, too aberrant, and impossible.

From Locke's view, we might say that the mainstream or Trinitarian Protestants detached—in a quite un-Christian way—marriage from the full truth about our freedom. Locke restored that connection, but in a more heretical way: He disagreed with the orthodox view that to be personal is to be relational. To be relational is to be natural, and to be personal is to be free—or not a natural being. Locke wanted to separate the *person* from *logos*, not for the sake of God (as Luther did), but for the sake of the person. *Logos*, for Locke, is the impersonal, mechanistic necessity that governs NATURE, a process that has no place for persons and is hostile to personal existence. Socrates, the thinker, ended up negating personal experience or personal significance on behalf of allowing his mind to grasp the truth about natural necessity. But Locke, the thinker, affirmed the person—and the reality created by free persons—against nature. Locke rejected the Christian view that we are personal and relational by nature, but he accepted the Christian view—and added to the Christian view—that we are free persons. For him, our personal liberation comes from ourselves, and not God or created nature.

Locke agreed with St. Augustine that we are all free persons. And on this Christian foundation he joined Augustine in finding no truth in natural theology and civil theology. None of us exist for nature or for our countries, and it is degrading and enslaving for free persons to think otherwise. For the Christians before Locke, the person is a relational, embodied being, and so he is not only a part of nature and a part of his country, but more. For Locke, he is only more—he is only free. For Locke, the person is in no sense a relational—meaning natural or instinctual—being. The person is not a biological being or a political being. The person is free to exist for himself, and to relate to others on behalf of his own interests or on his own personal terms. He constructs himself out of nothing, and his main interests are sustaining his personal being indefinitely and pursuing his own happiness. So Ratzinger affirms the separation of church and state with the person in mind as a genuine modern achievement. But he rejects the liberal individualist view that freedom from the state is for "subjectivity," or not freedom for the relational life that is the church, the family, and so forth.[33]

So God, for Locke, is a person, but not a relational being. Locke typically presents God, for us, in the past-tense, or not as a living, giving God. God made us, but left us on our own to sustain ourselves as best we can as free persons. Each of us is as on our own as a person as God himself is. Locke's God is certainly not one who provides for other persons. To the extent that we can say God wants anything for us, we can say he wants us to make ourselves as free as he is. To think of ourselves as lovingly dependent on God degrades us and turns us into suckers. From our pope's view, Locke's theology is an early version of "the theology of liberation." God is not denied, but he has nothing do with the achievement of our liberation.

Locke certainly follows the Christians by carefully freeing marriage from political determination. In his account in his *Second Treatise on Government*, government is instituted *after* marriage and the family. One reason government exists is to enforce marital contracts, but the contents of said contracts are the free choice of husband and wife. A problem experienced by women in "the state of nature" concerns the interpretation of said contract. The contract is on "the common concern" of the husband and wife for the children. But inevitably each of these free persons will have "different understandings" and so "different wills" when it comes to the meaning of the term of the contract. In the event of disagreement, the "last determination" concerning the contract's determination has to be "placed somewhere." Its natural place is with the man, Locke explains, "as the abler and stronger."[34] Locke does not flesh out why men are abler and stronger by nature. We do know they are, in general, physically stronger, and they have the added advantage of not being hobbled by pregnancy.

Locke, as usual, does not regard this natural fact of male strength and freedom as normative. Women have the right to leave their husbands either by the terms of the contract or "natural right," and the children might go with either the husband or wife after separation according to the contract's terms—nature providing no guidance on that matter. Most importantly, after the establishment of government it is the "civil magistrate"—and not some willful showdown between the two parties to the contract—that provides a nonpartisan interpretation of the terms of the contract. The point of civil government for marriage is to secure the freedom of women as equal partners to the rights-based marital contract. So government, to say the least, cannot tell women what to do when it comes to being married or having or raising kids. Government does not exist to decide the purposes of marriage—those having been decided by nature and contract—it only exists for deciding "any controversy" that arises between husband and wife about the way they have decided for themselves to handle nature's giving them the common concern of the kids and any other interests they have freely chosen to pursue together.[35]

Locke does not describe the relationship between man and woman as one of love. One does not find completion through marriage to one's spouse. Each of us is already a self-sufficient person. Marriage is a contract to have regular access to one another's bodies. The typical result is children. And with children, Locke adds, comes the obligation—to which in this case he adds love—to raise them. So the marriage contract should hold until the children are raised. At that point, unless you are still enjoying the sexual exclusivity, there is no point in staying together. A childless couple—either because the kids are grown and on their own or just because they did not have any children—should be free to divorce unless they freely decide to stay together with some other common interest in mind.

We can say that Locke presumes the continuation of the family in a way that preserves the species. Children are the natural limit to liberation, as is the love parents or at least mothers will have for children once they have them. But Locke also says, quite plainly, that free persons should invent their way out of natural limitations whenever they can. What we are given by nature, his general view is, we are better off without. So Locke did not predict the era of contraception, but he has no principled argument against it. He would surely see it as a new birth of freedom for persons. They could enjoy one another's bodies without being saddled by shared responsibilities. He might well welcome a world in which people so freely choose to have children or not be stuck with them as a byproduct of sex. Insofar as possible, Locke does not want us thinking of ourselves as men and women, and he wants to free women, especially, of the duties nature seems to impose on them through sexual differentiation. He does not want women to be compelled to be more relational than men.

It is hard to know what Locke would say today in the face of the birth dearth that plagues advanced or highly personal and relatively nonrelational nations. It is also hard to know what his response would be to the use and abuse of his personal principles producing a society where men find it too easy to detach themselves from their familial responsibilities and where there are so many lonely single moms. His intention, in fact, was to make the world better for women and children by overcoming patriarchal prejudice. He might be criticized for having a residual Darwinian or "sociobiological" faith in the persistence of natural instinct in securing the species, for, in other words, not knowing the extent to which his prophetic words would have such a deeply personal effect. He assumed that fecundity and prosperity in freedom would go hand in hand. His "labor theory of value" was based on the principle that numbers of people were more important than acres of land in determining a prince's powers.[36] He may not have appreciated fully that technological development would make "mental labor" so powerful that physical productivity would decline in significance as much as it has. It has not, of course, declined so much that we cannot acknowledge that we need more productive young people than we will have to take care of all the old people who are seemingly hanging around a lot longer than nature intends. Perhaps today Locke—seeing the connection between belief in a providential, relational God and personal fecundity—would be a lot more orthodox, more Trinitarian, when it comes to religion. What Locke's theory fails to account for is that a free society depends on personal love—love for the personal, relational God and those made in his image—generating dignity for relational service or charity. Our demographic crisis would not be so bad if it were not for the alarming decline of voluntary caregiving, especially but not only between one generation within a family and the next.

But, in principle, Locke would have to accept his version of the Augustinian point that the free person cannot be held responsible for the perpetuation of the species or the family. It is not his or her problem. The personal concern is with one's own being. And the person might even conclude that there is no point in generating replacements if I have no intention of being replaced.[37]

OUR INCREASINGLY LOCKEAN (OR HERETICALLY CHRISTIAN) COUNTRY

So it is on Lockean principles that even our Constitution of 1787 never refers to men or women, but only to persons. Our Constitution is as blind on gender or sex as it is on race or class or religion. And it is on those Lockean principles that women eventually became free to participate fully in public and economic life with men. Women were freed from the specific bodily burdens of being women to be free and equal persons. Through most of the history of our country, we had a kind of mixture of Lockean and more relationally or orthodox Christian views of who we are. The laws of the states, which were the laws that governed marriage and almost all of ordinary life, were not all that particularly Lockean. And so marriage was a relational union recognized by law, divorce was between difficult and impossible, adultery discouraged and chastity promoted, and the connection between being married and being parents was strong. Under these state laws, the various forms of orthodox Christianity were encouraged to inculcate their personal and relational understandings of who we are as believers. Our nation—despite the Lockeanism of the Founders—basically remained a nation of families. On that score, our nation remained more Puritanical than Lockean, our restless men were civilized by our loving women rather than being the solitary adventurers or self-absorbed, apathetic individualists that Tocqueville describes as dangerous democratic possibilities.

But over time even state law was progressively Lockeanized—divorce became easier, adultery and chastity were viewed with growing indifference, and the tie between being married and being parents became increasingly tenuous. Marriage became, increasingly, a contract in one's own interest that could be voided when one's interest changed. The pace of these changes accelerated little more than a generation ago, when the Supreme Court embarked on the project of using the Fourteenth Amendment as a weapon to transform the details of state and local life with the Lockean view of personhood or autonomy in mind.

Here are three big points our Court has made on who we are as free persons: In *Lawrence v. Texas* (2003) (the case that struck down a law prohibiting homosexual sodomy), the Court explained that the word liberty in the due process clause of the Fourteenth Amendment may be used to expand personal liberty for every new generation. It is a weapon to free persons from what used to be thought of as corresponding duties, whether necessary and proper, natural, divine, political, or merely relational. A second point from *Lawrence*: the Constitution's protection of personhood requires honoring all intimate, consensual choices—including casual sexual encounters—by any two autonomous beings, persons who are not essentially male or female, who are not defined by their biology. Finally, eleven years earlier, in *Planned Parenthood v. Casey* (1992), the Court told us that the reason abortion cannot be illegal is that the state cannot command women to be reproductive machines for the state or impose any substantial impediment on women defining themselves as free persons however they please. Each woman, the Court went on, is mysteriously freed from being bound to nature, politics, or the family so that she might become whomever she chooses to be.

It seems to me that our Court has done well in thinking through what it means to be personal under the law, but not what it means to be relational. It can be criticized for "deconstructing" marriage as an institution indispensable for our flourishing as who we really are. But that criticism does not have much weight if we really are as free as Locke, on the foundation of one part of Christian doctrine at the expense of others, believes. Obsessing over the relational cost of emptying marriage of its content is not a personal problem. Our transhumanists—or Lockeans on mega-steroids—believe that they can escape biological necessity by imposing their personal or technological will on a nature that is no respecter of persons and that does not think in terms of husbands or wives or kids. The world to come through their personal efforts will have no need of them.

RECONCILING NATURE AND THE PERSON?

Against the working out of these Lockean (or personal and nonrelational/nonnatural) trends, our philosopher-pope is attempting to revive a kind interreligious affirmation of the naturalness of the family, based on the naturalness of being either a man or a woman. Citing the Chief Rabbi of France, he says

> that the attack we are currently experiencing on the true structure of the family, made up of father, mother, and child, goes much deeper. While up to now we regarded a false understanding of the nature of human freedom as one cause of the crisis of the family, it is now becoming clear that the very notion of being—of what being human really means—is being called into question.[38]

The question *is* whether we are, as persons, men or women. Rabbi Gilles Berheim believes that Simone de Beauvoir's "famous saying" about not being born—but becoming—a woman is what we mean when we make "gender" the foundation of our "new philosophy of sexuality." From this view, a person's sex is not "a given element of nature" that must be accepted. Nor is it *something* that should any longer be "chosen for us by society." It is "a social role we choose for ourselves." Each of us, as our Court really did say, is mysteriously free to choose our own personal identity, to choose, for example, whether or not to think of oneself and act as a man or woman. That means, as the pope explains, that my "bodily identity" need not be a "defining element" of who I am as a human being. To be personal is to be free from biological determination. *My* identity need not be a biological identity. Our "gender" existentialism is the working out of the Lockean injunction to free ourselves, as persons, from our relational, instinctual, natural, and patriarchal illusions. My "social role" originates in my personal consent, in my free choice of what is best for me personally. Freed from the oppression of nature and society (meaning politics), I can be my own person.

The idea that to be a person means not to have a (relational) "nature," the pope knows as well as anyone, is a Christian heresy, a distortion of the early Church Fathers' discovery of the personal *logos*. The pope does not make the rhetorical error of saying explicitly that his existentialist opponents are merely bad Christians, or lax and oxymoronic Christians without Christ. He does do that implicitly by moving immediately to show the incompatibility of existentialist or "gender" personhood with the actual "biblical creation account." The truth is that "being created by God as male and female pertains to the essence of the human creature." The creature—the person—has a given essence. So the created or personal "duality" is not nature vs. freedom but male and female. It is because each of us is a created whole—or not some mixture of animal nature and liberated person—that being male and female is intrinsic to each of us. The idea that our bodies are worthless materials—merely natural resources—to be overcome by our free willing is actually a denial of personal creation. And so it is actually a denial of the reality of the person. If there is no natural support for personal "essence" in the personal logos that animates all of being, then there is no real content to the person's claim for particular significance.

So the defense of the family as an institution essential for who we are as relational beings—and as essential especially for children becoming the dignified beings they were created to be—is really a defense of "man himself," of who we are as relational persons, "about what it takes to be authentically human." The question about personal authenticity turns out to be, can "man become himself by living for himself alone," with his "relationships" to others being contingent on his personal interests? Or is it really true that man only finds himself in "self-giving," in rising above the emptiness of personal isolation in openness through love and shared understanding to others? Locking oneself in oneself—and denying the realities of the body from birth and love to death—is, the philosopher-pope observes, really a way of avoiding suffering. But surely a man lives authentically only "by letting himself be changed through the suffering" given to we relational persons alone.[39]

We can say that the rhetorical strategy of anyone who defends the idea of marriage as based on who we are as beings with personal, relational *logos* is to defend nature against autonomy or the person as wholly unnatural or self-determining and to defend the person against deterministic, including Darwinian, accounts of nature. These defenses are provisional and always in some ways vulnerable. The defenders of same-sex marriage echo a real part of Christianity when they defend the person against natural and social imperatives, when they attempt to liberate personal will and even relational life from children. And the Darwinian criticisms of the pretensions of the liberated persons are, after all, in some ways defenses of natural and civil theology against the un-biological claims of personal theology. The Christian defense of marriage in its integrity really does require the recovery of the credibility of personal *logos,* of the foundation of the person in nature. We have to recover—on the levels of both natural science and the science of theology—a full account of what it means to be made in the image of the personal, relational *logos* who is the Trinitarian God.

NOTES

1. Joseph Cardinal Ratzinger, *Introduction to Christianity,* translated by J. R. Foster and Michael J. Miller (San Francisco: Ignatius Press, 2004), 137–50.
2. Ratzinger, *Introduction to Christianity*, 147–48.
3. Pope Benedict XVI, "The Regensburg Address," reprinted in Tracey Rowland, *Ratzinger's Faith*: *The Theology of Pope Benedict XVI* (New York: Oxford University Press, 2008), 199. The quote in the text is the pope quoting Manuel II.
4. John Paul II, *Man and Women and He Created Them: A Theology of the Body*, translated by Michael Waldstein (Boston: Pauline Books, 2006).
5. Josef Cardinal Ratzinger, *Eschatology, Death, and Eternal Life* (Washington D.C.: Catholic University Press, 1988), 215.
6. Ratzinger, *Introduction to Christianity*, 158–59.
7. Josef Cardinal Ratzinger, *Salt of the Earth,* trans. By Adrian Walker (San Francisco: Ignatius Press, 1997), 239.
8. Ratzinger, *Salt of the Earth*, 240.
9. Ratzinger, *Salt of the Earth,* 240.
10. David Bentley Hart, *Atheist Delusions: The Christian Revolution and Its Fashionable Enemies* (New Haven: Yale University Press, 2009), 138.
11. Ratzinger, *Introduction to Christianity*, 134.
12. Ratzinger, *Introduction to Christianity*, 27.
13. Ratzinger, *Introduction to Christianity*, 183.
14. Pope Benedict XVI, *God is Love (Deus Caritas Est): Encyclical Letter.*
15. See Josef Cardinal Ratzinger, *In the Beginning . . . : A Catholic Understanding of Creation and the Fall* (Grand Rapids: Eerdmans, 2004).
16. See my "Strauss, Straussians, and Faith-Based Students of Strauss," *The Political Science Reviewer* 36 (2007): 1–12.
17. See Walker Percy, *Lost in the Cosmos* (New York: Farrar, Straus, and Giroux, 1983).
18. St. Augustine, *The City of God,* Bk. XIX.
19. John Paul II, *Theology of the Body,* 146–55.
20. See Tracey Rowland, *Ratzinger's Faith*, 78–79.
21. John Paul II, *Theology of the Body*, 150.
22. Ratzinger, *Introduction to Christianity*, 265–66.
23. See John Paul II, *Theology of the Body*, 398–99.
24. John Paul II, *Theology of the Body*, 399.
25. The following analysis depends fundamentally on Christopher C. Roberts, *Creation and Covenant: The Significance of Sexual Difference in the Moral Theology of Marriage* (New York: T&T Clark International, 2007).
26. Thomas Aquinas, *Summa Theologiae*, 1a.98.a2.

27. Thomas Aquinas, *Summa Theologiae,* 2a2ae.152; 3a.41.a2.
28. Roberts, *Creation and Covenant*, 104.
29. Roberts, *Creation and Covenant*, 107.
30. Pope Benedict XVI, "The Regensburg Address," 169–71.
31. This account of the movement of modern marriage from sacrament to contract is fundamentally indebted to John Witte, *From Sacrament to Contract, Second Edition: Marriage, Religion, and Law in the Western Tradition*, second edition (Louisville: Westminster/John Knox, 2012).
32. Alexis de Tocqueville, *Democracy in America*, volume 1, part 1, chapter 2.
33. Ratzinger, *Salt of the Earth*, 240.
34. John Locke, *Second Treatise on Government*, chapter 7, section 82.
35. Locke, *Second Treatise*, chapter 7, section 83.
36. Locke, *Second Treatise*, chapter 5, section 42.
37. The authoritative account of the place of Locke in the development of modern political thought and, to some extent, American practice, is Scott Yenor, *Family Politics: The Idea of Marriage in Modern Political Thought* (Waco, TX: Baylor University Press, 2011).
38. Pope Benedict XVI, *Address by the Holy Father on the Occasion of Christmas Greetings to the Roman Curia.*
39. Pope Benedict XVI, *Address by the Holy Father.*

Chapter Two

The Household and the City in Classical Political Philosophy and in John Witte, Jr.'s Account of the History of Western Jurisprudence

Terence J. Kleven

William Shakespeare begins his Sonnet 116 with this statement: "Let me not to the marriage of true minds admit impediments."[1] The sonnet is on the topic of love, but because the usage in this line of the words "marriage" and "impediment" are taken from the wedding ceremony in the Anglican *The Book and Common Prayer* and also because in line eleven there is a reference to "rosy lips and cheeks," we perhaps assume that the sonnet is principally about marriage. But this is not Shakespeare's intent, or at least not his sole intent. The sonnet more precisely is about friendship and about the type of love true friends have for one another, of which marriage can and should be—we hope in most cases is—a primary example. Shakespeare's line, to be precise, is about the place of knowledge in our lives and in friendships, and it indicates that friendship cannot truly exist without the marriage of minds, without the existence of a profoundly common understanding of the nature of things. Shakespeare draws together in this sonnet, in a concise poetic line, a reminder that knowledge is needed for friendship. The best and truest kinds of friendship only exist when true minds are united, and he says that there is no limitation on this shared knowing and the harmony it creates. As a result of this common knowing, bodies can and may unite later; according to the natural and right order of things, the intellectual governs the physical. But bodies are not best united before friendship thrives nor before the friendship is both privately and publically acknowledged. Yet what is prior in the order of nature is not always prior in the order of sequence; the physical often precedes the intellectual even as our opinions of the good precede our knowledge of it. Our first and often most abiding experience of love is the physical affection of a mother's womb, breast, lap and voice and the way they cause us to awaken to the first great friendship of our lives. Yet even in this first friendship, the physical leads to reason inasmuch as the voice speaks to the infant's fledgling reason, however imperfectly, and the two minds unite, sometimes continuously, sometimes only haphazardly, in an ongoing context of need, want, and self-giving. Reason, what is prior in rank, replaces what is prior in sequence.

The most learned of the Arabic philosophers, al-Fārābī, Ibn Bājja and Ibn Rushd, would admire Shakespeare's line because they too noticed that when the potential intellect becomes actual it unites with other actual intellects. Pure actuality is unifying. Our greatest happiness is knowing and common knowing forms friendship. These Muslim philosophers would concur with Shakespeare's affirmation of the intellectualism of friendship and also his claim that, even in this mundane world, the impediments to harmony between us are of our own making and not those of wisdom. Shakespeare intends that marriage must live up to the standard of friendship and friendship in turn must live up to the standard of the sheer quality of common and unifying knowledge. The Arabic philosophers might wonder, however, how an Englishman on an island on the margins of the intellectual world of their time could come up with such philosophic accuracy.

If, as Plato and Aristotle claim, man is political by nature, then our knowledge of ourselves and others is discovered in our associations. In the jurisprudential tradition of Western political thought, these associations have come to be defined by a notion of individual natural right. Brian Tierney writes:

> "We hold these truths to be self-evident, that all men are created equal, that they are endowed by their Creator with certain inalienable Rights . . . " But of course Jefferson's self-evident truths about inalienable rights have not seemed evident to most of the human race over most of recorded history. All civilized societies have cherished ideals of justice and right order, but they have not normally expressed those ideals in terms of individual natural rights—it would be hard, for instance, to imagine a Confucian Hobbes or Locke. Moses gave Commandments to the children of Israel, not a code of rights. Plato and Aristotle saw no need to appeal to a concept of natural rights in formulating their political theories. Roman lawyers too were able to do without such rights in crafting their complex legal system. In considering the origin of natural rights theories we are faced with a historical problem, not a sort of revealed truth.[2]

Tierney proceeds to enucleate that historical problem over the next three hundred pages of his book, and with considerable illumination he reflects on both the strengths and limitations of our current usage of the notion of natural right. He traces the origin of the idea of natural right to the medieval Decretists, the canon lawyers of the Church. Our legal tradition has pre-modern roots. In contrast to the assertion that natural right was first known through the American Declaration of Independence and the French Declaration of the Rights of the Man and the Citizen he says: "In fact, though, this central concept of Western political theory first grew into existence almost imperceptibly in the obscure glosses of the medieval jurists."[3] This long history of the notion allows us to see more adequately, as Tierney argues, where we are today in our legal and political conceptions because, amongst the medieval canon lawyers, the notion of "right" was part of a larger framework of justice and not an isolated principle, as it often is today. He not only identifies a transition that has taken place in the notion of natural right, but he identifies two problems with our current usage of the term "right." First, we advocate today for a "luxuriant array of rights inhering in various classes of humans,"[4] and this "multiplication of innumerable particular rights can erode any sense of community and the common good, values that earlier rights theorists never lost sight of."[5] Rights today are individualistic, a defense of the naturally solitary individual, as Rousseau would articulate it, rather than ways of orienting ourselves to the common good of a community.[6] The second problem, he says, is that "in many parts of the world the most elementary rights are denied altogether to subject peoples."[7] This denial is not a problem of the notion of rights, but a failure to implement the notion. Thus, the two problems he identifies are not of the same species; the first acknowledges a weakness of the notion, the second identifies its strength but says that is not being applied. It is the first problem, the limitation of the notion of natural right, that may go unnoticed. Since rights today are multitudinous, there are confusions regarding which right actually exists, which right pertains in a particular circumstance and concerning how to adjudicate a ranking of rights.

According to Tierney, the consequence of these two problems is that, while the language of right is most effective in combatting "gross political oppression or the harshest forms of economic deprivation,"[8] yet "the language of rights is often abused today"[9] in its defense of such individualism and such an array of competing rights. We need to preserve, he says, what is best in this Western tradition of law and justice, but he asks how we ought to address the weakness with the notion itself?[10] We are left with the problem that "innumerable particular rights can erode the sense of community and common good." The word "natural," or what Jefferson preserved with the word "inalienable" has often slipped away, and almost any wish can be called a right. Is it possible that rights can be used to defend both the individual and the justice of the community? What are the associations which constitute a community? Is it necessary for the notion of right to function in harmony with these associations for a common good? Does jurisprudence need to attend at least to certain associations as well as individual rights?

These associations are various, although two of the most common are the household and the city. The terms "household" and "family" are in some measure interchangeable because marriage is essential to both, and to be sure, as a people we will have to apprehend and use a manageable notion, both legally and in popular opinion, of what marriage is. In this inquiry we will use the more general term "household" instead of "family" because it more adequately accounts for an association which we often refer to with the term "family" but which is not always as clearly delineated as we may think—in the guilds of the medieval world and in many economic situations still, families were and are often more than husband, wife, and biological children, and they include apprentices who work for the household and learn a trade. Furthermore, the household is sometimes irregular, such as Silas Marner and Eppie, an elderly man and his adopted daughter, in George Eliot's *Silas Marner*. In the Bible, the account of Abraham reveals the profound respect for marriage which he and Sarah share, a respect exemplified in Sarah's friendship with Abraham (Genesis 13:10–20 and 20:1–18), Abraham's deferral to the judgment of Sarah pertaining to Hagar (Genesis 16:2–6 and 21:9–14) as well as Sarah's deferral to Abraham (Genesis 16:5) and acknowledgement of his "lordship" (Genesis 18:12). What do we call this collection of people belonging to Abraham? As well as Sarah, there is the concubine, Hagar, the children of both Sarah and Hagar, and their grandchildren. After Sarah's death, Abraham takes a second wife, Keturah, and there is mention of the birth of six sons born to them (Genesis 25:1–2). Abraham also has other concubines and their children (Genesis 25:6). Although Abraham was monogamous, the full impact of the phrase in Genesis 2:24 that man and wife would be "one flesh" had not at that time excluded concubinage. If we are to persist with the term "family," at very least we would not be able to apply to every situation one ideal notion, even though the biblical variations do not extend to homosexual marriages. Nonetheless, we will primarily use the term "household" in this inquiry as a reminder that our western tradition recognizes some extension or variation within an ideal.

The second term in our analysis, the term "city," calls attention to a larger association than the household, but it is also smaller than the idea of "nation-state" because the "city" is in a geographically-limited dwelling place. Since Machiavelli, the "nation-state" or simply "state" has been the political association which has been the ideal governing political life. The substitution of "state" for "city" in the recent versions of the democratic state is one of the monumental changes from classical to modern political philosophy and one to which we need to attend if we are to sort out the relation between the household and the city and the topic of how the term "right" is used in each. Is the relation of the household to the state the same as the relation of the household to the city? And does marriage or the household need either one of these associations? To these aspects of the inquiry, we now turn.

THE *APORIA* (Ἡ ἈΠΟΡΊΑ)

We in the West have two main heritages regarding marriage, family, friendship and the political regime, that deriving from Greek philosophy and the Judaeo-Christian. Islam is a variation, even if a unique variation, primarily on the Judaeo-Christian heritage. We have treated marriage and household in Islam elsewhere and we will not focus on Islamic jurisprudence in this essay.[11] Moreover, in this analysis we do not deny that there are alternatives in the Orient which we could explore, and these accounts, too, may have more of a contribution to make to our inquiry than we might think. The Hindu religion, for example, seems to be similar to the Sabeans mentioned in the Bible (Job 1:15, Joel 3:8, Isaiah 45:14) and in the Qur'ān (2:62, 5:6, and 22:17), and even if the most important document of the Sabeans, the *Nabataean Agriculture*, is full of strange notions which are impossible by nature, they also held opinions, such as the eternity of the world, which were argued by philosophers, notably Aristotle, as well as promulgated by the Hindus.[12] Be this as it may, our focus on the intellectual alternatives of Jerusalem and Athens is not without recognition that the Oriental alternatives may well pertain to the central *aporia* we explore here.

Aristotle says the following in regard to the relation between the household and the city:

> And it [that is, the end of the things we do that we want on account of itself, and the rest on account of this one] would seem to belong to the one that is most governing and most a master art, and politics appears to be of this sort, since it prescribes which kinds of knowledge ought to be in the cities, and what sorts each person ought to learn and to what extent; also we see that the most honored capacities, such as generalship, household economics, and rhetorical skill, are under this one. Since this capacity makes use of the rest of the kinds of knowledge, and also lays down the law about what one ought to do, and from what one ought to refrain, the end of this capacity should include the ends of the other pursuits, so that this end would be the human good. For even if the good is the same for one person and for the city, that of the city appears to be greater, at least, and more complete both to achieve and to preserve; for even if it is achieved for only one person that is something to be satisfied with, but for a people or for cities it is something more beautiful and more divine. So our pursuit aims at this, and is in a certain way political.[13]

Although Aristotle places household economics as an honored pursuit and acknowledges that the good of the individual may be the same as the good of the city, he concludes that the art which is the most governing and the most a master art, the art which is most beautiful and divine, is the political art. Thus, household economics, with its aspects of marriage and family, is subordinate to and governed by the political art. Why does Aristotle give the magisterial place to the art of governing the city and why are other associations so vital to life subordinate to it?

This Aristotelian formulation persists, at least in some measure, in the medieval world. In the tenth century, over twelve hundred years after Aristotle's comments, the Islamic political philosopher, al-Fārābī (d. 950 AD), concurs with Aristotle's remarks. Al-Fārābī writes:

> Human beings are [one] of the species that cannot complete their necessary affairs nor gain their most excellent state except by coming together as many associations in a single dwelling-place. Some human associations are large, some medium, and some small. The large association is an association of many nations coming together and helping one another. The medium is the nation. And the small are those the city embraces. These three are perfect associations.
>
> Thus the city is first in the rankings of perfections. Associations of villages, quarters, streets, and houses are defective associations. Of these, one is very defective, namely, the household association. It is part of the association in the street, and the association in the street is part of the association of the quarter. And this latter association is part of the civic association (*al-ijtimā' al-madanī*). The associations in quarters and associations in villages are both for the sake of the city. However, the difference between them is that quarters are parts of the city, while villages serve the city. The civic association is part of the nation, and the nation is divided into cities. The unqualifiedly perfect human association is divided into nations.[14]

The questions to ask of both Aristotle's and al-Fārābī's formulation are: Why is the city the most perfect political association and why are smaller political associations than the city, especially that of the household, defective? These examples of Greek and Islamic political thought criticize the exaltation of the household, along with marriage and family, as the highest political associations, and Aristotle in particular maintains that the highest art is the art of governing a city, of which marriage and the household are subordinate associations. At the same time, this emphasis on the priority of the city and the other two perfect associations, all of which are "associations in a single dwelling-place," is not equivalent to the universal and homogenous state, or what we have come to refer to as "globalism." Al-Fārābī acknowledges that globalism is a characteristic of religion. According to Aristotle and al-Fārābī, the city has boundaries and a central aspect of these boundaries is geographical.[15]

Our other heritage is Judaeo-Christian. John Witte, Jr., deserves our attention at this point because his book *From Sacrament to Contract: Marriage, Religion, and Law in Western Tradition*[16] as well as numerous other publications provide several of the best summaries available of the history of marriage and the household in Western tradition in general and in the history of jurisprudence in the United States in particular. In the article entitled "The

Meaning of Marriage," Witte makes the following quotation from Justice Stephen F. Field in the 1885 anti-polygamy case of *Murphy v. Ramsey*.[17] Field writes:

> For, certainly, no legislation can be supposed more wholesome and necessary in the founding of a free, self-governing commonwealth . . . than that which seeks to establish it on the basis of the idea of the family, as consisting in and springing from the union for life of one man and one woman in the holy estate of matrimony; the sure foundation of all that is stable and noble in our civilization; the best guarantee of that reverent morality which is the source of all beneficent progress in social and political improvement.[18]

Such a statement could not have been written without the long-standing impact of the Bible on our civilization, worked and reworked through centuries of Patristic theology and practice, as well as reformulations in Medieval canon law and Protestant church and civil law. Field's statement directly subordinates the justice of the commonwealth as well as the strength and progress of our civilization to their foundations in marriage and in the family that the marriage produces. Even though Field's judgment was made in 1885, a similar account of the relation between the household and the state would not be uncommon in recent evaluations of the insufficiency of legal support for the institutions of marriage and family in our national life. Field's statement is directly contrary to the Aristotelian and al-Fārābīan subordination of marriage and household to the city. To be precise, however, in Field's statement marriage and family are not juxtaposed to the city in the classical sense used above, but to the "commonwealth" and "civilization," associations both larger than the household and the city. Field's statement in support of these foundations is intended to promulgate legal support for marriage and family, for how can institutions so vital to the commonwealth and civilization be sustained if they are taken for granted or neglected? Field's formulation makes marriage and household prior to the city.

In the juxtaposition of these quotations from Aristotle, al-Fārābī and Justice Field, we have the formulation of a central *aporia* which emerges from our two heritages. This essay is an inquiry into their respective accounts of the relation between the household and the city, and of their entanglement with accounts of natural right. Although Witte does not address the topic which I have posed in citing passages such as these from Aristotle and al-Fārābī, there are aspects of Witte's account which provide reasons to conclude that the classical subordination of marriage and household to the city is not as much a contradiction to the Judaeo-Christian heritage as it first appears.[19] Is it possible at one and the same time to affirm that marriage and household are necessary foundations for civilization and that they also need governance by the city for their flourishing and for their proper service to the city? Marriage and the household may be "the sure foundation of all that is stable and noble in our civilization," but that does not mean that they are all that is noble, nor that they are a sufficient condition to bring about justice and common good. In whatever way our argument will lead us, these quotations pose a central *aporia* of contemporary morality and political life.

WITTE'S ACCOUNT OF MARRIAGE AND THE HOUSEHOLD IN CHRISTIAN HISTORY

Witte's legal scholarship identifies four perspectives on marriage which were used by Christians to explain Christian marriage. He writes:

> Marriage is a *contract*, formed by the mutual consent of the marital couple, and subject to their wills and preferences. Marriage is a *spiritual association*, subject to the creed, code, cult, and canons of the religious community. Marriage is a *social estate*, subject to special state laws of property, inheritance, and evidence, and to the expectations and exactions of the local community. And marriage is a *natural institution*, subject to the natural laws taught by reason and conscience, nature and custom.[20]

These perspectives are, according to Witte, complementary, but they do have competing claims to ultimate authority over the form and function of marriage. Roman Catholicism emphasized the natural, spiritual and sacramental perspectives. In particular, sacramental theology, which is articulated most clearly in Patristic and Medieval canon law and reaffirmed by the *Tametsi* decree issued at the Council of Trent in 1563, dominated Christian teaching until the sixteenth century.[21] As a sacramental union, marriage was and is understood to be permanent. Roman Catholic theology and canon law also emphasized the priority of celibate life over marriage in the requirement of a celibate priesthood. Protestants emphasized the natural and social perspectives. Although most Protestants rejected the sacramental perspective, they retained many aspects of Medieval canon law such as, for instance, the protection of free consent of both parties and the perpetuation of Old Testament laws prohibiting the marriage of relatives. Many Protestants did not require an ordained minister to conduct the marriage service, but they designated that this duty could be fulfilled by a local magistrate and the ceremony could be conducted outside the church building. Since for Protestants marriage was not sacramental, divorce was more acceptable, even if strongly discouraged, and many Protestant denominations required an examination for fault in order to impose disciplinary sanctions, such as the period of time the divorced individuals had to wait before remarriage or the exclusion from full participation in the sacraments. This Protestant theology of marriage and family persisted from the sixteenth to the eighteenth centuries.[22]

In the founding and the unification of the United States, laws in particular geographical regions reflected the political jurisdictions of the areas. Gradually throughout the United States, there is a "protestantization" of marriage law. The first settlement of pilgrims at Plymouth had neither educated nor ordained clergy; marriages were conducted and ratified by recognized civil or religious authorities. These practices persisted in Calvinist communities throughout New England. Divorce was settled by local civil courts. In areas where the Anglican Church was strong, the Anglicans maintained that marriage had to be performed in a church by a priest and divorce proceedings were to be heard and adjudicated by the civil legislature. Before the territories of Louisiana, Florida, Texas, New Mexico, and California became part of the United States (between 1803 and 1848), they were under the jurisdiction of Spain, and thus were under the canon law of the Roman Catholic Church.[23] Witte explains that after the acquisition of these territories, laws of marriage in these states came under the jurisdiction of the Congress of the United States, and after statehood, under local state government. Some aspects of the Roman Catholic teachings were rejected by these states, but in general Christian accounts of marriage persisted. This increasingly Protestant account of marriage in the legal history of the United States led to a greater emphasis of the contractual nature of marriage. At this point in his analysis Witte cites the examples of two statements by two leading jurists of the nineteenth century who insist that, although marriage is a contract, it is more than a contract. Joseph Story, the leading jurist of the nineteenth century, issued the following statement in 1834:

> Marriage is treated by all civilized societies as a peculiar and favored contract. It is in its origin a contract of natural law. . . . It is the parent, and not the child of society; the source of civility and a sort of seminary of the republic. In civil society it becomes a civil contract, regulated and prescribed by law, and endowed with civil consequences. In most civilized countries, acting under a sense of the force of sacred obligations, it has had the sanctions of religion superadded. It then becomes a religious, as well as a natural and civil contract.[24]

Although Story's intent is to integrate the natural, contractual and religious perspectives and to support marriage as the "seminary of the nation" and the "parent of society," the contractual remains dominant in this statement. The second quotation Witte makes at this point in his article is that of Justice Field, quoted above. Field's statement is not obviously contractual, but it is written fifty-one years after Story's and there is no reason to think that contractualism was any less important to the definition of marriage and household in the jurisprudence of the United States than it was previously. Although both of these nineteenth century jurists express the high regard they have for this institution of marriage and for the household it produces, their accounts present primarily the civil perspective, which is, as they both recognize, easily dominated by the contractual.[25]

Witte explains that this emphasis in jurisprudence in the United States is derived from the prominent writers of the Enlightenment who introduced a strongly contractual model for marriage.[26] He recognizes that the contractarian account is adumbrated by John Locke in 1690 in his *Two Treatises of Government*, and it gradually becomes the dominant Western model. Over time, the previous legal accounts of the marriage, infused as they were by one version of Christian teaching or another, were overturned. Such requirements as parental consent, church consecration, sacramental blessing by a priest, formal witnesses at a marriage, and consignment of all property to the husband as the head of the household became no longer necessary by law. Witte argues that in the twentieth century these and subsequent changes in traditional marriage were made in the United States in a succession of two waves, one from 1910 to 1940, the other after 1965.[27] Witte credits the first with genuine and necessary aspects of reform, such as affirmation of the right of women to have custody over children in cases of divorce, greater protection of women and children from abuse, and more educational opportunities for children, boys and girls alike.

Witte is more critical of the second wave. "The early Enlightenment ideal of marriage as a permanent contractual union designed for the sake of mutual love, procreation, and protection is slowly giving way to a new reality of marriage as a terminal sexual contract designed for the gratification of the individual parties."[28] The second wave is exemplified by the Uniform Marriage and Divorce Act of 1987. This Act defined marriage as "a personal relationship between a man and a woman arising out of a civil contract to which the consent of the parties is essential." This Act, Witte says, requires only minimal formalities for licensing and registration, and it rejects any need for parental consent, church consecration, sacramental blessing or witnesses in church. The Uniform Marriage and Divorce Act is based upon a Supreme Court decision which claimed that marriage is "one of the 'basic rights of man.'"[29] Witte argues that this principle of the freedom of marital contract leads to a more general right of sexual privacy.[30] In *Eisenstadt v. Baird*[31] and *Roe v. Wade*[32] there is an increasing emphasis on the independence of each individual in the marriage and, in particular, the right of the individual woman to make decisions whether to give birth to or to abort a child. This contractarian account of marriage is also further exemplified in the Uniform Premarital Agreement Act which has been adopted by nearly half of the states today.[33] This agreement allows the parties to contract, prior to marriage, all matters pertaining to the marriage, including property rights and even a future separation agreement. Witte's judgment that marriage is now a "terminal sexual contract" is indeed appropriate.[34]

Although many of these Court decisions reflect an attempt to provide greater protection for women and children, Witte says the reality is not always so simple. The stress on individualism, on the private decisions of each partner and on the free contract to remain or leave, leads to a greater fear of the decisions of one's spouse and to greater insecurity before, during and after marriage. Children cannot help but lose in this precarious environment. To recall an older contractarian defender, marriage and households in the state of nature are all too often, as Hobbes says, "nasty, brutish and short."

Witte says that there are five lessons to be learned from a study of the history of Western jurisprudence regarding marriage and household, all gained from practices deeply embedded in Western tradition. First, he says we need to preserve the variety of perspectives on marriage, the *natural*, the *spiritual*, the *social*, and the *contractual*, so that marriage entails all of these. Marriage needs more than one perspective, more than one forum. These fora, he says, are church, state and household, and marriage requires all of them in proper relation to one another. Marriage is inherently a communal enterprise which requires couples, magistrates, parents, ministers and friends working in cooperation for the common good, both of the couple and of the community. Witte notes that certain states, such as Denmark, England, India, and South Africa, "grant semi-autonomy to Catholic, Hindu, Jewish, Muslim, and Traditional groups to conduct their subjects' affairs in accordance with their own laws."[35] This recommendation is a profound recognition that religions cannot truly be themselves unless they are allowed jurisdiction to govern their own communities. Second, he says the affirmation of the importance of an engagement, or betrothal, followed by a waiting period, was not only a time for the couple to reflect on their decision but "it was also to invite others to weigh in on the maturity and compatibility of the couple."[36] Third, he says that the older tradition of distinguishing between annulment and divorce, which has become obsolete in the current practice of "no-fault" divorce, has led to the refusal of any legal or religious authority to make any decision on fault, with the result that there is often stigmatization by both parties. Legal decisions can vindicate one's place in the community.[37] Fourth, he says that it is necessary to balance norms of marital formation and dissolution. Witte says that stern rules of marital dissolution, which seek to prevent divorce, require stern rules of marital formation. Communities need standards for marital formation, which will prevent the need for dissolution, as much as they need stern laws against dissolution.[38] Fifth, he says that the Western tradition has always recognized that households have multiple forms. The household may often be husband and wife and children but it may also be a single parent with children, a parent or parents with adopted children, and even an extended family of kin or even "servants, students, sojourners" and it may embrace more than one generation. The purpose is the mutual care and nurture of all.[39] In this section, Witte used the term "household" consistently, as we did in the second section (The *Aporia* (ἡ ἀπορία)) of this essay.

AN ANSWER TO THE *APORIA*

How do these five recommendations pertain to our lead inquiry on the relation of marriage and household to the city? Notice that in each of the five lessons that Witte enucleates, there is a movement away from individualism toward a recognition that marriage and also the household are most healthy when they are in vital relation to a community, to associations larger than themselves and ones that are able to govern the marriage or household in certain ways. Marriage needs, in Witte's language, the perspectives or fora offered by associations such as church, the household, and state; the community needs to be invited to weigh in on the proposed marriage; religious and civil authorities of the community need to adjudicate the causes of divorce in order to exonerate the innocent; the community needs to identify a proper proportion in the severity or ease of both marital formation and dissolution; and the community needs to recognize multiple forms. In short, private good only truly flourishes when it is conjoined with common good, when a legal and political tradition recognizes the proper place of both. When individual rights are allowed to dominate, when rights are defined by the private interests of the individual, the community loses and, in fact, the community cannot be properly created. Tragically, the individual also loses. With our notion of "rights" we have moved to the extreme of the defense of the private over the public, and we need legal decisions that will bring the two together again. The perspective of the contractarian model of marriage, if used exclusively, leads to the deepening isolation of the individual. But marriage and family are not simply private decisions involving individual assent—although they are that; they are also more perfectly formed and wholesomely preserved within the common good of the larger community. This community connection is why the community's laws, its representatives, and even its generally accepted opinions need a role in governing marriage. According to al-Fārābī, the city is not the only complete good, but both marriage and family cannot act independently of it.

Al-Fārābī makes a statement in the paragraph I quoted which is germane to our argument here. He says: "Human beings are of the species that cannot complete its necessary affairs nor gain its most excellent state except by coming together as many associations in a single dwelling-place."[40] To be sure, this is another way of saying that "Man is political by nature" and that we cannot obtain our greatest happiness on our own. Marriage and households are associations outside the individual, and are indeed needed, according to al-Fārābī, for individuals to complete themselves. Marriage and family are two of the most intense experiences in which we learn that we cannot live to ourselves and that we must adjust to others. Love and friendship are not simply the legal manipulation of my individual rights for my own benefits. Marriage, and even eros itself, is vacuous if marriage is entered into as a "terminal sexual contract." It is odd that our legal system, which is, according to the definition what any just laws should be, a way of governing our relations with one another, now functions repeatedly in the areas of marriage and family to defend the solitariness and private wants of the individual. The social contract is not achieved by the privatization of right.[41]

Marriage and household depend on larger associations. The individuality promulgated in marriage, even by the religious, is one more version of the individuality—and solitariness—encouraged by the privatization of right, so clearly demarcated in legal decisions of our courts. However imperfect the history of legal formation has been regarding marriage and the household in Western tradition, the current plethora of legal ways to protect individualism is not the only nor even the best recipe for happiness. The exaltation of marriage as the most god-like form of association easily falls prey to the assertion of private rights against the world and a defense of sheer self-interest, by one or the other of the partners against the other, or by the two of them against the community. We would do better to start with the premise that man is political by nature and see how to build associations in proper relation to and rank with one another, in law and in everyday life, than we would by starting with the premise that we are solitary agents who need protection from one another. Furthermore, our intoxication with the erotic seems to go hand-in-hand with the fact that our lives are ultimately regulated and inundated by the unerotic—contractualism is as unerotic as could be. How could we ever imagine the marriage of true minds in friendship ever to be circumscribed by the contractual? Intellectual eros is the paradigm of all eros and the reason Shakespeare has a poem to write.

Indeed, we would be better to cultivate our friendships and to find ways of nurturing friendships in marriage in the same way that Shakespeare indicates in the first line of sonnet 116. Loving requires knowing and knowledge is virtue. A renewed study of the Bible shows us that however high and glorious the Bible's standard of Good is, the Bible is an exceedingly practical book which often as not profoundly recognizes imperfect situations. When Jesus is asked whether divorce is permissible, knowing he is being tested with a virtually impossible question, he refers to the Mosaic law in Deuteronomy 24:1 which allows divorce because of the hardness of human hearts; at the same time, Jesus says that it is a higher standard not to have hard hearts (Mark 10:1–12). The book of Ruth reveals at once

1. the serious friendship the widowed Ruth has with her widowed mother-in-law, Naomi,
2. Ruth's hard work in supplying for her own and Naomi's material needs,
3. Ruth's desire for physical love with a man she admires, and
4. her respect for family and family inheritance in order to raise up children for the preservation and prosperity of future generations of that family.

What a complicated—but interesting—set of associations for her to navigate, but are these associations really all that different from what all of us face? The solution for Ruth in order to fulfill her own and the happiness of others is levirate marriage. Levirate marriage may be surprising to us, but Ruth is not unhappy in finding that her own good is at the same time a common good, and the common good, allowed and embodied in an allegiance to levirate law, lead to her private good. There are numerous other biblical examples for our edification. St. Paul instructs Timothy that bishops should be "husbands of one wife" (I Timothy 3:2), which verse in itself neither requires celibacy of the priesthood nor of bishops nor requires divorce for priests in the Roman world with more than one wife. The Bible astonishes, not because it is historically limited, but because it is so alive with real-life challenges and solutions.

Aristotle and al-Fārābī not only claim that there needs to be a reciprocal relation between marriage, household and the city, they argue that the city is more excellent and more divine than marriage and the household. They do so because the gifts that are scattered throughout the citizens of the city are good for the whole as well as for the smaller associations which are parts of the whole. Even more precisely, according to both Aristotle and al-Fārābī the gifts of prophecy and philosophy are possessed by some and not by all, even if these gifts are providentially given to the whole city. Human natures are different; no one husband and wife have all that they need for their own completion nor for the flourishing of their children. A father, for example, cannot be a hockey coach, a musician, an English teacher, a craftsman, a doctor, a philosopher and a priest all at once, even if children would do well to have some training in or at least exposure to each art. We need others. What is "defective" about marriage for al-Fārābī is not that it is wrong but that it is incomplete. The respective intellectual and moral virtues of the citizens of the city complement each other, and individuals, even those possessed of the best intentions of a husband and a wife working together, are not enough. This more complete political association means that married couples must recognize that friendship is not fostered in the assertions of the rights of the individual; it is unusual indeed if we conclude that our greatest admirations of others in friendships emerge from a defense of our private rights against others. Assertions of private will and contractarianism are strange notions in that sacred domain of "the marriage of true minds," that is, of the sacred territory of friendship. Moreover, nature will not in the end allow us to use notions of individual right to define marriage and household according to our private choosing; what is unnatural will have a limited duration and will not be the cause of happiness. Marriage and the household will need commonly accepted laws to sustain them. They will need the support of the community, and the aim and the measure of their prosperity will be their contribution to the first of the complete communities, the city. The classical tradition, which I have represented in a few quotations of Aristotle and al-Fārābī, concurs with and supplements Witte's analysis of the need for laws which relate marriage and the household to the larger community. The individualization and privatization of the notion of right is not found in either of our heritages, the Greek philosophical or the Judaeo-Christian. Jurisprudence in the United States, as well as elsewhere, needs a reorientation along the lines of these three scholars.

NOTES

1. William Shakespeare, *The Norton Anthology of Poetry,* third shorter edition, Alexander W. Allison, *et al.*, eds., (New York: W.W. Norton & Company, 1970), 90.
2. Brian Tierney, *The Idea of Natural Rights*, Studies on Natural Rights, Natural Law, and Church Law 1150–1625, Emory University Studies in Law and Religion, volume 5, gen. ed. John Witte, Jr., (Grand Rapids, MI: William B. Eerdmans, 1997), 1.
3. Ibid., 344.
4. Ibid., 346.
5. Ibid.
6. The foundational texts for the modern republic stress individual right. Rousseau says: "Our first duties are to ourselves; our primary sentiments are centered on ourselves; all our natural movements relate in the first instance to our preservation and our well-being. Thus, the first sentiment of justice does not come to us from the justice we owe but from that which is owed us; and it is again one of the mistakes of ordinary educations that, speaking at first to children of their duties, never of their rights, one begins by telling them the opposite of what is necessary, what they cannot understand, and what cannot interest them." Jean-Jacques Rousseau, *Emile or On Education*. Introduction, translation, and notes by Allan Bloom, (New York: Basic Books, 1979), 97. Rousseau's book was first published in 1762.
7. Tierney, *Idea of Natural Rights*, 346.
8. Ibid., 347.
9. Ibid.
10. Ibid.
11. Terence J. Kleven, "Family Virtues in Islam and Christianity: Building Communities in Harmony," *Theological Review of the Near East School of Theology*, 34 (2013): 50–67.
12. Leo Strauss, *Persecution and the Art of Writing*, (Chicago: The University of Chicago Press, 1980), 124–26.
13. Aristotle, *Nicomachean Ethics*, trans., glossary and Introductory Essay by Joe Sachs, (Newburyport, MA: Focus Publishing, 2002), 1094a 8–1094b 12.
14. Al-Fārābī, "The Political Regime," Charles Butterworth, trans., in *Medieval Political Philosophy: A Sourcebook*, second edition, Joshua Parens and Joseph C. Macfarland, eds., (Ithaca, NY: Cornell University Press, 2011), 37.

15. For a concise and lucid summary of what is at stake in the debate over the priority of either the city or the universal and homogenous state, see George Grant, "Tyranny and Wisdom," in *Technology and Empire: Perspectives on North America* (Toronto: House of Anansi, 1969), 81–109.

16. John Witte, Jr., *From Sacrament to Contract: Marriage, Religion, and Law in the Western Tradition*, second edition, (Louisville, Kentucky: Westminster John Knox Press, 2012). The first edition was published by Westminister John Knox Press in 1997. The second edition is used in all references to this book below.

17. John Witte, Jr., "The Meaning of Marriage," *First Things*, 126 (2002): 30–41.

18. Ibid., 34.

19. One set of changes that is made between the first and second editions of Witte's book is the addition in the second edition of three chapters at the beginning of the book, the first on the "Classical Foundations of Western Marriage," the second on the "Biblical Foundations of Western Marriage," and the third on the "Patristic Foundations of Biblical Marriage."

20. Witte, "The Meaning of Marriage," 30. See also Witte, *From Sacrament to Contract*, 2.

21. Witte, "The Meaning of Marriage," 32.

22. Ibid., 31.

23. Ibid., 33.

24. Ibid., 34.

25. Witte's account of Story's contractual account is also found in the second edition of his book. Witte, *From Sacrament to Contract*, second edition, 302–4.

26. Witte, "The Meaning of Marriage," 35.

27. Ibid., 36.

28. Ibid.

29. Ibid., 37.

30. Ibid.

31. *Eisenstadt v. Baird*, 405 U. S. 438 (1972).

32. *Roe v. Wade*, 410 U. S. 113 (1973).

33. Witte, "The Meaning of Marriage," 37.

34. Witte's analysis of these two Acts in the second edition of his book remains the same as in the article cited. See Witte, *From Sacrament to Contract*, 315–23.

35. Witte, "The Meaning of Marriage," 38.

36. Ibid.

37. Ibid., 40.

38. Ibid.

39. Ibid.

40. Al-Fārābī, 37.

41. For a sustained criticism of the contractarianism of John Rawls, see George Grant, *English-Speaking Justice*, Arthur Davis and Henry Roper, eds., *Collected Works of George Grant*, volume 4, 1970–1988, (Buffalo, NY: University of Toronto Press, 2009), 190–268. The significance of the thought of John Rawls to generations of scholars in the United States is observed in the fact that he was a Harvard professor, and in 1979 he was appointed a Conant University Professor, Harvard's highest professional post.

Chapter Three

The Triumph of the Right of Intimate Association

William C. Duncan

The Supreme Court does not talk about marriage very much. Even when it is deciding a case where marriage is apparently the subject matter, the Court may say little about it. So substantive discussions about the meaning and nature of marriage are somewhat scarce in the body of Court opinions and thus stand out.

If our only resource for understanding the meaning of marriage were these formal opinions, what would we believe marriage to be?

The few Nineteenth Century cases provide a reasonably consistent answer. That answer, perhaps reflecting a broad social consensus on the question, was stable and arguably influential well into the twentieth century. The Court did not, however, address the question in any significant way for about ninety years after an 1888 decision, *Maynard v. Hill.*

Something eventful, however, happened in that intermission. Someone observing Act One of the Court's treatment of marriage, and then picking up again in Act Two, quickly realizes that a very fundamental change has occurred—as if the two parts of the play are in fact two separate plays, but both with the same title.

ACT ONE

The question of the nature of marriage was obviously important to the Court's polygamy cases. For instance, this passage from 1883:

> For certainly no legislation can be supposed more wholesome and necessary in the founding of a free, self-governing commonwealth, fit to take rank as one of

> the co-ordinate States of the Union, than that which seeks to establish it on the basis of the idea of the family, as consisting in and springing from the union for life of one man and one woman in the holy estate of matrimony; the sure foundation of all that is stable and noble in our civilization; the best guaranty of that reverent morality which is the source of all beneficent progress in social and political improvement.[1]

Probably the most famous statement from a Court decision about the meaning of marriage is this passage from the *Maynard v. Hill* case:

> It is also to be observed that, whilst marriage is often termed by text writers and in decisions of courts a civil contract. . . . It is something more than a mere contract. The consent of the parties is of course essential to its existence, but when the contract to marry is executed by the marriage, a relation between the parties is created which they cannot change. Other contracts may be modified, restricted, or enlarged, or entirely released upon the consent of the parties. Not so with marriage. The relation once formed, the law steps in and holds the parties to various obligations and liabilities. It is an institution, in the maintenance of which in its purity the public is deeply interested, for it is the foundation of the family and of society, without which there would be neither civilization nor progress.[2]

The meaning and nature of marriage was not nearly so central to the facts of *Maynard* (which dealt with the validity of a legislative divorce), but the Court used the occasion to opine at some length. The Court include extensive quotes from earlier state cases whose inclusion is instructive. For instance, the Court endorsed as "well expressed," a passage from an 1863 decision by Maine's Supreme Court:

> When the contracting parties have entered into the married state, they have not so much entered into a contract as into a new relation, the rights, duties, and obligations of which rest not upon their agreement, but upon the general law of the State, statutory or common, which defines and prescribes those rights, duties, and obligations. . . . It is not, then, a contract within the meaning of the clause of the Constitution which prohibits the impairing the obligation of contracts. It is, rather, a social relation, like that of parent and child, the obligations of which arise not from the consent of concurring minds, but are the creation of the law itself; a relation the most important, as affecting the happiness of individuals, the first step from barbarism to incipient civilization, the purest tie of social life and the true basis of human progress.[3]

The Court also invoked a Rhode Island opinion:

> *marriage,* in the sense in which it is dealt with by a decree of divorce, is not a contract, but one of the domestic *relations.* In strictness, though formed by contract, it signifies the *relation* of husband and wife, deriving both its rights and duties from a source higher than any contract of which the parties are

> capable, and as to these uncontrollable by any contract which they can make. When formed, this relation is no more a contract than "fatherhood" or "sonship" is a contract.[4]

The Court also cites Joseph Story's conflicts treatise in which he observed that marriage, "appears to me to be something more than a mere contract. It is rather to be deemed an institution of society."[5]

Maynard and its authorities and *Murphy* were consistent with the Court's earliest substantive discussion of marriage, in the *Dartmouth College* opinion written by Chief Justice John Marshall in 1819. One of the questions raised in that case was the scope of the Constitutional prohibition on laws impairing the obligation of contract. It was argued that a broad interpretation of that law would outlaw legislative divorces since such divorces disrupt a marriage contract. Chief Justice Marshall's response is significant. He said the contracts clause would only apply to contracts related to property and similar rights, not to legislative divorces. Why not? Because, the Chief Justice argued, the power of legislatures to grant divorces "enable some tribunals, not to impair a marriage contract, but to liberate one of the parties, because it has been broken by the other."[6] Crucially, the opinion continues: "When any state legislature shall pass an act annulling all marriage contracts, or allowing either party to annul it, without the consent of the other, it will be time enough to inquire, whether such an act be constitutional."[7]

Much of the content of marriage in our laws can be discerned by looking at the exit requirements. Thus, the traditional fault grounds of abuse and adultery signal an understanding that marriage should be safe for spouses and that they are to be faithful to one another. So too with these Supreme Court musings on the nature of marriage in the context of discussions of divorce and polygamy.

The picture of marriage that emerges from these nineteenth century cases is of a social institution, a union of a man and a woman, which, though formed by the consent of the parties is more than a dickered bargain. It has broad social significance beyond the spouses and is specifically linked to the bearing and rearing of children ("foundation of the family and of society"). It affects the happiness of the individuals involved in it and creates obligations for them that the parties themselves cannot merely create or escape at will.

While the Court did not return to a discussion of marriage for some time, this understanding of marriage was clearly still a vital part of the law. States court decisions in the nineteenth and twentieth centuries spoke in very similar terms. For instance, an 1847 Pennsylvania case explained:

> The great end of matrimony is not the comfort and convenience of the immediate parties, though these are necessarily embarked in it. . . . The paramount purposes of the marriage—the procreation and protection of legitimate children, the institution of families, and the creation of natural relations among

> mankind; from which proceed all the civilization, virtue, and happiness to be found in the world.[8]

In the 1891 revision of his influential treatise, Joel Bishop defined marriage as "the civil status of one man and one woman legally united for life, with the rights and duties which, for the establishment of families and the multiplication and education of the species, are, or from time to time may thereafter be, assigned by the law to matrimony."[9]

Two noteworthy Supreme Court decisions did briefly reference marriage in a way that would be important later. In *Meyer v. Nebraska*, 1923, the Court held that the states lacked power to prevent a parent's choice to have their children taught in a language other than English in schools. In passing, the Court said the "liberty" protected by the Fourteenth Amendment included the ability to "to enjoy those privileges long recognized at common law as essential to the orderly pursuit of happiness by free men" and specified, among others, "the right of the individual . . . to marry, establish a home and bring up children."[10] Notice that this is a "right" (singular) to marry and establish a home and bring up children rather than three separate "rights." Then, in 1942, the Court invalidated a mandatory sterilization law, saying: "We are dealing here with legislation which involves one of the basic civil rights of man. Marriage and procreation are fundamental to the very existence and survival of the race."[11]

In both cases, the Court's passing references to marriage hearkened back to the understanding of marriage from the more fulsome Court discussions—connecting marriage and procreation and ascribing to it a broad social purpose.

ACT TWO

The Court's most famous marriage case was decided in 1967.[12] In it, the Court invalidated Virginia's law criminalizing interracial marriage on two grounds. First, the Court noted the obvious problem with the statute—that it employed a racial classification and thus ran afoul of the Fourteenth Amendment's guarantee of equal protection of the laws without regard to race. Almost as an afterthought, the Court also noted the anti-miscegenation law infringed on a fundamental right to marry. Curiously, the decision spoke very little about the meaning and nature of marriage. The opinion includes five pages of analysis of the implications of the Equal Protection Clause for the racial classifications that formed the core of the challenged statute. By contrast, the section of the opinion addressing the right to marry was just two paragraphs, 177 words, long. In it, the Court cited two cases as authority for the "freedom to marry": *Skinner* and *Maynard*. The Court's due process analysis was still focused on the racial classification at issue:

> To deny this fundamental freedom on so unsupportable a basis as the racial classifications embodied in these statutes, classifications so directly subversive of the principle of equality at the heart of the Fourteenth Amendment, is surely to deprive all the State's citizens of liberty without due process of law. The Fourteenth Amendment requires that the freedom of choice to marry not be restricted by invidious racial discriminations. Under our Constitution, the freedom to marry, or not marry, a person of another race resides with the individual and cannot be infringed by the State.[13]

Just a few terms before, however, the Court discussed marriage in more detail and planted the seeds of a more radical shift from previous understandings. In *Griswold v. Connecticut*,[14] the Court invalidated a law that prohibited the use or distribution of contraceptives to married couples. Marriage was central to the Court's holding because the precise constitutional violation identified by the Court was an interference with marital privacy. So, Justice Douglas' opinion concludes with some comments about marriage:

> Marriage is a coming together for better or for worse, hopefully enduring, and intimate to the degree of being sacred. It is an association that promotes a way of life, not causes; a harmony in living, not political faiths; a bilateral loyalty, not commercial or social projects. Yet it is an association for as noble a purpose as any involved in our prior decisions.[15]

This passage has the feel of an afterthought, coming as it does at the very end of the opinion. It is marked by a vagueness that does not make it seem an appropriate foil for the robust descriptions in the earlier decisions. It does, though, hint at ideas about marriage that will become full-blown in later cases. For instance, the "hopefully." Marriage, here, is not a union or joining since we can at best hope it endures. More important is the weight-bearing term "association." Too much can be read into the term as it is used here. In the previous paragraph, Justice Douglas had invoked an earlier decision protecting the membership rolls of the National Association for the Advancement of Colored People (NAACP) on right of association grounds.[16] The analogy is, of course, a little awkward as the language in this passage suggests. The reference to an association seems to be tentatively offered only to draw the analogy to another privacy-based decision of the Court. The seed was planted, however, and the shift from marriage as a union to marriage as an association will develop fully in the next decade.

The key decision is the Court's second foray into contraception regulations, *Eisenstadt v. Baird*. This time, the case involved a prosecution under a Massachusetts law prohibiting distribution of contraceptives to unmarried people. The Court struck down the restriction though the doctrinal reason for doing so is a little murky. The key finding appears to be that the Court could see no rational reason for the law's "different treatment accorded married and unmarried persons."[17] This is itself a crucial commentary on the nature of marriage—that it's not essentially different from non-marriage, even perhaps a fleeting relationship.

The Court went further and included its own conception of marriage, expanding on this equation of married and unmarried couples. Justice William Brennan, writing for the majority says:

> If under *Griswold* the distribution of contraceptives to married persons cannot be prohibited, a ban on distribution to unmarried persons would be equally impermissible. It is true that in *Griswold* the right of privacy in question inhered in the marital relationship. Yet the marital couple is not an independent entity with a mind and heart of its own, but an association of two individuals each with a separate intellectual and emotional makeup. If the right of privacy means anything, it is the right of the *individual,* married or single, to be free from unwarranted governmental intrusion into matters so fundamentally affecting a person as the decision whether to bear or beget a child.[18]

The legal analysis of this passage has come in for some well-deserved criticism. H. Jefferson Powell points out: "one thing that cannot be said, with a straight face and expecting to be taken seriously, is that if the right of marital privacy means 'anything,' it must be a right belonging to individuals regardless of marital status. The Court's assertion to the contrary was sheer cynicism."[19] Elsewhere he says the passage "was proof that the difference between reasoned judgment and authoritarian *diktat* had become obscure."[20] This criticism rings true as a matter of constitutional analysis.

Perhaps, though, the two cases are more reconcilable if we take seriously Justice Brennan's account of marriage. If marriage is not more than the association of two persons then the right of marital privacy in *Griswold* is just a fancy way of referring to an individual right to contraception that, in that case, was being exercised by two individuals acting in concert. If marriage and non-marriage are essentially alike, then it might not be crucial to recognition of a new right that it is being exercised by individuals in either of the two arrangements. Michael Sandel argued that in *Eisendtadt*, the right of privacy "prevented intrusion into decisions of certain kinds" as opposed to preventing intrusion into the bedrooms of married couples.[21] But if marriage itself is just a different kind of decision, then that distinction is not all that salient. Marriage, the Court says, is just an association of two separate individuals. In *Griswold*, two separate individuals were denied contraception. So too in *Eisenstadt*. The constitutional concern is precisely the same—denial of contraception. Sure in the first case the two individuals were associated in a "hopefully" enduring relationship called marriage, but this is of no more moment than that the first case arose in Connecticut and the other in Massachusetts.

In support of this reading, the Supreme Court talked about *Eisenstadt* the next term in *Roe v. Wade*, which invoked the former's language about individual rights.[22] In fact, the *Roe* Court held: "Several decisions of this Court make clear that freedom of personal choice in matters of marriage and family life is one of the liberties protected by the Due Process Clause of the Fourteenth Amendment."[23] Which decisions? *Loving v. Virginia* and the cases it cited in support of a right to marry and *Eisenstadt*. What can this mean other than that marriage has constitutional significance only as a manifestation of individual choice? The Court invoked this passage from *Roe* in its next major contraception case in which it importantly recognized a positive right: "the same test must be applied to state regulations that burden an individual's right to decide to prevent conception or terminate pregnancy by substantially limiting access to the means of effectuating that decision."[24] That case involved a challenge to a New York law prohibiting advertisement of contraceptives, sales of contraceptives to minors, and a requirement that adults acquire contraceptives by prescription. The Court invalidated each of the requirements.

Further evidence of the Court's new understanding of marriage came in its treatment of marriage in the spousal consent to abortion case. There, the Court held that since the state cannot prevent an abortion "during the first stage . . . the State cannot delegate authority to any particular person, even the spouse, to prevent abortion during that same period."[25] As William Van Alstyne has noted, the Court endorsed the proposition "that one who has conceived a child in marriage with his wife has no more standing to claim an interest in the well-being of the child thus conceived than the most casual male acquaintance with whom she may have had an equally casual one night affair (namely virtually none at all)."[26] This, of course, is consistent with a view of marriage that sees it as little more than a choice to associate for an indeterminate amount of time.

Complete confirmation comes in the Court's second right to marry case where the Court flatly says the Court has "routinely categorized the decision to marry as among the personal decisions protected by the right of privacy."[27] It adds: "the decision to marry has been placed on the same level of importance as decisions relating to procreation, childbirth, child rearing, and family relationships."[28]

In subsequent decades, the Court discussed marriage substantively a couple more times, making explicit its understanding of marriage. The final case in the right to marry trilogy, for instance, listed "important attributes of marriage": "expression of emotional support and public commitment," "an exercise of religious faith as well as an expression of personal dedication," an expectation of consummation, and a way to access government benefits.[29]

Then, when the Court reiterated its support for abortion on demand in 1992, it included descriptions of marriage that tie the elements discussed in the cases since *Griswold* and *Eisenstadt* together. In the first, the plurality refers to "constitutional protection to *personal decisions* relating to marriage" and other issues.[30] After quoting *Eisenstadt*, the opinion says:

> These matters, involving the most intimate and personal choices a person may make in a lifetime, choices central to personal dignity and autonomy, are central to the liberty protected by the Fourteenth Amendment. At the heart of liberty is the right to define one's own concept of existence, of meaning, of the universe, and of the mystery of human life. Beliefs about these matters could not define the attributes of personhood were they formed under compulsion of the State.[31]

Here, marriage is a choice with profound personal meaning; indeed it is among those select choices through which individuals may create their own concept of meaning and of the universe!

As important for what it concludes is what the Court's view of marriage excludes. On this point, *Casey* is particularly instructive. In a later passage, the Court addresses the question of whether a married woman seeking an abortion may be required to *notify* her spouse of the decision. The Court says such a requirement is unconstitutional and that its conclusion "rests upon the basic nature of marriage."[32] What is that "basic nature"? The Court answers with the marriage definition from *Eisenstadt*. It goes on to say that this *notification* requirement "embodies a view of marriage consonant with the common-law status of married women but repugnant to our present understanding of marriage and of the nature of the rights secured by the Constitution."[33] This is a stunning admission: the idea that marriage is anything more than a loose association of autonomous rights-bearers is "repugnant" to the Court's understanding of marriage; and it is a very loose association indeed in which one of the associates need not share her decision to abort their joint child with the other.

Table 3.1.

Act One	*Act Two*
Union	Association
Choice (Consent)	Choice (Contingent)
Social Significance	Expressive Purpose
Creates Obligations	Prioritizes Autonomy
Linked to Children	Children Optional
Man and Woman	

Taking these descriptions together, from *Eisenstadt* to *Casey*, a drastically different picture of marriage emerges. Marriage now is a choice of two autonomous individuals to associate, on a par with other relationship choices, and with a purpose of allowing the individuals to engage in two (parallel?) projects of self-expression or even self-creation. We might say it is something less than a mere contract. The dramatic difference in the two conceptions of marriage is illustrated by comparing the essential elements of each side-by-side in Table 3.1.

The element of choice is shared though it plays very different roles in each. In the first, the spouses choose to marry with the understanding that doing so creates obligations that will transcend the initial choice.[34] In the second, the choice is really all there is; it is attached to no particular consequences unless those consequences are also chosen.

The first item on each list, however, is most important. The core question of the meaning of marriage rests on whether it is an actual joining of two people into something that transcends their autonomous wills. Once that question is answered, the other elements follow. An association of indeterminate length is unlikely to have a profound social significance though it can certainly be an instrument of expressive individualism (marriage, in this regard, is like a tattoo although perhaps more easily removed).

To take another example, the idea of marriage as a union surely derives from the literal biological joining of the married couple. This joining is a requirement for (though now perhaps somewhat attenuated in proximity by the possibility of assisted reproduction) the creation of children, hence the linkage. So what is the legal significance of the Court's understanding of marriage?

Writing in 1980, Kenneth Karst proposed an answer: an emerging right of "intimate association."[35] Drawing on *Griswold* and its successors, he predicted that the Court would begin extending constitutional status to "a close and familiar personal relationship with another that is in some significant way comparable to a marriage or family relationship" which "may take the form of living in the same quarters, or sexual intimacy, or blood ties, or a formal relationship, or some mixture of these" but could also include "close friendship, with or without any such links."[36] Such protection is justified because, "It is the *choice* to form and maintain an intimate association that permits full realization of the associational values we cherish most."[37] The breadth of the protection, he argues, makes sense since, "[f]ormal associational status plainly is neither a necessary nor a sufficient condition for the realization of the values of intimate association."[38] He cited an opinion of Justice Thurgood Marshall dissenting from denial of *certiorari* in a case where a custodian and librarian living together in an adulterous relationship were fired from their jobs,[39] as a "statement of things to come"[40] since it identified "rights to pursue an open rather than a clandestine personal relationship and to rear their child together in this environment."[41]

Though this was a logical prediction it never seemed to pan out in the Court's subsequent decisions. The Court did say, in a 1984 case, that there was a "constitutionally protected 'freedom of association'" that included "choices to enter into and maintain certain intimate human relationships" since doing so would, among other things, "safeguard the ability independently to define one's identity" but seemed to suggest that traditional family relationships were the kinds of relationships protected by this right.[42] Then, a few years later the Court even said this right was not necessarily "restricted to relationships among family members."[43] But this seeming vindication of Professor Karst's prediction was more apparent than real since no decision ever struck down a law on the basis that it denied that right to intimate association. This is probably not surprising given that, by this time, virtually all non-family intimate relationships were legally tolerated. (An important exception was the sodomy law challenged in *Bowers v. Hardwick* but the majority in that case did not address the intimate association claim, though the dissent argued it was implicated.)[44]

Yet, there is more than one way to create a constitutional right. The Supreme Court in the 1980s appeared unwilling to create a robust right to intimate relationships that would be treated the same as its recognized right to marry. The prediction was that marriage would disappear or shrink in constitutional significance, but that is not the only alternative. What if instead we take an existing right and have it mean something else? What if, instead, the Court decided to treat the right to marry as a subset of the right of intimate association? All that would take is a redefinition of marriage as an intimate association, a redefinition which the Court had already accomplished. Thus, in 1996, the Court could say: "Choices about marriage, family life, and the upbringing of children are among associational rights this Court" has protected.[45]

All of which brings us to the subject of same-sex marriage, which the Court has now endorsed as a constitutional right, or more precisely, a constitutional mandate on the states, in June 2015.[46] Recall that the one element in the previous understanding of marriage the Court had not explicitly addressed is the requirement that it involve a husband and wife. It is that element that was on trial in the same-sex marriage cases. In other words, the *Windsor* and *Obergefell* cases completed the reversal in the understanding of marriage begun in *Griswold* and *Eisenstadt* and thus ensured the triumph of the right of intimate association.

To do so, the Court needed only take its understanding of marriage to the next logical step. If marriage is less than a mere contract with no broader purpose than to be used as a means for self-actualization and self-expression, why would the association of two men or two women not be accorded the same protection as the association of a woman and a man? The association need only be labeled a marriage in both cases for the court to fully embrace the right of intimate association, albeit under the old nomenclature of a right to marry.

The Court had already ventured some comments relevant to this possibility when it struck down the federal Defense of Marriage Act in 2013's *U.S. v. Windsor* decision.[47] There, the Court said marriage is the act whereby a couple can "affirm their commitment to one another before their children, their family, their friends, and their community"[48] and the government's conferral of "dignity" and "status";[49] a "status" that "is a far-reaching legal acknowledgment of the intimate relationship between two people, a relationship deemed by the State worthy of dignity in the community equal with all other marriages."[50] Here are some of the hallmarks of the new definition: marriage is the "intimate relationship between two people" with an expressive purpose. The Court only added, perhaps building on its recognition of an affirmative entitlement in *Carey v. Population Services*, that marriage was also the government's vehicle for effectuating that right to intimate association (a type of pseudo-social significance—the public interest in endorsing private choices).

What followed that decision in the lower courts is particularly instructive. While previous same-sex marriage litigation had focused on equal protection claims (the laws target the protected class of sexual orientation) or rational basis arguments (it is irrational for the state to treat same-sex couples differently from opposite-sex couples in its marriage laws), the focus of the flood of litigation following *Windsor* shifted to fundamental rights arguments.

Now this would seem an inauspicious approach at first. The controlling Supreme Court precedent to that point on the recognition of un-enumerated rights required that such rights, narrowly defined, be rooted in the history and tradition of the nation[51] and the obvious novelty of same-sex marriage would seem an insurmountable obstacle to such a finding. Some of the lower courts quickly found a way around this obstacle—holding the previously recognized right to marry encompassed intimate associations that had never been labeled as marriages before. For instance, the Tenth Circuit posited the proper reading of the right to marry required "a broad[er] level of generality" and faulted the state for "downplay[ing]" the "personal aspects" of marriage "including the 'expression of emotional support and public commitment.'"[52] The quotation, of course, is from *Turner*, which the opinion discusses at length.[53]

Similarly, the Fourth Circuit said that the "right to marry is an expansive liberty that may stretch to accommodate changing societal norms" and is "a matter of choice" and "the right to make, decisions regarding personal relationships."[54] The court said "civil marriage . . . allows individuals to celebrate and publicly declare their intentions to form lifelong partnerships, which provide unparalleled intimacy, companionship, emotional support, and security. The choice of whether and whom to marry is an intensely personal decision that alters the course of an individual's life."[55]

Indeed, these decisions and others like them, are premised on the associational understanding of marriage. For instance, this passage from an Alaska District Court opinion which cites *M.L.B.*, *Casey*, and *Griswold*:

> The Supreme Court has never described or defined marriage as a right that is dependent upon the particular facts of the case before it or a right belonging to a particular group; on the contrary, its discussion of marriage has consistently been "in broad terms independent of the persons exercising it." The choice of whom to marry is an "associational right" that is "of basic importance in our society" and is "sheltered by the Fourteenth Amendment against the State's unwarranted usurpation, disregard, or disrespect." Our society places immense value on marriage because it "involve[s] the most intimate and personal choices a person may make in a lifetime, choices central to personal dignity and autonomy. . . . In *Griswold v. Connecticut*, the Supreme Court described in detail the autonomous essence of marriage and the private choice involved when entering such a commitment.[56]

When the Court heard arguments in *Obergefell*, it was an open question whether the Court would follow these kinds of decisions and accept the redefinition of marriage from a union to an association as a *fait accompli*. The Court did so and the triumph of the right to intimate association was completed as the Court discarded the last remnant of the old wisdom about marriage.

In *Obergefell*, the Court adopted the associational model of marriage with gusto. The opinion began by describing what same-sex couples were seeking in attempting to secure a new definition of marriage as a liberty, a right "to define and express their identity."[57] Underscoring this point, the opinion later says that the failure to secure the title of marriage for their relationships had created a specific kind of deprivation: "A truthful declaration by same-sex couples of what was in their hearts had to remain unspoken."[58] Marriage, the Court says, "has evolved over time" but has now been recognized as a fundamental "interest of the person." [59] In identifying what the majority believed was the essence of marriage, Justice Kennedy described it as "a personal choice . . . inherent in the concept of individual autonomy."[60] Indeed, "[t]he nature of marriage is that, through its enduring bond, two persons together can find other freedoms, such as expression, intimacy and spirituality."[61] Marriage, he argues, is unique "in its importance to the committed individuals."[62] Marriage, to the Court is not necessarily related to children since that's "only one of many" aspects of the institution.[63] The state, says the majority, uses marriage to allow couples to "aspire to the transcendent purposes of marriage and seek fulfillment in its higher meaning."[64] Thus, retaining the old understanding of marriage would "disparage [individuals'] choices and diminish their personhood."[65]

There were good reasons for the Court not to have taken that fateful step, however. Whatever its merits for allowing federal courts wide latitude in policing family law, it had significant drawbacks in theory and practice.

The intimate association view of marriage does not provide an adequate account of marriage. There is, for instance, significant research that confirms long observation that marriage can transform spouses.[66] Children of married biological parents appear to have very different experiences from those who are raised by single people or unmarried couples.[67] All of which suggests that, however imperfect, in many cases, marriage really can create a union that is fundamentally different than just the sum of two atomized parts.

Also, the triumph of intimate association, particularly in the Court's formulation in *Windsor*, which suggests a government duty to dignify adult choices, would likely give impetus to efforts to secure social, as opposed to merely legal, acquiescence in the new view. This would involve pressure on those who see merits in the discarded understanding of marriage through levers of employment, tax status, professional licensing, etc. Recent high profile examples suggest some of this is already at work among private actors, but Court endorsement of the idea that embracing the other conception of marriage is to embrace a "repugnant" notion would presumably embolden such persecution.

The association model also prioritizes the interests of adult parties over other interests, in particular the needs of children. The understanding of marriage as a union, springing from the real biological union from which children are created and which is at the center of marriage as previously understood, makes real the entitlement of children to know and be raised by their own mother and father in a relationship of real stability and commitment, or at least a married mother and father when biological parents are not able to care for the child. Fleeting associations or associations among same-sex couples cannot secure the same entitlement and, in fact, may prevent a real relationship with at least one of the child's parents.

On the other hand, the Court's full endorsement of the intimate association model could provide an important opportunity for non-governmental institutions, like churches, to champion the competing model more firmly rooted in experience and inherited wisdom. Indeed, among the most eloquent voices for the richer understanding of marriage as a union creating unchosen obligations that provide a stable foundation for adult happiness and child well-being is the Lutheran pastor Dietrich Bonhoeffer. In a letter from prison to his niece, he wrote,

> In your love you see only the heaven of your own happiness, but in marriage you are placed at a post of responsibility towards the world and mankind. Your

> love is your own private possession, but marriage is more than something personal—it is a status, an office. Just as it is the crown, and not merely the will to rule, that makes the king, so it is marriage, and not merely your love for each other, that joins you together in the sight of God and man.[68]

A renewed appreciation for this understanding could prevent a misstep for the Court this summer. If necessary, it could spur renewed efforts to secure the promise of marriage that is now threatened with displacement by the thin conception of intimate association.

NOTES

1. *Murphy v. Ramsey*, 114 U.S. 15, 36 (1885).
2. *Maynard v. Hill*, 125 U.S. 190, 211 (1888).
3. *Ibid.* at 211–212, quoting *Adams v. Palmer*, 51 Maine 481, 483 (1863).
4. *Ibid.* at 212, quoting *Ditson v. Ditson*, 4 R.I. 87, 101 (1856).
5. Joseph Story, *Commentaries on the Conflicts of Laws, Foreign and Domestic* (1834), §108.
6. *Dartmouth College v. Woodward*, 17 U.S. 250, 300 (1819).
7. *Ibid.*
8. *Matchin v. Matchin*, 6 Pa. 332, 337 (1847). *See also Head v. Head*, 2 Ga. 191, 205 (1847); *Wray v. Wray*, 19 Ala. 522, 525 (1851); *Hamaker v. Hamaker*, 18 Ill. 137, 141 (Ill. 1856); *Baker v. Baker*, 13 Cal. 87, 103 (Cal. 1859).
9. Joel Prentiss Bishop, *New Commentaries on Marriage, Divorce, and Separation*, vol. 1 (1891), §11. See also A. Parlett Lloyd, *A Treatise on the Law of Divorce* (1887), 18; James Schouler, *Law of the Domestic Relations* (1905), §11; Joseph R. Long, *Treatise on the Law of Domestic Relations* (1905), §3; Frank Keezer, *The Law of Marriage and Divorce* (1906), §8.
10. 262 U.S. 390, 399 (1923).
11. *Skinner v. State of Okl. ex rel. Williamson*, 316 U.S. 535, 541 (1942).
12. *Loving v. Virginia*, 388 U.S. 1 (1967).
13. *Ibid.* at 12.
14. 381 U.S. 479 (1965).
15. *Griswold v. Connecticut*, 381 U.S. 479, 486 (1965).
16. *NAACP v. Alabama*, 357 U.S. 449 (1958) (State of Alabama could not require NAACP to turn its membership rolls over to the Attorney General in a dispute over the organization's compliance with corporate registration laws).
17. *Eisenstadt v. Baird*, 405 U.S. 438, 447 (1972).
18. *Id.* at 453, emphasis in original.
19. H. Jefferson Powell, "The Humanity of Law" *Villanova Law Review* 55 (2010), 1161, 1173.
20. H. Jefferson Powell, "On Not Being 'Not An Originalist,'" *University of St. Thomas Law Journal* 7 (2010), 259, 268.
21. Michael J. Sandel, "Moral Argument and Liberal Toleration: Abortion and Homosexuality," *California Law Review* 77 (1989), 521, 528.
22. 410 U.S. 113, 169-70 (1973).
23. *Ibid.* at 169.
24. *Carey v. Population Services International*, 431 U.S. 678, 688 (1977).
25. *Planned Parenthood of Central Missouri v. Danforth*, 428 U.S. 52, 69 (1976).
26. William Van Alstyne, "The Unbearable Lightness of Marriage in the Abortion Decisions of the Supreme Court: Altered States in Constitutional Law," *William & Mary Bill of Rights Journal* 18 (2009), 61, 67.
27. *Zablocki v. Redhail*, 434 U.S. 374, 384 (1978).
28. *Id.* at 386.

29. *Turner v. Safley*, 482 U.S. 78, 95-96 (1987).
30. *Planned Parenthood of Southeastern Pennsylvania v. Casey*, 505 U.S. 833, 851 (1992).
31. *Id.* at 851.
32. *Ibid.* at 896.
33. *Ibid.* at 898.
34. F. H. Bradley, "F. H. Bradley," in *Conservative Texts: An Anthology* (Roger Scruton ed., 1991), 40, 58 n.1 ("Marriage is a contract, a contract to pass out of the sphere of contract.").
35. Kenneth L. Karst, "The Freedom of Intimate Association," *Yale Law Journal* 89 (1980), 624.
36. *Ibid.* at 629.
37. *Ibid.* at 637 (emphasis in original).
38. *Ibid.* at 647.
39. *Hollenbaugh v. Carnegie Free Library*, 439 U.S. 1052 (1978) (Marshall, J., dissenting from a denial of certiorari).
40. Karst at 673.
41. *Hollenbaugh* at 1055.
42. *Roberts v. United States Jaycees*, 468 U.S. 609, 617–20 (1984).
43. *Board of Directors of Rotary International v. Rotary Club of Duarte*, 481 U.S. 537, 545 (1987).
44. 478 U.S. 186, 202 (1986) (Stevens, J., dissenting).
45. *M.L.B. v. S.L.J.*, 519 U.S. 102, 116 (1996) (holding a court fee for appealing the State's termination of parental rights was unconstitutional).
46. *Obergefell v. Hodges*, 576 U.S. __ (2015).
47. *U.S. v. Windsor*, 133 S.Ct. 2675 (2013).
48. *Ibid.* at 2689.
49. *Ibid.* at 2692.
50. *Ibid.*
51. *Washington v. Glucksberg*, 521 U.S. 702 (1997).
52. *Kitchen v. Herbert*, 755 F.3d 1193, 1211 (2014) (*quoting Turner v. Safley*, 482 U.S. 78, 95–96 [1987]).
53. Turner also gets a star turn in the Ninth Circuit's same-sex marriage case. *Latta v. Otter*, 771 F.3d 456, 471–72 (9th Cir. 2014).
54. *Bostic v. Shaefer*, 760 F.3d 352, 376 (4th Cir. 2014).
55. *Ibid.* at 384.
56. *Hamby v. Parnell*, Case 3:14-cv-00089, slip op. at 12 (D. Alaska 2014) (footnotes omitted). The first quote is from *Kitchen*, the second from *M.L.B.*, the third from *Casey*.
57. *Obergefell*, slip opinion at 2.
58. *Ibid.* at 7.
59. *Ibid.* at 6.
60. *Ibid.* at 12.
61. *Ibid.* at 13.
62. *Ibid.*
63. *Ibid.* at 16.
64. *Ibid.* at 17.
65. *Ibid.* at 19.
66. *See* W. Bradford Wilcox, et al., *Why Marriage Matters* (3d ed. 2011), 20–22.
67. See Kristin Anderson Moore, Susan M. Jekielek, and Carol Emig, "Marriage from a Child's Perspective: How Does Family Structure Affect Children, and What Can We Do about It?" *Child Trends Research Brief* (June 2002); Mark Regnerus, "How Different are the Adult Children of Parents who Have Same-Sex Relationships? Findings from the New Family Structures Study," *Social Science Research* 41 (2012), 752, 764.
68. Dietrich Bonhoeffer, *Letters and Papers from Prison* (Eberhard Bethge, ed., 1953), 42–43.

Chapter Four

Free and Happy Bonds

Loving v. Virginia*'s Nineteenth Century Precedent on Marriage and the Pursuit of Happiness*

Adam M. Carrington

In the current debate over marriage law, great attention is given to the case of *Loving v. Virginia.*[1] That 1968 decision famously struck down laws banning interracial marriage as violating both the Equal Protection and Due Process clauses of the United States Constitution. While speaking to the Due Process Clause, Chief Justice Warren declared that "[t]he freedom to marry has long been recognized as one of the vital personal rights essential to the orderly pursuit of happiness by free men."[2] Warren's statement posited both a means and an end. Scholarly and judicial discussions consistently address the means: Warren's claim that marriage is part of the right to liberty guaranteed by the Due Process Clause.[3] But less attention is paid to the end that this liberty helps to fulfill—that persons act on their right to marry as part of the "orderly pursuit of happiness."[4] This lack of attention has left open the question of how marriage contributes to the pursuit of happiness, particularly from the judicial branch's perspective.

In this chapter, I examine the judicial branch's link of marriage and the pursuit of happiness. I do so by discussing how an important period of the American judiciary—one from which Warren drew—articulated the connection between the two. Building off Warren's use of precedent, I examine judicial opinions discussing this link in the decades surrounding the Fourteenth Amendment's 1868 ratification, spanning generally from 1848 to 1890. In so doing, I find within the judiciary of the time a coherent understanding of the nature of human happiness as realized in marriage. For the Court, marriage functioned as the deepest form of human community, one whose provision served an important role in the happiness of individuals and in the happiness of society. Beyond addressing the important judicial history behind Warren's assertion, I will show how this coherent understanding contributed to a judicial definition for the pursuit of happiness that interacts with contemporary discussions.

To explain this understanding, first, I show how state and federal courts declared marriage to be a private source of happiness particular to the individuals involved. The courts reasoned that marriage provided one of the deepest means for community that could facilitate happiness in the physical, material, and emotional needs it met. Based upon these claims, the courts then acted in several ways to protect happiness within marriages, including using the language of contract to ensure consent, taking steps to guard the health of marriages, and protecting—imperfectly—the individual rights of spouses. Second, I turn to the basis of Warren's claim that marriage was a "social institution," one also found in the latter-nineteenth century judiciary. The courts during that time connected marriage to a form of public happiness that stemmed from the institution's fulfillment of certain social goods. Here the nineteenth century cases described marriage as more than a contract. It was a "public institution" which created the next generation, lessened the burden of the state to provide, and cultivated the character of citizens necessary for republican self-government. I then conclude by noting how contemporary marriage jurisprudence retains the connection between marriage and happiness, finding continuity and discontinuity with the particular claims found in the nineteenth-century vision.

THE PURSUIT OF HAPPINESS AS JUDICIAL CONCEPT

One reason for the dearth of scholarship on the judicial understanding of marriage and the pursuit of happiness is textual. The Constitution does speak of liberty in the Due Process Clause. The term "pursuit of happiness," however, appears nowhere in the text. Instead, the words come most famously from the Declaration of Independence when it asserts that all "are endowed by their Creator with certain unalienable Rights, that among these are Life, Liberty and the pursuit of Happiness." Still, courts have consistently viewed the pursuit of happiness as judicially cognizable, including cases on issues as diverse as education, employment, and assisted suicide.[5]

Furthermore, judicial bodies previous to the Warren Court connected marriage in particular to happiness's pursuit. The Chief Justice recognized this fact. In his discussion of marriage as pursuing happiness in *Loving*, Warren cited two cases. The first case was the 1942 decision *Skinner v. Oklahoma,* where the Court struck down a state law allowing for the sterilization of persons convicted multiple times of "felonies involving moral turpitude." This opinion receives the most scholarly attention as *Loving*'s judicial precursor.[6] But while this opinion speaks of a liberty right, it makes no mention of the pursuit of happiness. Warren's claim on this matter came from the second cited case, the lesser known 1888 Supreme Court decision in *Maynard v. Hill.* Warren in fact cited *Maynard* twice, both to define marriage as pursuing happiness and to describe marriage as a "social institution."[7] The decision in *Maynard* concerned the inheritance rights of the children of a couple who divorced while the father was acquiring land in the Oregon territory.[8] Though primarily a matter of statutory interpretation, the Court's decision spent considerable time discussing marriage's legal nature and function, in so doing drawing upon decades of state and federal court precedent. Thus, Warren's choice of *Maynard* was important as that case's description of marriage consciously built upon the judicial consensus regarding marriage and the pursuit of happiness which had come to be in the decades surrounding the Fourteenth Amendment's ratification. Therefore, I will look to *Maynard* as well as many state and federal cases preceding it to better understand the precedential origins upon which Warren's *Loving* opinion drew. Thereby, I will show the era's consistent though multi-faceted judicial understanding of marriage and the pursuit of happiness.

MARRIAGE FOR PRIVATE HAPPINESS

In *Maynard,* the U.S. Supreme Court's reference to happiness came in quoting state court precedent. Re-stating the Maine Supreme Court opinion of *Adams v. Palmer*,[9] Justice Stephen Field declared marriage to be "a relation the most important, as affecting the happiness of individuals."[10] This argument was common to state and federal courts in the time broadly surrounding the Fourteenth Amendment's ratification. In the 1848 case of *Sheffield v. Sheffield,*[11] for example, the Texas Supreme Court stated that "the mutual comfort and happiness of the parties are the principle, though not the only, objects of the engagement."[12] In *Perry v. Graham,*[13] the Supreme Court of Alabama declared that marriage "may be deemed as much more valuable than money, as it more permanently affects the happiness and prosperity of the parties."[14] The U.S. Supreme Court itself argued that marriage was the *primary* means to secure happiness. In the 1874 case of *Randall v. Kreiger,* Justice Swayne declared "[t]he happiness of those who assume its [marriage's] ties usually depends upon it more than upon anything else."[15]

How Marriage Contributes to the Private Pursuit of Happiness

The courts at the time went on to articulate just what this happiness looked like. At its core, this conception of happiness saw marriage as creating and maintaining a form of community. The courts during this period viewed marriage doing so by creating a deep and expansive union of two persons. This union comprised an emotional and intellectual bond as well as a combining of financial assets. An Arkansas court thus declared that "[t]his bond of union between husband and wife contemplates not only a union of hearts, but a union of property and all other interests."[16] In fact, several courts called upon the Biblical language that in marriage two would become "one flesh"[17] to articulate the breadth and depth of the union marriage created.

The courts then discussed the particulars of this union, paying attention to how each contributed to the happiness of those involved. Common to today's discussions, the courts saw this bond as often involving romantic love. In *Sheffield v. Sheffield,* the Texas court argued that this "most important of human transactions" was regarded as "the basis . . . of the domestic affections."[18] A Washington Territory court noted that "[i]t seemed, in civil cases, conclusively to presume every husband to be truly devoted, body, soul, spirit, and estate, to cherish his own wife as his own flesh."[19] The courts saw this love as a powerful part of human happiness. As is often declared in recent cases, the courts further reasoned that marriage constituted an important means to secure this happiness by the commitments made to each other—publicly and formally declaring mutual and exclusive love.[20]

Love was not a necessary component, however, and the courts articulated other means to happiness which marriage procured, regardless of the romantic affection involved. A Tennessee court, for instance, said that in marriage the spouses "mutually promise cohabitation and a continual care to promote the comfort and happiness of each other."[21] Both cohabitation and care aided greatly in happiness. Cohabitation, for example, aided happiness as part of an accepted avenue for sexual intercourse,[22] as "[o]ne object of marriage undoubtedly is the pleasure of association with a female."[23] This particular means, of course, was hoped to have some connection to the possible love between spouses spoken of before, though such a prerequisite was not inquired into by the courts. Nonetheless, as a source of pleasure, the courts saw such relations between the sexes as a means to happiness. Moreover, courts understood cohabitation to provide opportunities for other forms of intimacy. An Alabama court criticized a husband for "viewing the marriage relation as merely physical and sexual" and that instead he should consider his wife to be "a companion in life."[24] Companions, the courts reasoned, shared in common their entire lives not just particular, isolated aspects. Thus, other cases spoke of the privacy of the home giving a place for greater mutual trust and a person in whom to confide. One Tennessee court, for example, spoke of "the frankness and freedom of a confidential intercourse, so proper to this relation."[25] Here happiness involved the ability to openly share with another one's thoughts, fears, and hopes in a context protected by the marriage relation. Cohabitation also formed an important prerequisite for the other means for happiness mentioned, namely "continual care." Such care included provision of material needs such as food, clothing, and shelter. An Alabama court noted that a "duty owed from the husband to the wife . . . is that of maintenance"[26] for her in these matters. Cohabitation and continual care, therefore, provided material as well as emotional supports which the courts tied directly to human happiness.

In making these claims, the courts said much regarding the meaning of happiness's pursuit. Primarily, these judicial bodies saw human happiness as greatly tied to its social nature. Human beings were not meant to live alone. Instead, they were meant to live in community; and marriage formed one of the most basic, and intense, communities in human experience. The courts furthermore argued that, within these communities, human happiness involved seeking both pleasure and security—life itself and some conception of the good life. The community formed by marriage gave its participants a context in which to gain both: Pleasure in the form of physical and emotional intimacy, security in a lasting context for these pleasures as well as for physical provision. All of these aspects offered the prospect of happiness that the courts found unequaled in other spheres of human life.

Court Enforcement

We must remember, however, that the right being protected by the courts was the pursuit of happiness, not its attainment. The courts articulated broad ways in which marriage could fulfill human happiness. Yet these judicial bodies saw a more limited sphere for what could be legislatively commanded and judicially applied toward that end. The courts therefore responded to this understanding by discerning what could be done by law, then sought to protect these means for pursuing happiness within marriage to the extent considered appropriate.

One Flesh, One Contract

First, the courts could not enforce the union of persons as "one flesh" in all its forms. While praising love as important to marital happiness, they could obviously not demand it judicially. Furthermore, though sexual relations were considered so important to marriage, suits attempting to enforce conjugal rights received swift dismissal as outside the courts' power.[27] The courts could, however, provide legal recognition to the couples' "oneness" regarding property. In the Indiana court case of *Noel v. Ewing,* a case cited by the Supreme Court in *Maynard,* the Indiana court stated that marriage "merged the legal existence of the parties into one."[28] The debts of one became the debts of the other, as did the previously separate estates. This legal union comprised a picture of the other forms of union the court recognized as applying to marriage. The courts therefore assumed, for example, that while cohabitation continued, husbands were legally considered to consent to contracts made by the wife "for the supply of articles suitable to their means and station in life."[29] The items procured by the wife were for common use paid for from common funds, regardless of who actually made the money.

Second, the courts protected happiness in marriage by considering it as a kind of contract. *Sheffield v. Sheffield,* for example, referred to marriage as a "contract" to then state that through it "the parties have pledged themselves . . . for their own happiness."[30] This description protected the pursuit of happiness in several ways. For one, describing marriage in terms of contract connected its pursuit of happiness to consent. In *Maynard v. Hill*, the Supreme Court noted that "marriage is often termed by text writers and decisions of courts as a civil contract, generally to indicate that it must be founded upon the agreement of the parties."[31] *Randall v. Krieger,* also from the Supreme Court, declared "[m]arriage is an institution founded upon mutual consent. That consent is a contract."[32] The Supreme Court arguments here, furthermore, consciously drew upon state cases such as *Maguire v. Maguire*, a Kentucky Court of Appeals decision which argued that "[m]arriage [is] in one sense, a contract—because, being both stipulatory and consensual, it cannot be valid without the spontaneous concurrence of two competent minds."[33] These claims further revealed the courts' understanding of the right to pursue happiness and its relation to marriage. Happiness's pursuit was deeply connected to the concurrence of the will found in consent. In seeking to fulfill other components of happiness in marriage, this union must first be based upon the acquiescence of the parties. The motives to get married could vary. Some may marry for love, others for social status, still others for financial security. Regardless of the reasons, to protect the pursuit of happiness the courts demanded that the persons entering marriage freely agree to such a union.

In speaking of happiness and consent, however, the courts did seek to define necessary conditions in which consent could be given, again as a means of protecting the happiness of those who might marry. *Maguire v. Maguire* stated that the "concurrence" in entering marriage must come from "two competent minds." Competency could be denied for reasons permanent and temporal. Those considered severely mentally ill, for instance, could not contract for marriage as they were not considered of "sound mind" to truly understand the contract entered. Among other temporal reasons was the age of those getting married. *Shafher v. State of Ohio,* from the Ohio Supreme Court, declared "the blessings of the marriage relation can only be realized when entered into with the utmost freedom of choice, and between persons of matured judgment and discretion."[34] The Ohio court here declared that persons could be too young to judge whether or not they truly desired to enter marriage. In addition, this case's defense of "the utmost freedom of choice" showed that other traditional contractual protections, such as those guarding against coercion, fraud, or distress, applied to marriage as well.

Beyond protecting consent, the language of contract meant a broad range of persons could enter it. In particular, it meant that marriage was open to more than merely those with a religious affiliation. In *Maynard v. Hill,* the U.S. Supreme Court declared that as a civil contract, marriage "does not require any religious ceremony for its solemnization."[35] Non-religious as well as religious persons could enter into marriage in a form recognized by the government. In fact, Pennsylvania's supreme court argued in 1866 that as marriage "is a civil contract" it "does not require any particular form of solemnization before officers of church or state . . . " instead only requiring evidence of consent between the parties either by signatures or by witnesses.[36] While other states required more formal ways of substantiating a marriage, across the states the language of contract kept matrimony open to those capable of making a contract regardless of religious affiliation.

Protecting the Marriage Bond

A third step the courts took involved enforcing laws that protected the marriage relationship from threats either to its stability or to the individual rights of spouses. Threats to marriage's stability included a long line of state cases which declared that spouses could not act as witnesses against each other. Allowing such testimony would harm the trust and support that privacy afforded to husband and wife. A Tennessee case discussed above stated that "[t]o enforce or permit the husband or wife, to publish and prove before the court, the conduct and conversation of the other, made known to the witness in the frankness and freedom of a confidential intercourse, so proper to this relation, would be, as we think, of injurious consequences to the happiness of families."[37] The court in this case continued that "the consciousness that this [witnessing against a spouse] might be done, would be productive of reserve, distrust and anxiety in the minds of persons sustaining this important relation."[38] For the courts, this distrust and its consequent anxiety would do much harm to the happiness of the marriage relationship. Twenty years later, the same state court confirmed that such action "would tend to destroy that bond of mutual confidence and unquestioning trust that is essential to the peace and happiness of this most sacred of all domestic relations."[39] Here the court recognized several important ways in which marriage related to the pursuit of happiness. The breadth and depth of the marriage union often required a level of confidence and trust beyond that of other relationships. To live in constant fear that a person so intimately connected would be forced to divulge any and all information he or she knew would certainly harm the happiness of those involved. It could strain if not sever an important part of what made the community found in marriage so important to fulfilling our social nature. Thus an Arkansas court declared in a case denying spousal testimony that "to break down or impair the great principles which protect the sanctities of that relation [marriage] would be to destroy the solace of human existence."[40]

Contrary to more modern views, courts also saw the happiness of marriages protected by making it difficult to obtain a divorce. In *Sheffield v. Sheffield,* for example, the court argued that "the happiness of married life greatly depends on its indissolubility . . . ."[41] The reason the court gave pertained to the effect the ease or difficulty of obtaining divorce had on spouses. Easy divorce, the court claimed, led to more difficult marriages and a more vicious character in those involved. The opinion explained that "the prospect of easy separation foments the most frivolous quarrels and disgusts into deadly animosities."[42] Here the court recognized the clashes that often occurred in marriages. But to allow an easier dissolution of the marriage would place the couple on more antagonistic footing and make them less virtuous in their actions toward each other. Small feuds could fester and build to the poisoning of the entire relationship, both parties knowing that the union could be easily, legally ruptured. The requirement to stay married, the court argued, could breed the opposite effect: "when they know they must live together, except for causes prescribed by the law, they learn . . . 'to soften, by mutual accommodation, the yoke which they know they can not shake off; they become good husbands and wives from the necessity of remaining husbands and wives; for necessity is a powerful master in teaching the duties it imposes.'"[43] In this way the courts saw the maintenance of marriage bonds as protecting happiness by preserving the permanence needed to keep short-sighted responses from causing lasting damage. But even more, the courts saw preserving these marriages as cultivating certain virtues in spouses that aided in pursuing happiness. The necessity of continued union would teach husband and wife to better fulfill their roles in ways conducive to each other's felicity. They might, the court reasoned, be less selfish, more accommodating, and even more loving from the knowledge that they must find a way to make the relationship work.

The Rights of Spouses

Other protections were not of the marriage relationship itself but of the individuals involved. The courts upheld the concept that persons as individuals held the rights to be protected in their persons and their property regardless of the perpetrator. Thus, in *Maynard,* the court spoke of restraints on government deriving from "a regard for certain fundamental rights of the citizen which are recognized in this country as the basis of all government . . . ."[44] But in recognizing fundamental rights as the basis of all government, they empowered in the same way that they restrained. Governments could not act to infringe on fundamental rights. But what government did do—what was its basis for existing—was to act to protect such rights from violation by other persons. At times, this meant government stepping in to protect the rights of one spouse against another. In protecting these rights, again, the courts consistently saw themselves as defending the pursuit of happiness.

Some of these protections took the form of contract language to protect property. In these protections, the court followed state laws that increasingly undid the controversial concept of coverture. In coverture, wives were seen to give up their legal rights and obligations to their husbands upon marriage. Though cases asserting coverture still occurred in this period, by the late 1860s they were becoming rare, subverted by the courts and by state laws.[45] The courts applied laws, for example, protecting wives against coercion from their husbands. In one Colorado supreme court case, the court enforced a law "requiring the wife's private examination and acknowledgment of the wife" before her estate could be conveyed so as "to protect her from any coercion of the husband."[46] Protections also existed against fraud regarding property, where spouses showing fraud on their partner's part could void the sale of an estate.[47]

Other protections involved the life and liberty rights of an endangered spouse. In the same cases that denied the general power to compel spousal testimony, the different courts as one noted important exceptions. These "well known exceptions" were those "having relation to the personal security and protection of the wife"[48] or, put another way, "for the protection of the wife in her life and liberty."[49] If there were accusations that the husband had violated a woman's right to life through assault or bounded her liberty by physical restraint, then the wife could testify so as to defend herself against such violations.

Wives in particular received protection within the marriage relationship from threats to their person and to their liberty.[50] Divorces were generally granted—beyond desertion and infidelity—for "extreme cruelty" perpetrated against the wife. Many of these cases pertained to physical harm. The dockets are tragically full of instances of physical abuse.[51] Following the law, the courts allowed a dissolution of the marriage when a consistent pattern of such abuse was reasonably proven, again as a protection of the rights to life and liberty of the woman aggrieved.

But in a number of cases the courts recognized more extensive protections that went beyond physical abuse. One example came in the Nevada case of *Reed v. Reed.* The court there discussed the statute granting divorce for extreme cruelty, noting that "[t]his is the general language of the books, and it will be observed that physical injury alone seems to merit consideration, whilst the subtle torture of mental anguish, unless occasioned by personal violence done or apprehended, is entirely overlooked."[52] But the court itself was unwilling to overlook such attacks upon a spouse, adding, "[t]here may be extreme cruelty without the slightest violence."[53] In so doing, the court returned to the goal of protecting happiness's pursuit. The court based the problem of such "mental anguish" in the result that "the happiness of a life may be destroyed by a course of conduct which could furnish no ground for apprehending bodily harm or injury."[54] The supreme court of Michigan, too, joined in this application of extreme cruelty beyond physical violence. That court called a focus on physical violence alone to be "relics of barbarism in English law" which, "ignores the human soul, with all its susceptibilities of suffering tortures more intense than physical pain, and more certainly destructive of health and life."[55] Here we see the courts connecting verbal abuse to an attack on the health and life of the spouse, even saying that such attacks were at times more destructive than physical abuse. So defining life and health gave expansive protection to both, one understandable in light of the pursuit of happiness. For spouses received protection for life and health not only as mere survival; they received such protection as necessary for finding and maintaining happiness.[56] Thus an Arkansas court, though with significant condescension, stated that "[w]here it appears probable that no cure is to be expected, and that the evil will continue in its intolerable aspect, the happiness of a life is too sacred for sacrifice, although the subject may be an humble, hard working woman, without the refinements of education and culture."[57]

In these varied instances, we see the courts recognizing the great place that marriage holds in the pursuit of happiness by individuals. In so doing, they also provided a picture of what happiness itself meant in their reasoning. Marriage provided a possible means to deeply fulfilling community, community that social human beings found important to pursuing their happiness. They also saw the problems that could exist in marriage for happiness, namely threats to the person and property of women. The courts therefore sought to protect the happiness of the marriage relationship itself and the happiness of the individuals involved. Though far from perfect in enforcing needed protections, the court did provide a robust understanding of the pursuit of happiness for individuals entering marriage.

MARRIAGE FOR SOCIETAL HAPPINESS: A PUBLIC INSTITUTION

The courts' reasoning on happiness and marriage as well as its willingness to act regarding them did not end with its effect on the individuals involved. Beyond its relation to individual happiness, Chief Justice Warren in *Loving* also recognized "that marriage is a social relation subject to the State's police power."[58] In doing so, he again cited *Maynard v. Hill.* However, the Chief Justice did little to explain the Loving Court's understanding of marriage as "a social relation." Yet *Maynard,* along with other courts of its time, elucidated this position at length. Again, the courts here connected marriage with community. But this time the community was the broader political community, not the community formed by those getting married. The courts saw marriage as conducive to the happiness of the greater public, of the people in their role as citizens. Indiana's supreme court, for example, argued that marriage "is essential to the peace, happiness, and well-being of society"[59] while a neighboring Kentucky body called marriage a "domestic relation of its citizens which is most essential to its prosperity, moral power and happiness."[60]

How Marriage Served Public Happiness

Marriage served the happiness of the political community in a number of ways. Firstly, a political community's happiness necessitated that such a community exist. Marriage played a crucial role in creating and continuing this existence. Regarding creation, in the 1851 Supreme Court case of *Gaines v. Relf*, Justice Catron asserted that "[t]he great basis of human society throughout the civilized world is founded on marriages."[61] The political community looked to marriage for its beginnings, as it formed the first community from which all others originated. Maine's Supreme Court explained that marriage constituted "the purest tie of social life" which was "the first step from barbarism to incipient civilization."[62] Marriages were the purest social tie in part because they were the first, creating the most basic community. This most basic community gave rise to families with the creation of children and then to political community through the combination of families. Thus *Maynard* declared that marriage "is the foundation of the family and of society."[63] At the same time, political communities depended on marriages to continue their existence once founded. For it was through marriages that the next generation of citizens was created. In *Prewit v. Wilson,* Justice Stephen Field quoted Joel Bishop's famous work on marriage law, saying that marriage results, among other things, in "life to unborn children."[64] This point alone made marriage of great public importance, as a California court declared that "children are not born for the benefit of the parents alone, but for the country."[65] Children were not sons and daughters only; they were citizens whose very existence was necessary for the survival of the political community and thus for its happiness.

Second, a political community's happiness included its citizens possessing basic provisions of food, clothing, and shelter. As citizens were also in many cases spouses, marriage played a major role in this goal as well. In the 1887 case of *Murray v. Murray,* Alabama's supreme court spoke of "[t]he duty of the husband to provide maintenance for his wife."[66] This maintenance included the basic needs of food, clothing, and shelter in a fashion reasonably aligned with the man's financial state. Failure to provide such maintenance was considered a violation of the obligations of the marriage contract. Provision or lack thereof affected the happiness of the individuals involved, as previously discussed. But the court said the man's actions did more than violate obligations of a private contract. Instead, the opinion declared of such maintenance "it is not only a duty to her [his wife], but he owes it to the public, lest she become a charge upon it."[67] The husband's provision for his wife pertained to his role as a citizen as well as a spouse. Without the support provided by the husband for the wife, the woman would be left without means to survive. Absent those means, her maintenance would become the task of the state government. This situation would affect the political community's happiness by shifting resources to such care and away from other means to the public good.

Third, and perhaps most important to the courts, the political community's happiness was furthered in the formation of its citizens' moral character. Indiana's supreme court, for example, said that marriage "is a great public institution, giving character to our whole civil polity"[68] while North Carolina's supreme court argued that marriage "is an institution which is essential to . . . the preservation of human virtue."[69] The courts thought such virtuous morality a pressing concern beyond communal happiness. On it depended the very existence of society. Supreme Court Justice Stephen Field, who wrote the *Maynard* opinion, argued in another case that "in our intercourse with fellow men, certain principles of morality are assumed to exist without which society would be impossible."[70] Society would be impossible without a moral baseline because such a society would hold no regard for the rights of its participants. Contracts would be ignored to the detriment of property. Life and liberty would suffer along with property through rampant crime. As discussed before, the courts of the time regularly asserted that the protected exercise of individual rights was a central reason for the existence of society and of government. Thus a proper morality was considered "the source of all beneficent progress in social and political improvement."[71] Through such morality, society would be possible as such a society generally would respect the rights of its members.

Marriage's moralizing effect stemmed greatly from how it instructed persons to respect individual rights and thus to live in a free society. As noted before, the courts reasoned that marriage constituted, "the first step from barbarism to incipient civilization."[72] It appears that the pre-marital condition's barbarism, for the court, lay in the individual's sole consideration of his own interests apart from any considerations of justice or the rights of others. Marriage constituted the crucial first step away from this situation. From this first community persons created and learned how to live in broader communities, considering not only their own rights but those of their spouses, children, and fellow citizens.

The courts made the connection between marriage, morality and political society most clearly in the era's polygamy cases. In *Davis v. Beason,* the U.S. Supreme Court upheld a law denying the vote in the Idaho territory to those who practiced or supported polygamy. The Court, with Field writing, argued that polygamy tended "to degrade woman, and to debase man."[73] Both the degradation and the debasement connected to individual rights. Polygamy as practiced in this context involved one man entering into marriage with several women at the same time. In so doing, polygamy undercut a fundamental principle of American government: equality. A marriage where one sex was exclusive to a single participant but not the other was seen to deny the equality of men and women in a fundamental way. From this denial of equality resulted the asserted degradation of women and the debasement of men. Women were degraded in that they were reduced to unequal status—slave-like status—with rights unequal to their husbands. Men were debased in learning to act toward their wives like slave-masters—like tyrants. This state of affairs certainly threatened individuals' rights and thus individual happiness throughout the political community.

Moreover, the U.S. Supreme Court articulated the public consequences of such circumstances in the famous polygamy case of *Reynolds v. United States.* In that case the U.S. Supreme Court denied an appeal against polygamy laws on the basis of the First Amendment's Free Exercise Clause. Chief Justice Waite argued that "according as monogamous or polygamous marriages are allowed, do we find the principles on which the government of the people, to a greater or less extent, rests. Professor Lieber says, polygamy leads to the patriarchal principle, and which, when applied to large communities, fetters the people in stationary despotism, while that principle cannot long exist in connection with monogamy."[74] The courts saw a deep connection between the habits cultivated in the home and the character of those same persons acting in their capacity as citizens. Monogamy encouraged the concept of equality. That which is equal to another has no inherent right to violate that other's rights. Polygamy, on the other hand, bred despotic principles in the home, teaching spouse and child supposedly-inherent inequalities that the courts feared could easily be transferred to the public square, as "upon it [marriage and family] all the social and domestic relations are based."[75] The Supreme Court strikingly put the effect of polygamy this way: that "[t]he organization of a community for the spread and practice of polygamy is, in a measure, a return to barbarism."[76] In its attack upon the education of equal rights, polygamy for the courts served the perverse role of undoing the very civilization marriage was supposed to create and sustain.

Court Responses: Protection of Public Happiness

In these ways, the courts of the period saw marriage as a close-knit community essential to the creation and maintenance of the greater political community. Like its observations regarding the happiness of those getting married, the courts understanding here led to judicial action to further marriage's public role. A Texas court, for example, said the state should pass and apply marriage laws in ways that "will best promote its own social happiness and welfare."[77]

To promote social happiness, first the courts greatly qualified their own language of marriage as a contract, declaring it to be not a civil contract merely. In *Maynard,* the U.S. Supreme Court stated that "it is something more than a mere contract."[78] In *Adams v. Palmer,* the Maine court declared that "marriage, though in some of its aspects resembling a contract, is rather to be regarded as a social relation; a status with duties, rights and obligations established by the law of the State."[79] Declaring marriage to be a social relation and a status moved it far from the realm of a normal contract. The court in *Palmer* compared it to another social relation, one which in that time marriage constituted the necessary moral pre-requisite, saying that marriage was "a social relation like that of parent and child."[80] This comparison held significant ramifications for understanding consent, which the courts' contract language had sought to protect. Persons may consent to becoming parents. However, that consent did not extend to prescribing what duties should and should not be fulfilled as parents. Laws could and did specify what would be demanded of parents in regard to their children regardless of whether the parents consented to those demands. Children, after all, were for the country as well as the parents. Thus the court said of parenting that "the obligations . . . arise not from the consent of concurring minds—but are the creation of the law itself."[81] In the same way, marriages were created, as were children, by the consent of concurring minds. However, due to its significant ramifications for societal happiness, the laws could proscribe and prescribe much regarding its duties and its continuance.

The enforcements of family law for the sake of republican self-government were many in this period. The courts enforced husbands' provision for spouses, both in the marriage and when granting separations and divorces of which the wife was not at fault.[82] Care in particular should be provided for the child, with "the happiness and welfare" of the child taking precedence in the allotment of alimony.[83] The courts also sought to uphold marriage laws thought to protect and cultivate the morals of the persons involved. Polygamy, of course, was prohibited for the reasons already discussed. Sex outside marriage, cohabitation without marriage, as well as other violations of marriage's privileged place were prohibited and punished.[84]

In these ways, the courts saw themselves as protecting an institution essential to the public happiness of the political community. More than merely a means to individual happiness, marriage would help to create and sustain human civilization, doing so by procreation, education of children, and the cultivation of the virtues necessary for self-government.

CONCLUSION

In citing *Maynard,* Chief Justice Warren's *Loving* opinion touched upon a long-standing vision, one that saw marriage as part of happiness's pursuit. In large part, *Loving* followed this vision. Warren wrote of marriage in terms of a consenting contract, declaring that "[u]nder our Constitution, the freedom to marry, or not marry, a person of another race resides with the individual."[85] Furthermore, he described marriage as a kind of public institution, citing *Maynard* as he argued that "[m]arriage is . . . fundamental to our very existence and survival."[86] The public nature of marriage here pointed toward the connection between marriage and procreation; marriage was fundamental to our existence and survival because marriage led to the creation and education the next generation of citizens. Therefore, although *Loving* struck down bans on interracial marriage, it still assumed much of the relationship between marriage and happiness found in the nineteenth century.

This understanding again came under review in *Obergefell v. Hodges,* the seminal 2015 decision requiring states to grant marriage licenses to same-sex couples. In his majority opinion, Justice Anthony Kennedy declared that "[t]he history of marriage is one of both continuity and change."[87] Where did the pursuit of happiness rest along the continuity and discontinuity line? In discerning the line between continuity and change, Kennedy quoted *Loving* to reiterate that "marriage is 'one of the vital personal rights essential to the orderly pursuit of happiness by free men.'"[88] The Court, therefore, continued to affirm the connection between marriage and happiness's pursuit. Regarding how marriage aids the pursuit of happiness, Kennedy certainly sees important forms of discontinuity with *Loving* and the nineteenth century. Kennedy, for example, argues that marriage can no longer be defined by gender or, consequently, by child-bearing and education.[89] Yet Kennedy does see significant continuity as well. Marriage remains a means to fulfill the human need for community, both in material and spiritual ways.[90] It remains a contractual commitment of consenting adults. Kennedy even quotes *Maynard* to say that "marriage is a keystone of our social order,"[91] though that order is built more on affirming liberty as "individual autonomy" [92] than realizing certain societal expectations of procreation and cultivating virtue. Most of all, marriage remains a bond of love, now seen as one of marriage's core elements.[93]

Thus, as the newer definition of marriage continues to take judicial form, *Loving* and its nineteenth century precedent remain important parts of the ongoing discussion. For even though the question of gender's relation to marriage now appears judicially settled, the courts will seek where to draw Kennedy's continuity/discontinuity line on other marital matters. As it was with the question of gender, the arguments put forth in *Loving* and the other cases discussed above will remain important parts of the judicial debate. For in addressing these particular issues, the courts will continue to consider, not only what defines marriage, but how such a bond contributes to a permanent fixture of human life: the pursuit of happiness.

NOTES

1. See *Obergefell v. Hodges* 576 U.S. ____ (2015) (Kennedy, J., Opinion of the Court) (Slip Op. at 11–13). *Latta v. Otter* 771 F.3d 456 (2014); *Bostic v. Schaefer* 760 F.3d 352 (2014); *Whitewood v. Wolf* 992 F.Supp.2d 410 (2014); *United States v. Windsor* 133 S. Ct. 2675 (2013), at 2691.
2. *Loving v. Virginia* 388 U.S. 1 (1967), at 12.
3. See Jamal Green, "Divorcing Marriage from Procreation," *The Yale Law Journal* 114 (2005): 1991–1992; Andrew M. Roth, "Sociological, Political, and Legal Contexts Regarding the Current Debate on Gay Marriage," *Public Affairs Quarterly* 12 (1998): 355–356; Peter Wallenstein, "The Right to Marry: Loving v. Virginia" *OAH Magazine of History* 9 (1995).
4. Many of the works cited above do include the pursuit of happiness section of Warren's quote but focus their analysis on the claim to a Due Process liberty right. Another work mentioning the connection is Priscilla Yamin, *American Marriage: A Political Institution* (Philadelphia: University of Pennsylvania Press, 2012).
5. See *Meyer v. Nebraska* 262 U.S. 390 (1923); *Missouri v. Cummins,* 71 U.S. 320 (1867); *Washington v. Glucksberg* 521 U.S. 702 (1997). See also *Waugh v. Mississippi* 237 U.S. 589 (1915); *Meisel v. U.S.* 412 U.S. 954 (1973).
6. Ariela Dubler points to this case as constituting the "origins of the modern, judicially created right to marry" tracing its logic forward to the *Loving* case. See "Sexing *Skinner:* History and the Politics of the Right to Marry," *Columbia Law Review* 110 (2010), 1350.
7. *Loving,* 388 U.S. at 7.
8. The husband had moved to the Territory, obtained land, and then divorced his wife. The government cancelled half the land grant upon the divorce, since the amount awarded was based upon his married status. Later, the heirs to the wife sued to obtain the cancelled land as part of her estate. The Supreme Court affirmed a lower court ruling against the heirs, arguing that, under pertinent statutes, the man had not occupied the land in question long enough to obtain full ownership. See also Steven H. Hobbs, "Love on the Oregon Trail: What the Story of *Maynard v. Hill* Teaches us about Marriage and Democratic Self-Government," *Hofstra Law Review* 32 (2003): 111–144.
9. *Adams v. Palmer* concerned whether a man's second wife could recover her dower upon the death of her husband. The Maine court ruled in the woman's favor, declaring her husband's divorce from his first wife to be legal, thus legitimating her own marriage and vesting a right to the dower to her.
10. *Maynard v. Hill* 125 U.S. 190 (1888), at 211.
11. In this case, the Texas court denied a plea for a divorce because neither side proved desertion, infidelity, or any other legal grounds for ending the marriage.
12. 3 TX 79 (1848), at 86.
13. This case concerned whether a slave given to a woman before her marriage went to her husband upon her death or back to the woman's family.

14. *Perry v. Graham* 18 Ala. 822 (1851), at 826. See also *Adams v. Palmer,* calling marriage "a relation the most important, as affecting the happiness of individuals." See *Adams v. Palmer* 51 Me. 480 (1863).

15. *Randall v. Kreiger* 90 U.S. 137 (1874), at 147. This case concerned a widow seeking to reclaim land sold through a lawyer under power of attorney during her husband's life. The woman claimed the land as part of her dower. The Court denied her claim, saying that she gained her husband's estate upon his death and that the land, legally sold, was not part of his estate.

16. *Robinson v. Eagle and His Wife* 29 Ark. 205 (1874), at 207. This case concerned a dispute about the relationship between the common-law conception that the husband and wife's estates merged in marriage and a then-new provision of the Arkansas constitution keeping the wife's estate separate.

17. *Campell's Adm'r and Heirs v. Gullatt;* 43 Ala. 57 (1869), at 67; *Lanier v. Lanier* 52 Tenn. 462 (1871); *Goodrum v. Georgia* 60 Ga. 509 (1878).

18. *Sheffield v. Sheffield* 3 Tex. at 86. This case denied a divorce claim because infidelity had not been proven, alleged abandonment had not gone on for the required three years, and the otherwise mere desire of the spouses to divorce was not therefore enough to end the marriage.

19. *Phelps & Phelps v. Steamship Company of Panama* 1 Wash. Terr. 533 (1877). This case predominately considered the jurisdiction of an injury claim by a woman on a ship. In addition, the court determined that the husband joining the suit did not aid or harm it and that damages awarded should not be diminished simply because the husband could care for the woman.

20. See *Obergefell v. Hodges* 576 U.S. ____ (2015); *United States v. Windsor* 133 S. Ct. 2675 (2013).

21. *Doc Lonas v. TN* 50 Tenn. 287 (1871), at 308.

22. *Latham v. Latham* 77 Va. 307 (1878), at 346; *Ex parte Boscowitz* 84 Ala. 463 (1887), at 465–466.

23. *Long v. Long* 77 N.C. 304 (1877), at 311.

24. *Wood v. Wood* 80 Ala. 254 (1885), at 256.

25. *Brewer v. Ferguson* 30 Tenn. 565 (1851), at 566.

26. *Murray v. Murray* 84 Ala. 363 (1887), at 365.

27. The courts even refused to grant divorces for desertion on this ground. See *Southwick v. Southwick* 97 Mass. 327 (1867).

28. *Noel v. Ewing* 9 Ind. 37 (1857), at 49. This case concerned how state law abolishing dower connected with a widow's claims after her husband died. See also *Maynard,* 125 U.S. at 213.

29. *Litson v. Brown* 26 Ind. 489 (1866).

30. 3 TX at 85–86.

31. *Maynard,* 125 U.S. at 210.

32. 90 U.S. 147.

33. *Maguire v. Maguire* 37 KY 181 (1838), at 183–184. This case denied a woman's divorce claim on jurisdictional grounds.

34. 20 Ohio 3 (1851), at 6. This case concerned a claim of bigamy by a man married at age 16 and again at age 18. The court voided the first marriage because cohabitation had not occurred while the man was of age.

35. *Maynard,* 125 U.S. at 210.

36. *Commonwealth v. Stump* 53 Pa. 132 (1866), at 136.

37. *Doc Lonas* 30 Tenn. At 566.

38. Ibid., 30 Tenn. At 567.

39. *State for the Use of Sarah Barker v. Jas. MCauley* 51 Tenn. 424 (1871), at 433.

40. *Collins v. Mack* 31 Ark. 684 (1877), at 689. At the same time, interestingly, the courts did not extend the same protection to non-marital romantic relationships. In the 1867 case of *Flanagin v. Arkansas,* for instance, the supreme court of that state declared that in such cases one person could be forced to testify against another. *Flanagin v. Arkansas* 25 Ark. 92 (1867), at 95–96.

41. *Sheffield,* 3 Tex. at 86.

42. Ibid.

43. Ibid.
44. *Maynard,* 125 U.S. at 205.
45. One of the latest was *Cole v. Van Riper* 44 Ill 58 (1867). Even this case was suspect, as the court's application of coverture was contested by an 1861 statute protecting a wife's independence authority to own property.
46. *Keller v. Klopfer* 3 Co. 132 (1876), at 135.
47. See a mention of this in *Kennedy, &c. v. Ten Broeck, &c.* 74 Ky. 241 (1876), at 250.
48. *Brewer*, 30 Tenn. at 566.
49. *Missouri v. Berlin* 42 Mo. 572 (1868), at 577. See also *Cole v. Cole* 23 Iowa 433 (1867), at 438.
50. Some cases existed protecting the husband. In *Carpenter v. Carpenter,* for example, a Kansas court granted the husband a divorce because the wife, without justification, sent anonymous letters accusing her husband of infidelity with a married female co-worker. The court declared such action "intolerable cruelty" which even threatened the man's life due to the possible vengeance of the other woman's husband. See *Carpenter v. Carpenter* 30 Kan. 712 (1883).
51. See, for examples, *Glahn v. Glahn* 46 Ill. 144 (1867); *Burns v. Burns* 13 Fla. 369 (1869); *O'Neill v. O'Neill* 30 N.J. Eq. 119 (1878); *Briggs v. Briggs* 23 S.C. 377 (1886).
52. *Reed v. Reed,* 4 Nev. 395 (1868), at 398.
53. Ibid.
54. Ibid. In Pennsylvania, this same reasoning also applied to men seeking divorce. See *Jones v. Jones* 66 Pa. 494 (1871).
55. *Chaffee v. Chaffee* 15 Mich. 184 (1867), at 186–187.
56. For other cases along these lines see *Myrick v. Myrick* 67 Ga. 771 (1881); *Donald v. Donald* 21 Fla. 571 (1885); *Avery v. Avery* 33 Kan. 1 (1885).
57. *Haley v. Haley* 44 Ark. 429 (1884), at 435.
58. *Loving,* 388 U.S. at 7.
59. *Indiana v. Gibson* 36 Ind. 289 (1871), at 403.
60. *Maguire,* 27 Ky. At 185.
61. *Gaines v. Relf* 53 U.S. 472 (1851), at 534. Executors of a man's will refused to recognize a daughter of the deceased as a legitimate heir, since the woman's mother engaged in bigamy by marrying the deceased.
62. *Adams* 51 Me. at 485.
63. 125 U.S. at 211.
64. *Prewit v. Wilson* 103 U.S. 22 (1880), at 24. This case upheld the land transfer a man made to a woman in order to convince her to marry him. Afterwards, the man declared bankruptcy and creditors sued to nullify the land transfer as an attempt to defraud them. The Court upheld the land transfer since the woman had no knowledge of an attempt to commit fraud.
65. *Wand v. Wand* 14 Ca. 512 (1860), at 516.
66. *Murray* 84 Ala. At 365. In this case, the court denied a wife's claim to alimony from her husband when the two were not divorced but did claim that the husband could be legally forced to provide for her basic needs.
67. Ibid.
68. *Noel v. Ewing* 9 Ind. at 50.
69. *W.M. Sutton and His Wife v. J.A.J. Askew* 66 N.C. 172 (1872), at 185.
70. *Butcher's Union Company v. Crescent City* 111 U.S. 746 (1884), at 756.
71. *Murphy v. Ramsey* 114 U.S. 15 (1885), at 58.
72. *Adams,* 51 Me. at 485.
73. *Davis v. Beason* 133 U.S. 333 (1890), at 341.
74. *Reynolds v. United States* 98 U.S. 145 (1878), at 165-166.
75. *Gibson* 36 Ind. at 403.
76. *The Late Corporation of the Church of Jesus Christ of Latter-Day Saints v. United States* 136 U.S. 1 (1889), at 49.
77. *Shreck v. Shreck* 32 Tex. 578 (1870), at 587.
78. 125 U.S. at 211.

79. *Adams,* 51 Me. at 484.
80. Ibid., 51 Me. 485.
81. Ibid.
82. *Johnson v. Johnson* 20 Ill. App. 495 (1886).
83. *Chandler v. Chandler* 24 Mich. 176 (1871).
84. See *Davis v. Beason* 133 U.S. at 343 in its discussion of other sexual acts, including those sects who deny the existence of marriage but promote sexual relations amongst their members.
85. *Loving,* 388 U.S. at 12.
86. Ibid.
87. *Obergefell,* at 6.
88. Ibid., at 11.
89. "The constitutional marriage right has many aspects, of which childbearing is only one." *Obergefell,* at 16.
90. Kennedy argues that, in addition to economic help, marriage creates an "enduring bond" through which "two persons together can find other freedoms, such as expression, intimacy, and spirituality." See *Obergefell,* at 13.
91. *Obergefell,* at 16.
92. Ibid. at 12.
93. "Marriage responds to the universal fear that a lonely person might call out only to find no one there." *Obergefell,* at 14.

Chapter Five

On the Marriage of Dred Scott

David Ramsey

The Justices of the Supreme Court do not often refer to the Court's ruling in the *Dred Scott* case. When they do, it is often to illustrate the danger that an overly activist or politicized Supreme Court poses to the stability of the regime.[1]

Chief Justice Taney's opinion in the case is invoked to remind us that when judges seek to resolve decisive social issues on constitutional grounds independent of statutory support there can be tragic consequences, for the Court and the nation. Even less likely to receive attention from the modern Court is the dissent of Justice Curtis in that case. Yet Curtis' defense of Dred Scott's liberty includes important reflections on the significance of Scott's marriage to his claim of emancipation, a fact neglected by all eight of his fellow Justices, each of whom authored an opinion in the case. In the pages that follow, I argue that Justice Curtis' "argument from marriage" for the liberty of Dred Scott and his family derives from an Aristotelian understanding of politics, most notably the relationship between the varying modes of association within the natural household and his classification of regimes. I refer to this understanding as "Aristotelian" in part to assuage the concerns of classical political theorists who might otherwise question the care with which I approach the few passages from the *Politics* cited below, and in part because, while I am certain that there is a similar sensibility in the approach of both men to the political things, I remain uncertain to what extent Curtis was familiar with Aristotle's political writings. If, indeed, he turns out not to have known the *Politics* in any detail, I would suggest that far from making the appeal to Aristotle irrelevant, this similarity of approach might serve as evidence of the very stability within nature, and particularly human nature, that played so important a role in Aristotle's writings. Curtis seems to have seen in the peculiar circumstance of Scott's marriage and its subsequent fruit the grounds for showing or teaching how the American Constitution might be applied to resolve the tension—a tension that was growing increasingly manifest during his tenure on the Court—between the republican principles set down in the Constitution and the political compromises periodically hashed out by Congress to keep the Union from dissolving over the question of whether or not to continue accommodating the "peculiar institution" of slavery. Reconsidering Curtis' argument in light of the Supreme Court's recent decisions in *U.S. v. Windsor* and *Obergefell v. U.S.* allows students of American constitutionalism to anticipate some of the developments within the regime that are likely to follow from the novel account of marriage and the family laid out by Justice Kennedy in these cases. Curtis' argument from marriage suggests another way of explaining the manner in which the institution of marriage prepares the way for human liberty.

PUBLIC REASON: MAJORITY OPINION AND DISSENT

The Supreme Court is unique among the branches of the federal government in part because its most significant actions are almost always accompanied by a rational justification. The Court alone has adopted the convention of presenting its actions in the form of reasoned, written judgments. One might go too far, of course, in insisting that all discourse in the public square follow the example of the Court.[2] Without needing to defend any account of the place of the judiciary in the American political system which would exalt the Court as exemplar of "public reason," reasonable students of American constitutionalism may yet observe that the opinions issued by the Court have often served as models for our public discourse. Careful consideration of the Court's most enduring and consequential opinions may help us to better understand the manner in which the Constitution constrains, shapes and guides our politics. And further consideration of the Court's oeuvre suggests that her greatest failures have come in those cases where the arguments presented fail to persuade, or at least to appease, a majority of American citizens. As an example of the former, it is common today to point to Chief Justice Marshall's opinion in *Marbury v. Madison*.[3] As an example of the latter, it would be difficult to present a more prominent or easily recognized failure of judicial statesmanship than Chief Justice Taney's opinion in *Dred Scott v. Sandford*.[4] Though we must certainly look beyond the Court to appreciate the complexity of American constitutionalism, it is important to pause from time to time in order to survey the great variety of perspectives and ideas to which the Court has given voice in its opinions.[5] Indeed, study of the law offers this advantage, that within a single case we may find a number of important approaches to the same political problem. Dissents can often be just as important to our study as majority rulings. Sometimes heralding a departure from old precedent, a dissent joined by a plurality of Justices in the manner of Justice McReynolds' opinion in *National Labor Relations Board v. Jones & Laughlin Steel Corporation*[6] may help us to understand the significance of the new direction taken by the Court in Chief Justice Hughes' majority opinion. Sometimes such dissents, commanding a plurality of the votes on the Court, signal that an emerging majority on the Court has discovered some weakness in the precedent or that the views of the political community are beginning to change, in the manner of Justice Holmes' opinion in *Hammer v. Dagenhart.*[7] At other times, a lone dissenter might cry out against the folly of his colleagues, inspiring a future generation of lawyers to take up his argument and move the law in a new direction, in the manner of the dissents of Justice Harlan in *Plessy*[8] or Justice Brandeis in *Olmstead.*[9] In yet other instances, the absence of a dissenting opinion can facilitate the growth of problematic Court precedent, as the lower courts and the interested public are left to wonder what reasons Justice McReynolds, for example, might have had for failing to join the rest of the Court in *U.S. v. Curtiss Wright Export Corporation,*[10] or what Justice Butler might have said in defense of Ms. Buck's reproductive rights in *Buck v. Bell.*[11] The argument from marriage tucked into the middle of Justice Curtis' dissent in *Dred Scott v. Sandford* has been neglected by contemporary scholars, who tend to focus on the role that the opinion came to play in the abolitionist movement. But examining the argument from marriage for the liberty of Dred Scott in light of the Court's recent rulings on same-sex marriage allows us to draw out new points of comparison between the judicial temperaments and philosophies of Justices Curtis and Kennedy.

Of course few things are more likely to offend academic audiences today than suggesting some connection between the Court's recent rulings in *U.S. v. Windsor*[12] and *Obergefell v. Hodges*[13] and its rulings in *Dred Scott v. Sandford* and *Lochner v. New York.*[14] And yet the basis for doing so is clear, as the comparison does little more than suggest that questions regarding the constitutional status of slavery, workers' rights, and same-sex marriage have been divisive issues in American politics. What might make some uncomfortable with the suggestion that *Obergefell*, *Windsor*, *Lochner*, and *Dred Scott* should be studied together is the fear that doing so could suggest that the Court's recent same-sex marriage rulings are in some way destined to be looked upon with disfavor or held up for public ridicule by future generations. And indeed, in all four cases, the opinion of the Court rested upon a substantive interpretation and application of the due process clause.[15] This point has been most recently highlighted in Chief Justice Roberts' *Obergefell* dissent, an opinion which commanded the votes of four Justices on the Court.[16] Before we dismiss such comparisons out of hand, then, we would do well to remember that these things, the Court's rulings on constitutional controversies which loom large in contemporary politics, have been subject to change. Taney hoped to put the question of slavery to rest with his ruling in *Dred Scott,* but it is the arguments of the dissenters, McLean and Curtis, that enjoy popular support today. Opinions long regarded as little more than routine may represent important principles to future generations, and those principles embraced or rejected by one generation may be taken up again at a later date. To read the full range of opinions recorded by an earlier Court, then, is not merely a tool for understanding the constitutional controversies of the past. Doing so may also suggest to contemporary readers resources for better adjudicating contemporary debates.[17]

To point to one prominent example, a number of scholars have noted that we may be seeing in the Roberts Court something of a reconsideration of the principles advanced by the Court during the Lochner era, as its docket remains well stocked with cases giving it ample opportunity to expound upon the principles of economic liberty, and perhaps even a rebirth of Court protection for the liberty to contract.[18] There is some reason, then, to think that the reading of old opinions can inform analysis of contemporary political discourse. But it may also be the case that we are more inclined to learn from previous thinkers when we have some sense of who they were and what part they played in the politics of their time. There are, after all, many different moods of dissent, and many different temperaments on display in any given Court, and questions of character may have some bearing on the way in which written arguments should be interpreted. So before we turn to a consideration of the arguments presented by Justice Curtis in opposition to those put forward by those of his brethren in the Court's majority, before we turn to his words, we should first set down a few of his principal deeds.

MR. JUSTICE CURTIS[19]

It was President Millard Fillmore who appointed Benjamin Curtis to the Court in September of 1851. Curtis was highly regarded by a number of prominent American statesmen, among them Daniel Webster and Joseph Story. Story had instructed the young Curtis at Harvard Law School, and it was Story's seat on the Court, left vacant by the death of Levi Woodbury, which Curtis filled. Curtis established a reputation early as one of the first great American patent lawyers. From the beginning, he was engaged in the questions of how to accommodate the dynamism facilitated by the Constitution's protection of intellectual property rights within a stable constitutional and legal framework. During his first term on the Court, he authored the opinion of the Court in *Cooley v. Board of Wardens of the Port of Philadelphia,*[20] helping to resolve an important issue regarding the interplay of state and federal power over issues pertaining to interstate commerce which the Court had struggled to put to rest ever since Chief Justice Marshall's ruling in *Gibbons v. Ogden.* It is characteristic of Curtis' judicial disposition that, despite his views on the institution of slavery, which at times inclined toward the abolitionists, he faithfully enforced the fugitive slave laws when riding circuit in New England. His relations with other members of the Court, and especially Chief Justice Taney, were cordial or even warm. In brief, none of Curtis' contemporaries seem to have noted those signs of growing discontent which would lead him to resign from the Court in September of 1857, months after the *Dred Scott* ruling was handed down. Scholars have offered a number of explanations for his early departure from the bench. To begin with, Curtis never seems to have made peace with the requirements of his office to be away from home throughout so much of the year, and attempts to bring his wife and children with him to Washington during the Court's term proved impractical. On a related note, it appears that Curtis was troubled by the comparatively low level of his fixed salary while serving on the Court—his private practice having been quite lucrative—and though he attempted to make up for the loss in income by editing two highly regarded editions of his opinions, a two volume edition of his Circuit Court opinions published in 1854, and a twenty-two volume edition of the opinions of the Supreme Court published in 1856, the royalties from these works still fell short of making up the difference in his salary. Perhaps most tellingly, Curtis seems to have become disenchanted with the judicial office itself.[21] Having anticipated that the conferences of the Court would be possessed of an apolitical, leisurely and judicious mode of discourse, and that his work on the Court would be honored by the public, he grew increasingly distraught by the political machinations of his colleagues on the bench, and the heavy workload which they shared, taking perhaps too much to heart public criticism of his rulings. Curtis stands alone in the history of Supreme Court Justices for his decision to retire at such a young age from that tribunal, and that decision seems to have been set in motion by the internal discord on the Court which became evident in the weeks after Chief Justice Taney handed down his decision in the *Dred Scott* case. A disagreement between Curtis and Taney broke out[22] over whether or not Curtis would be allowed access to the written opinions of the Court in the case. It appears that the Chief Justice had been reluctant to draw further attention to the case, and that Curtis wanted to publish the opinions in pamphlet form as a means of bringing before the public eye the nature of the disagreement which had arisen on the Court. But lest Curtis' decision to leave the Court be given too much significance, leading to a characterization of the Taney Court as so politicized that the only option left to good men such as Curtis was to retire to private life, it is important to recall the generous words of Curtis' eulogy, upon the death of Chief Justice Taney, before the First Circuit Bar, a speech which bears no hint of the acrimony and mistrust evident in their post-*Scott* exchange of letters. The speech is effusive in its praise of Taney's abilities as a lawyer and administrator, concluding with a favorable comparison to Chief Justice Marshall:

> It is one of the favors which the providence of God has bestowed on our once happy country, that for the period of sixty-three years this great office has been filled by two persons, each of whom has retained, to extreme old age, his great and useful qualities and powers. The stability, uniformity, and completeness of our national jurisprudence are in no small degree attributable to this act. The last of them has now gone. God grant that there may be found a successor true to the Constitution, able to expound and willing to apply it to the portentous questions which the passions of men have made.[23]

Indeed, while it may very well be the case that Lincoln carried a well-worn pamphlet copy of Justice Curtis' *Dred Scott* dissent with him while debating Senator Stephen Douglas in 1858, drawing from the argument presented there to set the terms of public debate about the future of slavery in America,[24] Curtis' public conduct after leaving the Court shared far more in common with the Chief Justice than President Lincoln. While supporting the cause of the Union, he condemned Lincoln's suspension of the writ of *habeas corpus* and his assumption of additional war powers, and spoke out against the Emancipation Proclamation, going so far as to oppose Lincoln's re-election in 1864. Following Lincoln's assassination in 1865, he encouraged President Andrew Johnson to resist ratification of the Fourteenth Amendment, and with the assistance of William Evarts, shared the responsibility for preparing Johnson's defense in the impeachment trial. By developing plausible dissenting arguments in *Dred Scott,* Curtis may have sealed his legacy as an abolitionist and a Union man, just as the legacy of Taney would forever be sullied by his failure to put the slavery issue to rest with his arguments in the case. But a more discriminating analysis reminds us that such one-dimensional appraisals of both Justices must always fall short of the mark. The search for authentic understanding of history always involves a struggle to move beyond the monochromatic narratives of the schoolbook and the popular presentation. In an attempt to recover something of the vibrant color of the period, we turn now to one of the forgotten arguments of Justice Curtis' *Dred Scott* dissent, the argument from marriage to establish Mr. Scott's status as a free citizen of the United States.

THE ARGUMENT FROM MARRIAGE

The Constitution of 1787 provided little guidance for the Court when called upon to determine questions of U.S. citizenship and the scope of congressional power to regulate affairs in the Territories. These questions would need to be worked out through the course of regular politics. As national political divisions over the issue of slavery came to predominate in the politics of mid-nineteenth-century America, politicians decided to throw these issues to the Court. Both issues were on full display in *Dred Scott,* and Curtis and Taney ground their opinions in plausible interpretations of the textual evidence and the political practice which had accumulated over the intervening years. Modern readers tend to recognize and approve the views of Curtis, finding in them a semblance of the constitutional arrangements hashed out in the Reconstruction amendments. Taney's argument, on the other hand, proceeds in a manner similar to the approach of modern-day "originalists," keen to impart a sense of reverence for the American founders to the American public. He suggested that if we understand the self-evident truth propounded in the *Declaration of Independence* that all men are created equal to suggest that those of African descent are held to be the equals of whites, then we must also hold that our Founders, those "great men—high in literary acquirements, high in their sense of honor, and incapable of asserting principles inconsistent with those on which they were acting" were in fact profound hypocrites, as so many of them, Jefferson included, owned slaves. Since we would not want to disparage the reputation of the Founders, we must concede that the *Declaration* and Constitution were never intended to "embrace the negro race, which, by common consent, had been excluded from civilized Governments and the family of nations, and doomed to slavery."[25] In his dissenting opinion, Justice Curtis called these claims into question by pointing out that at the time of ratification of the Articles of Confederation, five states—New Hampshire, Massachusetts, New York, New Jersey, and North Carolina—had held that all free, native-born inhabitants, whether descended from African slaves or not, were citizens and, if possessed of the requisite qualifications, free to exercise the franchise of electors.[26]

Curtis might have concluded his argument at this point, declaring that "[t]his alone would, in my apprehension, be sufficient to decide the question."[27] But rather than conclude with the arguments from history and constitutional text, Curtis attempts another argument, one grounded in a peculiar fact upon which all parties had agreed, but from which none of his fellow Justices attempted to build an argument. The fact is this: that while residing in the Wisconsin Territory with Dr. Emerson, Mr. Scott "was married, with the consent of Dr. Emerson, to Harriet, named in the declaration as his wife, and that Eliza and Lizzie were the children of that marriage, the first named having been born on the Mississippi River, north of the line of Missouri, and the other having been born after their return to Missouri."[28] In light of these facts, the question of Mr. Scott's standing to sue for freedom in federal courts under diversity jurisdiction comes to be seen in a new light, as the Court must now determine whether any other state or country can, after the marriage in Wisconsin Territory, "refuse to recognize Mr. Scott as anything other than a free man suing for the liberty of himself, his wife, and the children of the marriage."[29] Following the course of international law, Curtis argues, a lawful marriage contract must be recognized as such by any foreign state or nation. By consenting to the marriage of his slave to another of his slaves while residing on free soil, Dr. Emerson had, in effect, manumitted his slave. Upon entering into the marriage contract with his spouse, certain rights and duties were bestowed upon the couple, and a change in status was effected, such that those who had once been the property of another were now granted the liberty to enter into a permanent and binding contract with one another. As Curtis notes, "it has been held by this court that a bequest of property by a master to his slave by necessary implication entitles the slave to his freedom, because only as a freeman could he take and hold the bequest."[30] By allowing Mr. Scott to enter into a marriage contract with Harriet while residing on free soil, Dr. Emerson allowed the despotic mode of association which would persist between himself and Mr. Scott upon their return from the territories to fall away, replaced by the new republican mode of spousal association formally recognized to exist between Dred and Harriet in their marriage contract. The despotic association of entirely distinguishable creatures, master and slave, was replaced by the association of equals, naturally distinguishable but complementary. Even if the law did not require that Dr. Emerson relinquish his dominion over his slave upon their return to Missouri, neither did it prohibit him from doing so. Nor would the law shy away from protecting the civil rights of spouses. Moreover, any attempt by the state of Missouri to impair the obligations of their marriage contract executed pursuant to laws governing the Territory would run afoul of the explicit prohibition of such laws in the Constitution's contract clause,[31] a clause which, at the time, was employed by the Court more than any other constitutional provision to invalidate state laws.

Thus far, then, the argument from marriage proceeds in this fashion: The slavery of Dred Scott ended when his master permitted him to marry Harriet on free soil. *It was marriage that made the slave free.*[32] It could also be argued that it was this act of marriage that introduced Scott into the citizenry of the United States. It is but one of the incidents of citizenship that citizens may contract with one another to marry. In so doing, the parties to the contract are imbued with certain civil rights and obligations belonging to that condition.[33] Once the marriage contract has been executed pursuant to state law, it is incumbent on all foreign governments—those of other states and nations—to acknowledge the new status of these citizens, and the rights and duties appertaining thereto, unless the marriage contract is proved to be fraudulent. The rights of the parties to the marriage contract are enforceable in courts of law, and any attempt on the part of a state to interfere with the operation of these contractual rights would violate the explicit prohibition of such laws by the Constitution's contract clause.

So as to prevent any confusion about these claims, Curtis summarizes his conclusions before moving on.[34] Reviewing these conclusions, we see that the argument from marriage plays a secondary or supporting role in Curtis' overall argument to establish the freedom of Scott. Curtis may very well have preferred the elegance of an approach to manumission which required all slaveholders residing in free territory to acknowledge such residence as an act of manumission, thereby vesting the primary responsibility for liberating slaves in the policymaking houses of Congress, with only a minimal role for the President and an even more constrained role for the courts. The decision of whether or not to establish freedom in the territories was fraught with political considerations—best to ensure that such decisions are made by the most numerous, deliberative and representative branch of the government. But if this is the case, why include the argument from marriage at all? While the argument that the Court should insist that the questions arising from such a case are best left to be resolved by the political branches is certainly compelling, this was not Curtis' solution. By laying out the argument from marriage, he demonstrated how the Court might also play a role in facilitating the manumission of slaves, working within the fact patterns of the cases coming before it to illustrate for the public the means of bridging the gap between despotic and constitutional rule within the household, and thereby gradually changing the character of the regime. Curtis is careful to clarify that the act of manumission in the present case is not an act of judicial will, but rather the consequence of the free choice of Dr. Emerson, who consented to the union. Moreover, Curtis insists that participation in the marital union is said to be one "which none but a free man can assume," chiefly because with it comes the lawful responsibility to nurture the fruit, the issue, which naturally follows from such a union. The law might establish paternity, but it would remain the obligation of the spouses to nurture and educate their children. The part to be played by the Court may be less apparent, but it is significant. By framing the marital relationship in terms of a contract between husband and wife, Curtis was placing the new mode of association between two former slaves and their master in terms that could be adequately comprehended under existing precedent. For "the law does not enable Dr. Emerson, or anyone claiming under him, to assert a title to the married persons as slaves, and thus destroy the obligation of contract and bastardize their issue and reduce them to slavery."[35] The condemnation of the judgment issuing from the Missouri Supreme Court in the case of *Scott v. Emerson*[36] follows logically from these formulations. Curtis rejects the decision of the majority in that case, quoting instead from the dissenting opinion of Chief Justice Gamble in that case:

> There is with me nothing in the law of slavery which distinguishes it from the law on any other subject, or allows any more accommodation to the temporary

> excitements which have gathered around it. . . . But, in the midst of all such excitement, it is proper that the judicial mind, calm and self-balanced, should adhere to principles established when there was no feeling to disturb the view of the legal questions upon which the rights of parties depend.[37]

It would seem that Curtis found in the dispassionate analysis of the Missouri Chief Justice something similar to the apolitical judicial temperament he strove to adopt when applying the fugitive slave laws while riding circuit in New England. Moreover, by quoting a dissenting Chief Justice to oppose the highly partisan and politicized formulations of Taney, we find in Curtis' dissent further evidence of his growing disenchantment with the temperament of his colleagues on the Court. When asked to defer to the judgment of the lower court on this question, Curtis insists that the issue of what laws of the United States were in operation in the Territory of Wisconsin belongs most properly, in the final analysis, to the U.S. Supreme Court, rather than to the supreme court of a slave state. When reviewing the status of congressional legislation over the Territories, Curtis, far from providing the substantive reading of the due process clause employed by Taney to rule the Missouri Compromise unconstitutional, traces the origin of congressional prohibition of slavery in the Territories back to the Northwest Ordinance of 1787, finding no constitutional obstacle to such oversight of territorial governance. Congress may prohibit slavery in the territories, and it is the proper role of the Court to correct the proceedings of any state tribunal refusing to give force to such a policy.

SUBSTANTIVE DUE PROCESS AND JUDICIAL REVIEW

Contemporary scholars of the Court do not spend much time thinking about what was happening on the Supreme Court when the *Dred Scott* opinion was handed down.[38] To the extent that the case is still covered in courses on constitutional law, it is often presented as one of the few clear instances when the Court was in the wrong, a prominent and convenient example of what one legal scholar has come to refer to as the anticanon.[39] Judges may have discretion, but they must remember to exercise it with great care. The power of judicial review is a perilous one, best used sparingly.[40] More recently, Gerald Rosenberg has added an empirical dimension to the argument, suggesting that the Court is far less capable of effecting permanent social change independent of the political branches than is commonly imagined.[41] The argument from marriage put forward by Justice Curtis in his *Dred Scott* dissent may serve as an important example to those now seeking to understand the significance of the Court's decision in *Obergefell.* With its decision, the Court sought to bring to an end the recent wave of state experiments with same sex marriage and pronounce the discovery of a new fundamental right.

Taken together with *Windsor*, we see a narrow majority of the Court employing a substantive interpretation of the due process clause to justify its exercise of judicial review, striking down recently enacted state and federal laws. In *Windsor*, the Court suggested that it would defer to the judgment of state lawmakers in future cases.[42] This approach had the advantage of building on the Court's recent revitalization of notions of federalism in a line of cases running from *U.S. v. Lopez* through *U.S. v. Morrison* and up to its recent ruling in *NFIB v. Sebelius*. In *Obergefell,* the same five Justices chose not to exercise the promised self-restraint, and with it the cautious approach to discovery of fundamental rights announced in *Washington v. Glucksberg,*[43] choosing rather to cast its weight behind what it deemed to be a new-formed societal consensus. While it remains to be seen whether or not the Court's reliance on a substantive interpretation of the due process clause in these recent cases is sufficient to put the political question to rest, history suggests that continued exercise of such a wide-ranging claim to authority on the part of the judiciary is likely to lead to difficulties, not the least of which are those identified by Cooley, Thayer, Bickel, and Rosenberg. Indeed, the dissenting opinions of Chief Justice Roberts, Justice Scalia, and Justice Alito in *Windsor* and *Obergefell* sound a chorus of these long-term institutional concerns. The lessons of *Dred Scott* must always lie before the Court.[44] Justice Curtis' effort to present the institutional arguments against the highly partisan excesses of his colleagues in that case, advocating in its place a more circumspect and dispassionate role for the judiciary as arbiter of the controversy and interpreter of law and precedent, may help to remind us of the important role played by dissent in the life of the law and, more broadly, American constitutionalism. Moreover, due consideration of the arguments presented by Curtis on that occasion reminds us that ours is not the first generation to find in marriage intimations of the truth about human liberty. Indeed, as we become aware of similar arguments put forward by members of the Court in every generation, whether from the authoritative position of a majority opinion or from the secondary vantage of a concurrence or dissent, the conclusion becomes inescapable that the marital relationship has always been, and will remain, an indispensable component of American liberty.

NOTES

1. Consider, for example, the following passage from Justice Scalia's dissenting opinion in *Planned Parenthood v. Casey*:

> There comes vividly to mind a portrait by Emanuel Leutze that hangs in the Harvard Law School: Roger Brooke Taney, painted in 1859, the 82d year of his life, the 24th of his Chief Justiceship, the second after his opinion in *Dred Scott.* He is all in black, sitting in a shadowed red armchair, left hand resting upon a pad of paper in his lap, right hand hanging limply, almost lifelessly, beside the inner arm

> of the chair. He sits facing the viewer, and staring straight out. There seems to be on his face, and in his deep set eyes, an expression of profound sadness and disillusionment. Perhaps he always looked that way, even when dwelling upon the happiest of thoughts. But those of us who know how the lustre of his great Chief Justiceship came to be eclipsed by *Dred Scott* cannot help believing that he had that case—its already apparent consequences for the Court, and its soon to be played out consequences for the Nation—burning on his mind. I expect that two years earlier he, too, had thought himself "call[ing] the contending sides of national controversy to end their national division by accepting a common mandate rooted in the Constitution." It is no more realistic for us in this case, than it was for him in that, to think that an issue of the sort they both involved—an issue involving life and death, freedom and subjugation—can be "speedily and finally settled" by the Supreme Court, as President James Buchanan in his inaugural address said the issue of slavery in the territories would be. . . . Quite to the contrary, by foreclosing all democratic outlet for the deep passions this issue arouses, by banishing the issue from the political forum that gives all participants, even the losers, the satisfaction of a fair hearing and an honest fight, by continuing the imposition of a rigid national rule instead of allowing for regional differences, the Court merely prolongs and intensifies the anguish.
>
> We should get out of this area, where we have no right to be, and where we do neither ourselves nor the country any good by remaining. (505 U.S. 833 at 1001–2)

2. John Rawls, *Political Liberalism* (New York: Columbia University Press, 1993), 235–40.

3. 5 U.S. 137 (1803) voided §13 of the Judiciary Act of 1789 as an unconstitutional extension of the Supreme Court's original jurisdiction, thereby establishing the principle that the Supreme Court may exercise judicial review of federal, as well as state, legislation.

4. 60 U.S. 393 (1857) ruled that U.S. citizenship under the Constitution of 1787 did not extend to persons of African descent, slave or free, and that Congress had exceeded its legislative power when it outlawed slavery in the territories north of 36'30" in the Missouri Compromise of 1820.

5. Melvin I. Urofsky, *Dissent and the Supreme Court: Its Role in the Court's History and the Nation's Constitutional Dialogue* (Cambridge, MA: Harvard University Press, 2015). See also Jamal Greene, "The Anticanon," *Harvard Law Review* 2 (December 2011): 379–475.

6. 301 U.S. 1 (1937) upheld provisions of the Wagner Act authorizing the National Labor Relations Board to prevent unfair labor practices in industry on the grounds that such practices could lead to strikes which would substantially affect the flow of interstate commerce. Taken together with the Court's ruling in *West Coast Hotel v. Parrish*, the ruling reflected a significant departure from the Court's recent rulings striking down key legislation in President Roosevelt's New Deal program, and likely persuaded Congress not to move forward with the President's efforts to "pack the Court" with new appointees. Justice McReynolds' dissent highlights "the departure from what we understand has been consistently ruled here," at 76.

7. 247 U.S. 251 (1918) It struck down, by a 5–4 vote, the Federal Child Labor Act of 1916, which prohibited the movement of goods produced by children under the age of 14, or by children between the ages of 14 and 16 working more than eight hours a day, across state lines. The Court found that the law was an attempt to regulate manufacture, not commerce, and as such exceeded Congress' legislative authority, encroaching on state police powers. Holmes' dissent was joined by Justice Brandeis and Clarke, the two most recent appointees to the Court, and presents an argument largely identical to that later employed by Chief Justice Stone in his unanimous opinion in *U.S. v Darby Lumber Co.* 312 U.S. 100 (1941) which overturned *Hammer*.

8. *Plessy v. Ferguson,* 163 U.S. 537 (1896) upheld a Louisiana statute "requiring railway companies carrying passengers in their coaches in that State, to provide equal, but separate, accommodations for the white and colored races." Justice Harlan's dissent from the Fuller Court's establishment of the "separate but equal" principle gave voice to what may now be one of the most commonly held American sentiments, that "our Constitution is color-blind, and

neither knows nor tolerates classes among citizens. In respect of civil rights, all citizens are equal before the law," at 559.

9. *Olmstead v United States,* 277 U.S. 438 (1928) allowed the use of evidence obtained through the use of wiretaps put in place without a warrant to secure conviction of a bootlegger on the grounds that the courts had never before required that law enforcement agents secure a warrant before obtaining evidence by means of eavesdropping. Justice Brandeis' dissent serves as the basis for the doctrine of a constitutional right to privacy today. Much like Sutherland's opinion for the Court in *Curtiss-Wright*, Brandeis' opinion served as a vehicle to introduce into *U.S. Reports* concepts developed long before he was appointed to the Court. Cf. Warren and Brandeis, "The Right to Privacy," 4 *Harvard Law Review* 193 (1890), and Sutherland, *Constitutional Power and World Affairs* (New York: Columbia University Press, 1918.

10. *United States v. Curtiss-Wright Export Corp.* 299 U.S. 304 (1936) elaborated upon general notions of sovereignty and ruling that the executive is imbued with inherent power to regulate foreign affairs, independent of any authorization from the text of the Constitution or congressional statute.

11. 274 U.S. 200 (1927) upheld a Virginia statute allowing superintendents of state mental institutions to order compulsory sterilization of those citizens, male and female, deemed 'mentally defective' and housed in state facilities, so long as the state followed the multi-step administrative appeals process established by the statute. Justice Holmes concluded his argument upholding the eugenics statute with the claim that "three generations of imbeciles are enough," at 207.) See also the essay by Lauren Hall, "Sterilization, Reproductive Rights and the Ninth Amendment," *infra.*

12. 570 U.S. _____ (2013) struck down Section 3 of the federal Defense of Marriage Act, which had amended the Dictionary Act so as to define the word "marriage" as a legal union between one man and one woman as husband and wife, and the word "spouse" as a person of the opposite sex who is a husband or a wife, on the grounds that the statute, colored as it is by animus or "a bare congressional desire to harm a politically unpopular group," and unsupported by any legitimate government purpose, constitutes a deprivation of the Court's substantive interpretation of the liberty of the person protected by the due process clause of the Fifth Amendment, at 20, 25–26.)

13. 576 U.S. _______ (2015) discovered a 14th Amendment requirement that states recognize citizens' fundamental right to same-sex marriage, and thereby striking down state marriage laws to the contrary as a violation of individual rights to due process of law and equal protection of the laws. This right is asserted to be "inherent in the concept of individual autonomy," (at 12) which the Court rightly expounds upon over time as rising "from a better informed understanding of how constitutional imperatives define a liberty that remains urgent in our own era" (at 19).

14. 198 U.S. 45 (1905) struck down a New York law regulating the working hours and conditions of bakers on the grounds that it violated the liberty of contract derived from the Court's substantive interpretation of the due process clause of the Fourteenth Amendment. The Court's ruling was ridiculed by Justice Holmes in a dissent which charged the majority with relying on principles derived from "an economic theory which a large part of the country does not entertain," going on to explain that "a Constitution is not intended to embody a particular economic theory, whether of paternalism and the organic relation of the citizen to the state or of laissez faire. It is made for people of fundamentally differing views," at 75–76.

15. Matthew Franck, "What Happened to the Due Process Clause in the *Dred Scott* Case? The Continuing Confusion over 'Substance' versus 'Process," *American Political Thought* 4 (2015) 120–48.

16. *Obergefell v. Hodges*, at 9–15.

17. Keith Whittington, "The Road Not Taken: *Dred Scott,* Judicial Authority and Political Questions," 63 *Journal of Politics* 365 (2001); Mark Graber, "Desperately Ducking Slavery: *Dred Scott* and Contemporary Constitutional Theory," 14 *Constitutional Commentary* 271 (1997) and *Dred Scott and the Problem of Constitutional Evil* (New York: Cambridge University Press, 2006).

18. Jedediah Purdy, "The Roberts Court v. America: How the Roberts Court is using the First Amendment to Craft a Radical, Free-Market Jurisprudence," 23 *Democracy: A Journal of*

Ideas 46 (2012). Cf. Anna Harvey, "Chapter 8: Misreading the Roberts Court," in *A Mere Machine: The Supreme Court, Congress and American Democracy* (New Haven: Yale University Press, 2013).

19. With the exception of a recently published biography (Stuart Streichler, *Justice Curtis in the Civil War Era: At the Crossroads of American Constitutionalism* [Charlottesville: University of Virginia Press, 2005]), Justice Curtis has received little attention from contemporary scholars, though he appears to have been highly regarded by the legal community throughout his career, and the literature indicates a number of prominent eulogies upon his death in 1874. The most helpful brief treatment of his judicial career is Richard E. Leach, "Benjamin Robbins Curtis: Judicial Misfit," 25 *The New England Quarterly* 507 (1952). The posthumously edited and published *Memoir of Benjamin Robbins Curtis, LL.D, with Some of His Professional and Miscellaneous Writings* (New York: Da Capo Press, 1879/1970) gathers some of Curtis' more interesting correspondence, including the exchange of letters with Taney in the wake of the *Dred Scott* decision, discussed below, which seems to have led to Curtis' decision to resign from the Court (I.209-242). The sketch that follows draws from a number of additional sources: William Gillette, "Benjamin Robbins Curtis" in Leon Friedman and Fred L. Israel, eds. *The Justices of the United States Supreme Court: 1789–1969,* vol II (New York: Chelsea House Publishers, 1979); Earl M. Maltz, "The Last Angry Man: Benjamin Robbins Curtis and the *Dred Scott* Case" 82 *Chicago-Kent Law Review* 265 (2007); Lucas E. Morel, "The Dred Scott Dissents: McLean, Curtis, Lincoln, and the Public Mind" 32 *Journal of Supreme Court History* 133 (2007); Dean Grodzins, "'Slave Law' versus 'Lynch Law' in Boston: Benjamin Robbins Curtis, Theodore Parker, and the Fugitive Slave Crisis 1850–1855." 12 *Massachusetts Historical Review* 1 (2010); Don E. Fehrenbacher, *The Dred Scott Case: Its Significance in American Law and Politics* (New York: Oxford University Press, 1978); Carl Brent Swisher, *Roger B. Taney* (Hamden, CT: Archon Books, 1961) and *The Taney Period,* vol. 5 of the *Oliver Wendell Holmes Devise* (New York: Cambridge University Press, 1974/2010); and Charles Warren, *A History of the American Bar* (Boston: Little, Brown & Co., 1911) and *The Supreme Court in United States History,* vol. 2 (Boston: Little, Brown & Co., 1923).

20. 53 U.S. 299 (1851). Upholding a Pennsylvania statute which required foreign vessels entering the port of Philadelphia to either employ a local pilot for purposes of navigating the port, or pay a fine equal to half the pilotage fee into a pension fund for the widows and orphans of local pilots, on the grounds that a congressional statute of 1789 left to the states the power to regulate pilotage in local ports until such time as Congress might adopt a more comprehensive regulatory scheme. In so ruling, Justice Curtis helped to resolve a question the Court had struggled to put to rest since Chief Justice Marshall's broad construction of Congressional power to regulate interstate commerce in *Gibbons v. Ogden* 22 U.S. 1 (1824), namely, whether or not states possessed power to regulate interstate commerce in the absence of a federal regulatory scheme.

21. Streichler, *Curtis in the Civil War Era* 145–50.

22. Though only the general outlines of the dispute are presented here, the pertinent correspondence makes for interesting reading (Curtis, *Memoir* I.192–263, esp. 212–29).

23. Samuel Tyler, *Memoir of Roger Brooke Taney.* (New York: Da Capo Press, 1872/1970). 515–16.

24. Morel, *Dred Scott Dissents* 134, 141; Jaffa, *Crisis* 276-303 and Appendix II; Streichler, *Curtis in the Civil War Era,* 120; Curtis, *Memoir* 1879/1970, I.354–55.

25. Ibid., at 410.

26. Ibid., at 572–73.

27. Ibid., at 599.

28. Ibid., at 599.

29. Ibid., at 599.

30. Ibid., at 600, citing *Legrand v. Darnall,* 27 U.S. 664 (1829). Upholding the provisions of the will of a Maryland slaveholder, Bennett Darnall, posthumously manumitting and bequeathing land to his son, Nicholas Darnall, whose mother had also been a slave of Bennett. The Court grounded its ruling that "a devise of property real or personal by a master to his slave entitles the slave to his freedom by necessary implication" in a Maryland case, *Hale v. Mullin,* which had first announced the rule.

31. "No State shall . . . pass any Bill of Attainder, ex post facto Law, or Law impairing the Obligation of Contracts" (Article I, Section 10, Clause 1).

32. It lies beyond the scope of the present work to develop in detail the many points of correspondence between an Aristotelian conception of political science and the words and deeds of Justice Curtis. But one might see in Curtis' argument from marriage a reminder of two of the approaches to development of such a science as laid out by Aristotle in Books I and III of the *Politics*. Consider first the treatment of the forms of association which precede the city: master and slave, parent and child, husband and wife (1259a35–1260b25). In each of these forms of association we find the principle of a different regime or mode of political rule. Drawing a further distinction between the end for which this authority is exercised—for the good of the ruler or the good of the ruled, we arrive at the initial classification of six regime types: monarchy/tyranny, aristocracy/oligarchy, constitutional or republican (politeia)/democratic (1279a23–1279b10). These initial reflections are further developed through consideration of the different senses in which citizenship might be understood, in which human beings might be understood as parts of a greater whole (1274b30–1279a22). Taken together, we find that the principal concerns of Books I and III of Aristotle's Politics are very much a part of Curtis' manner of addressing the question presented to the Court and the regime by the facts of Dred Scott's case. That Curtis alone of his colleagues emphasizes the significance of a change in the mode of association between two individuals as a means of illustrating the path toward a change in the regime's understanding of citizenship may suggest to some readers the merits of a more careful study of Curtis' words and deeds.

33. 60 U.S. 393, at 600.

34. First. The rules of international law respecting the emancipation of slaves, by the rightful operation of the laws of another State or country upon the status of the slave, while resident in such foreign State or country, are part of the common law of Missouri, and have not been abrogated by any statute law of that State. Second. The laws of the United States, constitutionally enacted, which operated directly on and changed the status of a slave coming into the Territory of Wisconsin with his master, who went thither to reside for an indefinite length of time, in the performance of his duties as an officer of the United States, had a rightful operation on the status of the slave, and it is in conformity with the rules of international law that this change of status should be recognised everywhere.

Third. The laws of the United States, in operation in the Territory of Wisconsin at the time of the plaintiff's residence there, did act directly on the status of the plaintiff, and change his status to that of a free man.

Fourth. The plaintiff and his wife were capable of contracting, and, with the consent of Dr. Emerson, did contract a marriage in that Territory, valid under its laws, and the validity of this marriage cannot be questioned in Missouri, save by showing that it was in fraud of the laws of that State or of some right derived from them, which cannot be shown in this case, because the master consented to it.

Fifth. That the consent of the master that his slave, residing in a country which does not tolerate slavery, may enter into a lawful contract of marriage, attended with the civil rights and duties which belong to that condition, is an effectual act of emancipation. And the law does not enable Dr. Emerson, or anyone claiming under him, to assert a title to the married persons as slaves, and thus destroy the obligation of the contract of marriage and bastardize their issue and reduce them to slavery. 60 U.S. 393, at 601.

35. 60 U.S. 393, at 601.

36. 15 Missouri Reports 576.

37. 60 U.S. 393, at 602.

38. One prominent exception is Mark Graber's *Dred Scott and the Problem of Constitutional Evil*, New York: Cambridge University Press, 2006.

39. Greene, "The Anticanon."

40. Cf. Thomas Cooley, *A Treatise on the Constitutional Limitations Which Rest Upon the Legislative Power of the States of the American Union* (New York: Da Capo Press, 1868/1972); James Bradley Thayer, "The Origin and Scope of the American Doctrine of Constitutional Law," 7 *Harvard Law Review* 129 (1893) and Alexander Bickel, *The Least Dangerous Branch: The Supreme Court at the Bar of Politics* (New Haven: Yale University Press, 1962). For

Cooley, the power of judicial review should be applied only in instances of clear violation of a constitutional provision. "The interference of the judiciary with legislative Acts, if frequent or on dubious grounds, might occasion so great a jealousy of this power and so general a prejudice against it as to lead to measures ending in the total overthrow of the independence of the judges, and so of the best preservative of the constitution. The validity of the law ought not then to be questioned unless it is so obviously repugnant to the constitution that when pointed out by the judges, all men of sense and reflection in the community may perceive the repugnancy. By such a cautious exercise of this judicial check, no jealousy of it will be excited and the public confidence in it will be promoted and its salutary effects be justly and fully appreciated" (168 and, more generally, 159–88). Thayer adds to this rule the corollary that "if what I have been saying is true, the safe and permanent road towards reform is that of impressing upon our people a far stronger sense than they have of the great range of possible harm and evil that our system leaves open, and must leave open, to the legislatures, and of the clear limits of judicial power; so that responsibility may be brought sharply home where it belongs . . . Under no system can the power of courts go far to save the people from ruin; our chief protection lies elsewhere. If this be true, it is of the greatest public importance to put the matter in its true light." Bickel, seeking to cast a veil (Cf. Edmund Burke, *Reflections on the Revolution in France* (Indianapolis: Hackett, 1987) 17) over the Court's bold exercise of judicial review in the desegregation cases, emphasizes the importance of what he terms the "passive virtues" of the Court: "The Court wields a threefold power. It may strike down legislation as inconsistent with principle. It may validate . . . legislation as consistent with principle. *Or it may do neither.* It may do neither, and therein lies the secret of its ability to maintain itself in the tension between principle and expediency." (69, emphasis in original).

41. Gerald N. Rosenberg, *The Hollow Hope: Can Courts Bring About Social Change?* (Chicago: University of Chicago Press, 1991). Rosenberg hedges these claims a bit, however, noting that "on an intuitive level, opposition from political elites is not conducive to court effectiveness. On the other hand, judicial isolation from many pressures allows courts to act when other institutions wish to but cannot. Surely it is naïve to expect courts to be able to solve political and economic problems that the other branches cannot. But it appears equally short-sighted to deny that since mid-century courts have played an important role in producing significant social reform" (30).

42. 570 U.S. ____ (2013) (slip op. 17-19) and (C. J. Roberts, dissenting, 3-4).

43. 521 U.S. 702, 720 (1997).

44. Graber, *Dred Scott,* 85–89.

Chapter Six

Back to the Future

Reynolds *Revisited and the Structure of the American Family*

Martha Rice Martini

> *"Abram's wife, Sarai, had borne him no children. She had, however, an Egyptian maidservant named Hagar. Sarai said to Abram: 'The Lord has kept me from bearing children. Have intercourse, then, with my maid; perhaps I shall have sons through her." Abram heeded Sarai's request." Gen. 16:1–2*

This chapter explores some potential consequences of the recent Supreme Court decision on same-sex marriage, *Obergefell v. Hodges* (2015). In particular, it takes up the question implied during oral argument by Justice Alito, "Why two?"[1] As Chief Justice Roberts notes in his later dissent, the majority offers no reason why the two-person element of the definition of marriage should be preserved once the man-woman element is jettisoned.[2] Since the union of one man and one woman is the simplest reproductive association, accounting for the dyad at the heart of traditional marriage, if marriage is no longer understood as gender-specific, why should it be understood as number-specific?[3]

This chapter will take up four cases: *Reynolds v. United States* (1878), *Employment Division, Oregon Department of Human Resources v. Smith* (1990), *Obergefell v. Hodges*, and *Brown v. Buhman* (2013), a U.S. District Court case, with appeal pending.

Its main focus is plural marriage in a religious context, indeed, as plural marriage came to light in *Reynolds* and continues in *Brown*. Therefore, these cases explore not only the expanding liberty interest under the Due Process Clause of the Fourteenth Amendment, evident in *Obergefell* and its antecedents, but also the Free Exercise Clause of the First Amendment. However, the conclusion and, in particular, the reasoning supporting that conclusion insofar as it derives from the Due Process Clause, appear applicable also to plural marriage outside a religious context, including various polyamorous associations.

REYNOLDS (1878)

George Reynolds, a resident of the Territory of Utah, was convicted of bigamy under a federal statute governing the Territories. Reynolds proved to the Court's satisfaction that at the time of his second marriage, he was a member of the Church of Jesus Christ of Latter Day Saints, and a believer in its doctrines, which included the duty of male members, circumstances permitting, to take more than one wife. Upon this proof, he asked the trial court to instruct the jury that if they found from the evidence that he was married a second time, having a first wife living, because of what he believed to be a religious duty, then their verdict must be "not guilty." Instead, the court instructed the jury that if they found from the evidence that Reynolds was married a second time, having a first wife living, the belief that he was not committing a crime did not excuse him from conviction. "Upon this charge and refusal to charge the question was raised, whether religious belief can be accepted as a justification of an overt act made criminal by the law of the land."[4]

The Court cites the First Amendment and the express charge against legislation "prohibiting the free exercise of religion." Noting that "religion" is not defined in the Constitution, the Court turns to "the history of the times in the midst of which the provision was adopted." After a learned inquiry touching the works of Madison and Jefferson, it concludes that while Congress has no legislative power over mere opinion, it was left free to reach actions "in violation of social duties or subversive of good order."[5]

Turning to the matter of plural marriage, the Court notes that it "has always been odious among the northern and western nations of Europe, and, until the establishment of the Mormon Church, was almost exclusively a feature of the life of Asiatic and African people." Moreover, the Court continues, a second marriage was always void at common law and, from the earliest history of England, was treated as an offense against society. "In the face of all this evidence," the Court concludes, "it is impossible to believe that the constitutional guaranty of religious freedom was intended to prohibit legislation in respect to this most important feature of social life."[6]

> Marriage, which from its very nature a sacred obligation, is nevertheless, in most civilized nations a civil contract, and usually regulated by law. Upon it society may be said to be built and out of its fruits spring social relations and

> social obligations and duties, with which government is necessarily required to deal.[7]

The only question remaining is whether those who make plural marriage a part of their religion are exempt from the operation of the statute. "Laws are made for the government of actions, and while they cannot interfere with mere religious belief and opinions, they may with practices." The Court notes laws against the religious practices of human sacrifice and the self-immolation of widows. So here. "Can a man excuse his practice to the contrary because of his religious belief? To permit this would be to make the professed doctrines of religious belief superior to the law of the land, and in effect to permit every citizen to become a law unto himself."[8]

Accordingly, the Court affirms Reynolds' conviction.

SMITH (1990)

Alfred Smith and Galen Black were fired from their jobs with an Oregon drug treatment clinic because they ingested peyote, for sacramental purposes, at their Native American Church. Peyote was a controlled substance under Oregon law, with no exemption for the sacramental use of the drug. When Smith and Black later applied for unemployment compensation, they were denied benefits. In a court action contesting that denial, they argued that their religious motivation for using peyote placed them beyond the reach of the criminal law.

While the Court agrees that the "exercise of religion" may include not only what is believed but what is done in service of what is believed, it concludes, quoting *Reynolds*, that it has never held that an individual's religious beliefs excuse him from compliance with an otherwise valid law prohibiting conduct that the government is free to regulate: "Can a man excuse his practices to the contrary because of his religious beliefs? To permit this would be to make the professed doctrine of religious belief superior to the law of the land, and in effect to permit every citizen to become a law unto himself."[9]

The Court notes that the only cases where it has held that the First Amendment bars application of a neutral, generally applicable law (as distinguished from a law specifically targeting a particular religion or religious practice) to religiously motivated action have involved not only the Free Exercise Clause, but the Free Exercise Clause in combination with other constitutional guarantees, such as freedom of speech or of the press. Because the case at bar does not present such a hybrid situation, "the rule to which we have adhered ever since *Reynolds* plainly controls."[10]

Accordingly, the Court affirms the denial of unemployment benefits.[11]

OBERGEFELL (2015)

James Obergefell and several others, members or former members of same-sex couples, brought suit in several states (Michigan, Ohio, Kentucky, Tennessee) asserting a constitutional right to same-sex marriage. Those suits were later consolidated and heard in aggregate at the Supreme Court.

The Court begins by invoking the Due Process Clause of the Fourteenth Amendment, which protects not only rights enumerated in the Bill of Rights, but also "certain personal choices central to individual dignity and autonomy."[12]

According to the Court, identifying these fundamental rights is a judicial duty that cannot be reduced to any formula, requiring "reasoned judgment." History and tradition may guide the inquiry but do not set its boundaries: "If rights were defined by who exercised them in the past, then received practices could serve as their own continued justification and new groups could not invoke rights once denied."[13]

Addressing this self-imposed duty, the Court identifies a fundamental right to marriage, citing *Loving v. Virginia* (1967), and other cases, in support. Noting that *Baker v. Nelson* (1972) held that exclusion of same-sex couples from marriage did not present a "substantial federal question," they now overrule that case, adducing "other, more instructive precedents."[14]

The Court cites four "principles and traditions" culled from their analysis. First, the right to marry is fundamental because personal choice regarding marriage is essential to individual autonomy. "There is dignity in the bond between two men or two women who seek to marry and in their autonomy to make such profound choices." Second, the right to marry is fundamental because it supports a unique, committed two-person union. "When sexuality finds overt expression in intimate conduct with another person, the conduct can be but one element in a personal bond that is more enduring." Third, the right to marry is fundamental because it safeguards children and families. "Without the recognition, stability, and predictability marriage offers, [the children of same-sex couples] suffer the stigma of knowing their families are somehow lesser." And fourth, the right to marry is fundamental because marriage is key to our social order. Couples excluded from marriage are consigned to a social instability that demeans them, teaching them that they're unequal in important respects.[15]

The Court carefully distinguishes *Washington v. Glucksberg* (1997), where several physicians and their patients claimed a fundamental right under Due Process to physician-assisted suicide. While the *Glucksberg* Court required "a careful description" of any fundamental right asserted, with specific reference to historical grounding, that approach is "inconsistent" with the Court's approach to fundamental rights regarding marriage. The Court concludes that the fundamental right at issue here is not the circumscribed right of same-sex marriage but "the right to marry in its comprehensive sense."[16]

After a passing nod to the Equal Protection Clause of the Fourteenth Amendment, said to be complicit with the Due Process Clause in supporting the right at issue, the Court concludes. "*Baker v. Nelson* must be and now is overruled and the State laws challenged by Petitioners in these cases are now held invalid to the extent they exclude same-sex couples from civil marriage on the same terms and conditions as opposite-sex couples."[17] In closing, the Court adds: "It would misunderstand these men and women to say they disrespect the idea of marriage. Their plea is that they do respect it, respect it so deeply that they seek to find its fulfillment for themselves. . . . The Constitution grants them that right."[18]

BROWN (2013)

Kody Brown, his legal wife, and three other women were charged under the Utah bigamy statute, which reads, "A person is guilty of bigamy when, knowing he has a husband or wife or knowing the other person has a husband or wife, the person purports to marry another person or cohabits with another person." Brown and the others, famous for the television show, "Sister Wives," are members of the Apostolic United Brethren Church, derived of early Mormonism, which teaches plural marriage as a core religious practice. The Browns moved for dismissal of all charges in a motion for summary judgment, arguing that the statute is unconstitutional.[19]

In an exhaustive and freewheeling opinion, larded with historical referents, the District Court begins by citing *Reynolds*. It would be an easy enough matter, the Court says, to find against the Browns, defaulting simply to *Reynolds*. But this it does not do. Instead, the Court divides the statute into two "prongs," the first treating of marriage understood as legally recognized marriage, and the second treating of religious cohabitation.[20]

The Marriage Prong

With respect to the first prong, the Browns make no claim to having entered into legal unions by virtue of their religious cohabitation. Instead, they claim to have entered into personal, religious relationships that they knew would not be legally recognized as marriage, even though they use marital terms to describe those relationships. The Browns assert a "fundamental liberty interest" under the Due Process Clause in choosing to cohabit and maintain plural romantic attachments, even if those attachments are characterized by some as plural marriage.[21]

The Court assumes that there is no fundamental right to plural marriage, understood as legal marriage to more than one person at a time, because

Glucksberg, for example, requires a person asserting such a right to "carefully describe" the right, and show how that right as described fits within the Constitution's notion of ordered liberty. Since plural marriage has never been part of our constitutional order, the Court concludes that any asserted right to plural marriage must fail under *Glucksberg*. Therefore, the Court finds the first prong of the statute constitutional under the Due Process Clause.[22]

Turning to the Free Exercise Clause, the Court says that the *Reynolds* Court was infected by the "entrenched nature of an orientalist mindset among ruling elites during the time period when *Reynolds* was decided." According to the Court, that mindset presumed the racial inferiority of Middle Eastern, African, and Asian cultures. Indeed, the Court asserts that the federal government targeted Mormon polygamy for elimination at a time when "the good order and morals of society served as an acceptable basis" for legislative enactment.[23]

After a lengthy excursus on relations between the United States and the early Mormon Church, the Court concludes that "[i]t would be ludicrous to suggest that the federal legislation at issue in [Reynolds] did not specifically target the LDS Church and its practice of polygamy." *If,* the Court says, it had been sufficiently established that the statute here were an extension of that earlier legislation, the Court would likely have found that the marriage prong of the statute was not a neutral law of general applicability under *Smith*, and so, applying heightened scrutiny, would have found that prong unconstitutional. But since this was *not* sufficiently established, the Court defers to *Reynolds,* finding the first prong of the statute constitutional under the Free Exercise Clause.[24]

Religious Cohabitation Prong

With respect to the second prong, the Court takes up a three-part analysis, reviewing each argument in turn: (1) Substantive Due Process under the Fourteenth Amendment; (2) the Free Exercise Clause of the First Amendment assuming the statute is *not* operationally neutral and of general applicability; and (3) the Free Exercise Clause of the First Amendment assuming the statute *is* operationally neutral and of general applicability.

1. Substantive Due Process under the Fourteenth Ammendment

The cohabitation prong of the statute reads: "A person is guilty of bigamy when, knowing he has a husband or wife or knowing the other person has a husband or wife, the person . . . cohabits with another person." The Browns assert "a fundamental liberty interest" under the Due Process Clause in choosing to cohabit and maintain plural romantic attachments. The Court agrees that the liberty interest described in *Lawrence v. Texas* (2003) is broad enough to encompass cohabitation under the statute: "Liberty presumes an autonomy of self that includes freedom of thought, belief, expression, and certain intimate conduct." *Lawrence*, in brief, protects consensual adult sexual activity from government interference absent evidence of injury or coercion. Because the cohabitation prong does not survive rational basis review under *Lawrence*, it must be stricken as a violation of substantive Due Process.[25]

2. *The Free Exercise Clause of the First Amendment: Type A Cases*

Subjecting the statute to analysis under the Free Exercise Clause, the Court asks whether, as in *Smith*, the cohabitation prong is operationally neutral and of general applicability, answering that it is not; noting that "few, if any [cohabitations] are prosecuted other than [religious cohabitations]." Likening this case to *Church of Lukumi Babalu Aye, Inc. v. City of Hialeah* (1993), where the Court found that although city ordinances against animal sacrifice were indeed facially neutral in their "artful" drafting, they nonetheless unconstitutionally targeted specifically the practice of the Santeria religion. So here. Notwithstanding its "artful" drafting, the statute unconstitutionally targets specifically the practice of the United Brethren, and similar groups. Accordingly, the statute must be justified by a compelling state interest and narrowly tailored to advance that interest.[26]

According to the Court, criminalizing religious cohabitation but not adulterous cohabitation (and, with respect to religious cohabitation, selectively prosecuting persons entering into a religious union with a woman under eighteen or those who have, as here, openly discussed their cohabitation with the media) demonstrates that the cohabitation prong, whatever its interest, is not narrowly tailored to advance that interest. Therefore, assuming the statute was *not* operationally neutral and of general applicability, the second prong of the statute must fail under the Free Exercise Clause.[27]

3. *The Free Exercise Clause of the First Amendment: Type B Cases*

But even if the statute *were* operationally neutral and of general applicability, the Court says that it could not survive a Free Exercise challenge under *Smith*. According to *Smith* and its progeny, even a neutral law of general applicability that touches religious practice may be found eligible for a court-ordered exemption if that practice is also in violation of other fundamental rights. Though *Smith*'s "hybrid rights" exception requires at least a "colorable showing" of infringement of some other fundamental right (that is, a fair probability of success on the merits), the Court here finds that the Browns make that showing on each of their companion constitutional claims, that is, Freedom of Association, Substantive Due Process, Equal Protection, and Free Speech; thus requiring heightened scrutiny. Therefore, even assuming that the statute *were* operationally neutral and of general applicability, the second prong of the statute must fail under the Free Exercise Clause.[28]

Accordingly, the Court grants *in part* the Browns' motion for summary judgment, ruling the cohabitation prong of the statute unconstitutional on several grounds; but, understanding "marry" on the marriage prong to mean "legally marry," ruling the marriage prong constitutional under *Reynolds*.[29]

CONCLUSION: REYNOLDS REVISITED

Surely the *Brown* Court is correct that laws against plural marriage understood as religious cohabitation cannot survive constitutional challenge after *Lawrence*, which protects the sexual privacy of consenting adults from meddling majorities. Analysis under *Smith* and its hybrid exception only serves to confirm that result. Cohabiting religious persons such as the Browns can adduce on their behalf not only the Free Exercise Clause, but also the liberty interest under substantive Due Process, and other rights, such as the right to free association.

The *Brown* Court concluded with respect to the first prong of the statute—the marriage prong—that if sufficient evidence had been presented demonstrating that the statute specifically targeted religions like the United Brethren, it would have failed under *Smith* even without recourse to "hybrid" analysis, that is, an exemption would have been required under the law. But that demonstration was never made.

With respect to analysis of the first prong under substantive Due Process, the Court could not identify any fundamental right that would survive a *Glucksberg* challenge, requiring, at a minimum, that the proposed right be "carefully described" and historically embedded in our constitutional order.

The *Brown* opinion, now under review, was written without benefit of *Obergefell.* After *Obergefell,* which waved it aside, *Glucksberg* is no longer an issue. The *Obergefell* decision rests on a right to marry simply, a comprehensive right, broad enough to encompass the marriage of persons of the same sex. If plural marriage is a stranger to *our* constitutional order, as *Reynolds* argued, the marriage of persons of the same sex was a stranger not only to our constitutional order but to *every* constitutional order until the last twenty years.

Chief Justice Roberts' dissent in *Obergefell* is worth pondering. He states that the majority randomly inserts the adjective "two" throughout the opinion, expressly noting how much of the majority's reasoning would apply with equal force to a claim for a fundamental right to plural marriage.

> If "[t]here is dignity in the bond between two men or two women who seek to marry and in their autonomy to make such profound choices," why would there be any less dignity in the bond between three people who, in exercising

> their autonomy, seek to make the profound choice to marry? If a same-sex couple has the constitutional right to marry because their children would otherwise "suffer the stigma of knowing their families are somehow lesser," why wouldn't the same reasoning apply to a family of three or more persons raising children? If not having the opportunity to marry "serves to disrespect and subordinate" gay and lesbian couples, why wouldn't the same "imposition of this disability" serve to disrespect and subordinate people who find fulfillment in polyamorous relationships?[30]

Why indeed?

The *Obergefell* Court stated that history and tradition do not set the boundaries when determining fundamental rights: "If rights were defined by who exercised them in the past, then received practices would serve as their own continued justification and new groups could not invoke rights once denied." Just as *Baker v. Nelson* was set aside by the *Obergefell* Court because it excluded same-sex couples from marriage, so *Reynolds* may be set aside by some future court in the name of the fundamental right to marry: "[*Reynolds v. United States*] must be and now is overturned, and the State laws challenged by Petitioners in these cases are now held invalid to the extent that they exclude [plural unions] from civil marriage on the same terms and conditions as [couples]."

As for George Reynolds, Kody Brown, and others in plural unions seeking to exercise the fundamental right to marry: "It would misunderstand these men and women to say they disrespect the idea of marriage. Their plea is that they do respect it, respect it so deeply that they seek to find its fulfillment for themselves."

How, after *Obergefell*, does the Constitution not grant them that right?

NOTES

1. Transcript of Oral Argument: *Obergefell v. Hodges,* at 17.
2. *Obergefell* v. *Hodges*, 135 S.Ct. 2584, (2015).
3. Robert P. George, "Is Polyamory Next?" *The American Interest*, August 25, 2015.
4. *Reynolds v. U.S.*, 98 U.S. 145, 162 (1878).
5. Ibid., at 164.
6. Ibid., at 165.
7. Ibid.
8. Ibid., at 166–67.
9. *Employment Division, Oregon Department of Human Resources v. Smith*, 494 U.S. 872, 879 (1990).
10. Ibid. at 882.
11. Congress responded to *Smith* by passing the Religious Freedom Restoration Act (1993), articulating what it understood to be the proper standard of review in Free Exercise Cases: Government shall not substantially burden a person's exercise of religion even if the burden results from a generally applicable law, unless that law serves a compelling state interest, and is narrowly tailored to advance that interest. That is, even a neutral law of general applicability that substantially burdens the religious practice of a defendant, must serve a compelling state interest and be narrowly tailored to advance that interest, *or* an exemption from that law must

be granted. RFRA was later ruled unconstitutional as applied to the states. *City of Boerne v. Flores* 521 U.S. 507 (1997).

12. *Obergefell* v. *Hodges*, at 2597. The Due Process Clause of the Fourteenth Amendment reads: "No State shall . . . deprive any person of life, liberty, or property, without due process of law[.]" The Court has interpreted this clause to include a "substantive" element protecting certain liberty interests against state deprivation no matter what process is provided.

13. Ibid., at 2598 & 2602.

14. Ibid., at 2598.

15. Ibid., at 2599–2602.

16. Ibid., at 2602.

17. Ibid., at 2602–2605.

18. Ibid., at 2608.

19. *Brown v. Buhman*, 947 F.Supp.2nd 1170 (2013), at 1176 & 1181.

20. Ibid., at 1181.

21. Utah's rich history conflating legal unions and religious unions has led to confusion of the two in law and lay parlance. "Until 1898, the doctrine of common law marriage could render a religious cohabitation a purported legal union[.]" Id. at 1206.

22. Ibid., at 1195.

23. Ibid., at 1184–1185.

24. Ibid., at 1190.

25. Ibid., at 1202.

26. Ibid., at 1217.

27. Ibid., at 1221.

28. Ibid., at 1222.

29. Ibid., at 1234.

30. *Obergefell* v. *Hodges*, at 2621–2622.

Chapter Seven

Sterilization, Reproductive Rights, and the Ninth Amendment

Lauren K. Hall

The debate over the status of Fourteenth Amendment jurisprudence is often framed in ideological terms, with conservatives advocating judicial restraint and an emphasis on procedural due process and liberals advocating for a substantive understanding of due process protections.[1] While there are notable exceptions on both sides, the general ideological lines are fairly stable. The case of *Buck v. Bell* (1927) challenges these ideological lines, with conservatives and progressives alike eschewing the substantive due process protections against state forcible sterilization laws, instead arguing for a bare and inhumane procedural due process that left seventy-thousand Americans barren and violated.[2] *Buck v. Bell* affirms the constitutionality of a state law granting power to sterilize individuals held in institutions. Carrie Buck was a young woman institutionalized for "feeble-mindedness" after she became pregnant out of wedlock. Holmes' decision in the case, that the state has the power to sterilize individuals without their consent, rests on the argument that Carrie Buck's due process rights consisted only in the bare institutional procedure by which she was evaluated and ultimately selected for sterilization. Holmes gives a ringing endorsement to the eugenics movement in his final sentence: "three generations of imbeciles are enough."

Apart from reducing due process protections to almost any form of procedure for taking away individual rights, the case also reflects the ideologically complex roots of reproductive rights in American jurisprudence. The decision to sterilize Carrie Buck relied on two assumptions: first, that reproduction, and family life broadly, rather than being sheltered in an intimate and private sphere, is in fact a public decision that can and should be controlled by the political process; second, that the Constitution, because it is silent on "bodily integrity" or privacy as such, offers no protection against the intrusion of the state into not only reproductive decisions, but into the very bodies of its citizens.[3] The assumption regarding the political nature of decisions about reproduction draws support from Progressive attitudes towards the family, seen most clearly during the eugenics era. The assumption regarding the propriety of judicial restraint is, on the other hand, most commonly attributed to political conservatives. In what follows, I argue that the ideological roots of eugenics in progressivism combined with the more conservative doctrine of judicial restraint led the Court to reject its duty as a protector of individual rights. I lay out a potential solution to this problem, one that does not rely on our acceptance of a simplistic substantive due process argument, but instead argues that the Constitution provides ample content for substantive due process claims through the Ninth Amendment, an almost wholly neglected area of legal thought.

A BRIEF HISTORY OF EUGENICS

The eugenics movement was an ideologically diverse movement in the late 1800s founded on the belief in the potential for a scientific management of society.[4] Excited about Darwin's recent discoveries about evolution, political activists like Margaret Sanger, scientists like Harry Laughlin, and politicians like Teddy Roosevelt believed that the solution to everything from poverty to crime lay in our genes and, for the first time, society could control those genes through the scientific control of reproduction.[5] The goals were laudable: to use science to eradicate the pain of poverty and the costs of criminal behavior. The eugenics movement did what democracies do so well: taking new scientific and technological ideas and applying them to modern social problems. Francis Galton described the goals of eugenics as twofold, to lower the birth rate of the "unfit" and to encourage the marriage and reproduction of "fit" individuals.[6] The policy means used ranged from controlling immigration and employment through minimum wage laws to access to contraception. While both conservative and progressive thinkers took part, many of contemporary progressives' favorite causes have their roots in eugenics policies aimed at eliminating the unfit from the population.[7]

One of the primary tools of "negative" eugenics was institutionalization of the unfit to prevent them from reproducing. As the practice spread, its costs grew, raising concerns that long-term institutionalization of large populations would put a strain on state coffers. This concern led to increasing support for technologies to prevent reproduction, including both birth control and sterilization. Feminists and eugenicists banded together to provide birth control for lower-class women. While feminists tended to support individual-level birth control, eugenicists preferred birth control that could be easily controlled in institutional settings and that could be made permanent, allowing the release of the "feeble-minded" back into society without danger of reproducing their kind. Sterilization, whether forced or voluntary, was an elegant solution to the problem of how to control the reproduction of institutionalized populations permanently.

The eugenics movement aligned itself well with the Progressive movement as a whole, since both shared a faith in science as an important tool for implementing government policies to carry out broad social and political change.[8] This combination of trust in scientific knowledge with a belief that the social is more important than the individual laid the foundation for the belief that the best way to achieve particular social ends is to use the power of social coercion over individuals guided by administrators and statisticians. Applying this technique to reproduction led to predictable results.

All told, the United States forcibly sterilized around 70,000 people in the twentieth century. Most of these procedures were performed in California.[9] Connecticut's forcible sterilization law was so popular that the Nazis used it as a template for their own sterilization of the Jews a few years later. The last forced sterilization under eugenics laws occurred in Oregon in 1981, but as late as 2010, the state of California admitted to sterilizing female inmates without their informed consent.[10] State and institutional control over reproduction was seen as commonsensical and laudable by diverse groups, and the population as a whole—at least in the first half of the twentieth century—supported these measures.

Despite such popularity, members of the elite were concerned about the constitutionality of large-scale eugenics policies. State control over individual reproduction, particularly forcible sterilization, seemed so clearly a violation of individual liberty that many states were afraid to instantiate large-scale eugenics policies.[11] The Court's opinion in *Buck v. Bell* (1927), written by the great Justice Oliver Wendell Holmes, Jr., laid these fears to rest, for a time. But today that ruling is often ridiculed for its failure to protect any kind of reproductive rights, instead arguing that "it is better for all the world if, instead of waiting to execute degenerate offspring for crime or to let them starve for their imbecility, society can prevent those who are manifestly unfit from continuing their kind." [12]

BUCK, SKINNER, AND FORCIBLE STERILIZATION

What is so surprising to a student of limited government is that the Constitution afforded so little protection for minorities and individuals against the interests of eugenically-minded majority factions, despite its clear goal of protecting individuals against government encroachment. If the Progressives, hoping to change human nature through scientific management of society, provided the impetus, the fatal blow to individual liberty was provided when Justice Holmes appropriated the conservative doctrine of judicial restraint to advance these Progressive ends. While the emphasis on Fourteenth Amendment protections is itself in some ways a remnant of the Progressive insistence that the private is in fact public, Holmes' argument that "there is no doubt that in that respect the plaintiff . . . has had due process of law" emphasizes the doctrines of procedural due process and judicial restraint. Even those like Jules Gerard who criticize the decision argue that the doctrine of judicial restraint made the outcome inevitable. [13] The belief that the only protection the Constitution affords is procedural due process stands in contrast to a natural law position that would have taken more seriously Carrie Buck's right to reproduce, though Holmes himself clearly rejects such arguments.[14]

Intuitively, insofar as the Constitution lays out a system of limited government, it seems that a bare procedural protection cannot be all that the Constitution afforded Carrie Buck, but it was all Holmes' interpretation of the Constitution offered. While the judiciary cannot protect against all instances of legislative injustice, it does seem reasonable that the Constitution's protections for individual rights should at least extend to bodily autonomy and the protection of intimate rights like reproduction. While the doctrine of judicial restraint sensibly defers to democratically elected legislatures, it must balance this deference against the commonsense interpretation of the Constitution as creating a structure for limited government and protecting a broad and not clearly defined private sphere. How then does (or can?) the Constitution protect the individual rights not specified in the document itself? If the Constitution does not defend our basic right not to be sterilized against our will, what *does* it do? To answer this question we need to look more closely at the arguments presented in *Buck v. Bell* and *Skinner v. Oklahoma*.

Carrie Buck's case and her fate are equal parts predictable and tragic: predictable, since her case was essentially fabricated to provide judicial legitimacy for the spread of eugenics laws nationwide;[15] tragic, because the outcome justified the institutionalization and sterilization of her entire family, including a sister who did not discover the cause of her sterility until the 1980s.[16] Carrie Buck was initially institutionalized for having a child out of wedlock. Her mother's prostitution arrests and Carrie's own birth out of wedlock were used as proof that her "degeneracy" was genetic. The later discovery that Carrie was probably the victim of rape or manipulation at the hands of her foster family and that her institutionalization was a cover-up to protect the family name make her case all the more tragic. The Court argued that the forcible sterilization of Carrie Buck (and her young daughter) was constitutional because she had the benefit of a legal procedure by which her fundamental right to reproduction was taken away. That legal procedure was not trial by jury, but instead the internal procedure of review by asylum officials and eugenicist doctors who determined which inmates were "unfit" and likely to pass on their infirmity, mental or physical, to the next generation.

Buck and her guardian (complicit with the state in earlier cases) argued that not only did the Due Process Clause protect her substantive right to reproduction, but also that the Equal Protection Clause was violated since the law applied only to those in institutions.[17] Holmes' famous argument rejects all individual reproductive rights claims in favor of social outcomes, comparing sterilization to vaccination and the draft, arguing that these are simply sacrifices one may be called upon to make for the good of the group: "We have seen more than once that the public welfare may call upon the best citizens for their lives. It would be strange if it could not call upon those who already sap the strength of the State for these lesser sacrifices, often not felt to be such by those concerned, in order to prevent our being swamped with incompetence."[18] Holmes relies on two important assumptions: first, that the fate of society is of greater priority than the fate of individuals, and second, that the right to reproduce is, rather than a foundational right, instead a "lesser sacrifice," felt little.

Holmes' opinion is quite short, and refers to precedent only in passing, making it difficult to place in either historical or jurisprudential context. After a brief summary of the case, the opinion itself is two short paragraphs, and his appeal to precedent is contained in the single sentence, "The principle that sustains compulsory vaccination is broad enough to cover cutting the Fallopian tubes." There is no further discussion of the decision he appeals to in *Jacobson v. Massachusetts* and no attempt to argue that the cases are parallel.

Jacobson itself is somewhat helpful, since it finds the origin of the power to vaccinate in the state's broad police powers, arguing that "according to settled principles, the police power of a state must be held to embrace, at least, such reasonable regulations established directly by legislative enactment as will protect the public health and the public safety."[19] It gives states wide discretion to protect the health and welfare of the community, even at the cost of individual freedom. It does, however, acknowledge some limits to the police powers, namely, that "no rule prescribed by a state, nor any regulation adopted by a local governmental agency acting under the sanction of state legislation, shall contravene the Constitution of the United States, nor infringe any right granted or secured by that instrument." Justice Harlan, citing the decision in *Crowley*, adds that "the possession and enjoyment of all rights are subject to such reasonable conditions as may be deemed by the governing authority of the country essential to the safety, health, peace, good order, and morals of the community." Thus, at the very least, Holmes would need to argue that forced sterilization violates no rights found in the federal

Constitution and that the restriction on Carrie Buck's freedom through forced sterilization is "reasonable" in the same way that vaccination of the unwilling against smallpox is "reasonable" given the risks to the public and the restriction of individual liberty resulting from vaccination.

While my emphasis in what follows will be primarily on whether there might be an interpretation of the Constitution that would protect Carrie Buck against state-sponsored sterilization, it also seems at least plausible that the restriction on liberty of forcible vaccination is different in both degree and kind from the kind of restriction Carrie Buck suffered on being permanently sterilized since sterilization involves the assured destruction of human potential and not merely the potential for harm. Vaccination assumes a small risk on the individual's part for benefits to both the individual and society in the immediate term. Sterilization instead requires substantial risk and the assured destruction of reproductive ability on the part of the individual for purely social benefits that only emerge in the long-term (if they emerge at all). Holmes' assurance that vaccination is similar enough to sterilization to cover the case requires a justification which is absent from his opinion.

Unfortunately, the only dissenting vote in *Buck* was not accompanied by a written opinion, and so we do not know on what constitutional grounds Justice Butler might have rejected the Court's decision. But it is possible to put forward an educated guess based on his opinions in other cases. Butler was a proponent of the expansive application of the due process clause to protect individual rights that has come to be known as substantive due process. He joined with the majority that protected the right to private education in *Pierce v. Society of Sisters* (1925), suggesting a willingness to support familial (and religious) rights against state-mandated public education.[20] And yet Butler was not an enemy of state interference, nor was he a champion of civil liberties.[21] If a respect for familial rights was his primary motivation, it seems odd that he did not set down his reasons for dissenting to serve as the possible basis for overturning the decision later.[22] Philip Thompson suggests that Butler's Catholicism probably played the decisive role in his dissent and may have been the reason he refused to record his dissent for posterity.[23] Holmes himself suspected as much, arguing that "Butler knows this is good law, I wonder whether he will have the courage to vote with us in spite of his religion."[24] Catholics in the U.S. were some of the most vocal opponents of forced sterilization policies and Catholic countries were some of the few holdouts against sterilization as a path to eugenic purity in Europe.[25] Whether Butler's dissent was motivated entirely by religion or also by due process considerations will never be known.

What does become clear, in both *Buck* and its progeny, is that the Fourteenth Amendment alone is insufficient to protect the right to reproduction from government interference. This failure is seen most obviously in *Skinner v. Oklahoma* (1942), which is where we find the most substantive discussion of the issues raised in *Buck*. While *Buck* was never overturned, state power of sterilization was called into question in *Skinner,* the first case to postulate a "right to have offspring."[26] Interestingly, *Skinner* ignores both the question of whether sterilization constitutes cruel and unusual punishment as well as that of whether it is in harmony with the requirements of due process of law. The major issue, according to the Court, is whether Oklahoma's use of sterilization violates the equal protection clause of the Fourteenth Amendment. The Court focuses on the way in which the Oklahoma statute differentiates between theft and embezzlement in its punishments. The decision is important because it, unlike *Buck*, emphasizes the centrality of reproduction to human life: "We are dealing here with legislation which involves one of the basic civil rights of man. Marriage and procreation are fundamental to the very existence and survival of the race. The power to sterilize, if exercised, may have subtle, far-reaching and devastating effects."[27] Crucially, the Court emphasizes the importance of reproduction for its importance to the race, not necessarily its importance to individuals. However, later in the decision Justice Douglas' majority opinion refers to reproduction as one of the "basic civil rights of man." This juxtaposition is characteristic of the family's unique roots in man's nature as well as its importance to civil society broadly.

The Supreme Court's decision in *Skinner* focuses on the equal application of the law. The decision in 1942 coincided closely with the realization of what eugenics had made possible in Europe. The concern was primarily that states might use policies grounded in eugenic theory to target ethnic and racial minorities, as in Germany. The concern that eliminating the power to reproduce violates an individual if unenumerated right is not discussed. Justice Douglas' opinion rejects the idea that there is any scientific basis for distinguishing between burglars and embezzlers, arguing, "We have not the slightest basis for inferring that that line has any significance in eugenics, nor that the inheritability of criminal traits follows the neat legal distinctions which the law has marked between those two offenses."[28] At the same time, the Court upholds the goals of the eugenics movement broadly, arguing, not that the eugenics movement was scientifically suspect, but that Oklahoma fails to root the distinction between grand larceny and embezzlement in any eugenic evidence. The implication remains that the state retains the right to control reproduction, so long as such control has justification in scientific theory. Crucially, *Skinner* does not overturn *Buck.* It distinguishes between the two cases, arguing that *Buck* does not violate the equal protection clause because it involves the trade-off between reproduction and freedom. Institutionalized persons who are sterilized can be safely released into society, making room for others to enter institutions for care. In *Skinner*, sterilization is not a condition of release, but simply an additional element of punishment, which makes the violation of equal protection even more egregious.

It is in Chief Justice Stone's *Skinner* concurrence that we find the first real questioning of the application of eugenic science to public policy. He begins by clearly upholding Buck: "Undoubtedly, a state may, after appropriate inquiry, constitutionally interfere with the personal liberty of the individual to prevent the transmission by inheritance of his socially injurious tendencies."[29] But he then goes on to question whether due process requires that an individual be given the opportunity to question whether his deficiencies are due to inheritable defects. The Court at least made the pretense in *Buck* of arguing that Carrie Buck's mother was feeble minded and that Carrie herself was degenerate for having a child out of wedlock. That the proof offered was doctored does not negate the argument that such proof was required. Oklahoma's law, on the contrary, does not require any process to demonstrate that an individual suffers from a hereditary form of criminality. The demands of due process would seem to require at least the demonstration of actual inheritable disease:

> And so, while the state may protect itself from the demonstrably inheritable tendencies of the individual which are injurious to society, the most elementary notions of due process would seem to require it to take appropriate steps to safeguard the liberty of the individual by affording him, before he is condemned to an irreparable injury in his person, some opportunity to show that he is without such inheritable tendencies.[30]

Justice Jackson's concurrence goes further, providing the first clear admission that eugenical policies may be entirely illegitimate, regardless of due process protections. Jackson argues,

> *There are limits to the extent to which a legislatively represented majority may conduct biological experiments at the expense of the dignity and personality and natural powers of a minority—even those who have been guilty of what the majority define as crimes.* But this Act falls down before reaching this problem, which I mention only to avoid the implication that such a question may not exist because not discussed. On it, I would also reserve judgment.[31]

Extending even further than Stone, Justice Jackson's argument is a first step toward the recognition of serious limitations on a eugenics movement because such a movement inherently violates the rights (though he does not use that term) of individuals. More importantly, Jackson makes two related arguments: 1) the majority cannot demand just anything from a minority and 2) even those convicted of crimes have rights that deserve protection. While neither of these views would be controversial to the framers of the Constitution, they were certainly non-obvious to the other Justices on the Court in both *Buck* and *Skinner*.

While it is easy to reject the decisions in *Buck* and *Skinner* as little more than extensions of the failure of eugenics as a scientific movement, the more important analysis requires thinking through why this interpretation of the Constitution failed to identify forced sterilization as a serious rights violation, *even if* there might have been widespread societal benefits.[32] From a natural rights perspective, Holmes' argument fails on numerous fronts. Holmes compares forced sterilization to the draft or to vaccination. A natural rights theorist might be able to defend the draft and forced vaccination as extensions of the right to self-defense. In both cases, the state calls upon a limitation of one's liberties for benefits in which that individual will share. There is no clear extension of a right in the forced sterilization case. Carrie Buck herself will not benefit directly from her own sterilization or those of other institutionalized persons.[33] Even if eugenical science were correct that benefits would accrue over many generations, Carrie Buck would be long dead before such utopian goals were reached.

Any doctrine of limited government would seem to require that state compulsion of citizens (apart from criminal punishments) be as minimally invasive as possible and that the individual share or have the potential to share in the benefits created by limitations on individual liberty. The case of sterilization clearly fails this test, since removing Carrie Buck's ability to reproduce does not secure her other rights in any other way. Instead, she has been permanently prevented from engaging in one of the foundational human experiences. The problem for legal scholars is that these foundational experiences and the rights that extend from them are not clearly laid out in the Constitution, nor are they enumerated in any detail, apart from the politically-relevant rights protected in the Bill of Rights. In what follows, I argue that application of the Ninth Amendment can help to bridge this gap.

PROTECTING A RIGHT TO REPRODUCTION: THE NINTH AND FOURTEENTH AMENDMENTS

Substantive due process claims involve moving beyond the procedural concerns cited by Holmes in *Buck* toward a theory of limitations on the *kinds* of laws that a majority may pass. On this reading of the Fifth and Fourteenth Amendments, some laws may be unjust because their substance is such that they violate individual rights in a fundamental way.[34] The major objection to substantive due process jurisprudence is that it allows the Court to create the substance of the law out of whole cloth, opening the way for an activist Court to strike down majoritarian law.[35] Critics of substantive due process like Gerard argue that while what happened to Carrie Buck was clearly unjust, "the Court was right to refuse to overturn it. The remedy for a lousy statute is to persuade the legislature to appeal it . . . it is immensely preferable to the alternative of empowering judges to strike down the substance of legislation under the supposed aegis of the Due Process Clause."[36] Leuchtenberg admits that "if others were to avoid the fate of Carrie Buck, they needed to look not to the U.S. Supreme Court, but to the people of the Commonwealth of Virginia, and their salvation was a long time coming."[37] It might seem from this reasoning that we are between a rock and a constitutional hard place. Either we accept the judicial activism of substantive due process jurisprudence, in that the "substance" of the due process clause is merely filled in by whatever passing fad or judicial desire happens to be in play that day, or we can advocate judicial restraint and allow tens of thousands of individuals to be sterilized without their consent because the Constitution does not explicitly lay out such protections in either its grant of powers or in the Bill of Rights itself.

This characterization strikes me as both too simplistic and extremely dangerous. If the Constitution does not protect the rights of individuals from invasive surgeries done without their consent, it hardly seems worth defending. Fortunately, the situation is neither as simple nor as hopeless as it first appears. *Skinner* and *Buck* are important for contemporary theorists not only because they are central to the under-recognized area of family rights, but also because they demonstrate the limitations of Fourteenth Amendment jurisprudence for checking the power of majority faction in the form of unjust decisions made by the people's representatives.

Buck and *Skinner* provide two test cases for considering how a moderate understanding of substantive due process would require neither capitulation to majority cruelty nor abandonment of the Constitution to judicial vicissitudes. In both cases the Fourteenth Amendment plays a central role in the Court's decision, though applied in different ways. What is missing from substantive due process discussions is what provides the *substance* of substantive due process in the first place, and that substance can be found in the amendment that is never mentioned in either of these cases. It is somewhat puzzling that none of the Justices authoring opinions in these cases mentions the Ninth Amendment or how it could be applied to limit state power in cases concerning foundational but heretofore unrecognized rights like that of reproduction. Indeed, we must wait for Justice Goldberg's concurrence in *Griswold v. Connecticut*, more than a generation after *Skinner,* for this argument to be advanced. Goldberg's concurrence provides the foundation for an understanding of substantive due process whose substance is provided, not by mere judicial opinion, but by the grounding provided by a moderate but foundational understanding of the Ninth Amendment.

The Ninth Amendment is frustratingly open-ended and vague: "The enumeration in the Constitution, of certain rights, shall not be construed to deny or disparage others retained by the people." On the one hand, the language of the Amendment suggests a wide vista for rights that might be protected by the Court from the interference of majoritarian legislation. On the other hand, it requires limits of some kind lest it undermine all legitimate political activity. In the case of a fundamental right like reproduction, it could be a crucial wedge. While its application in areas like reproduction seems obvious, as Goldberg argued in *Griswold*, Ninth Amendment jurisprudence has, by and large, been unsuccessful.[38] Yet sterilization laws, unlike later abortion laws, would have been the ideal context in which to introduce a robust and coherent understanding of the Ninth Amendment as providing a bulwark against state violation of individual rights.

In *Griswold*, Goldberg lays out a convincing foundation for future Ninth Amendment jurisprudence. "The language and history of the Ninth Amendment reveal that the Framers of the Constitution believed that there are additional fundamental rights, protected from governmental infringement, which exist alongside those fundamental rights specifically mentioned in the first eight constitutional amendments."[39] The existence of the Ninth Amendment alone requires that the Court take it seriously as part of the Constitution they are sworn to uphold.

> The Ninth Amendment to the Constitution may be regarded by some as a recent discovery, and may be forgotten by others, but, since 1791, it has been a basic part of the Constitution which we are sworn to uphold. To hold that a right so basic and fundamental and so deep-rooted in our society as the right of privacy in marriage may be infringed because that right is not guaranteed in so many words by the first eight amendments to the Constitution is to ignore the Ninth Amendment, and to give it no effect whatsoever.[40]

Finally, Goldberg rejects the claim that Ninth Amendment jurisprudence opens the door to judicial activism and allows judicial opinion to replace the Constitution. Quoting the Court in *Snyder*, Goldberg says judges will be limited by the "'traditions and [collective] conscience of our people' to determine whether a principle is 'so rooted [there] . . . as to be ranked as fundamental.'"[41] This argument fails to convince Goldberg's fellow justices, particularly Justices Black and Stewart, who directly criticize the Ninth Amendment approach in their dissents.[42]

Black and Stewart base their criticism of Goldberg's Ninth Amendment jurisprudence on the grounds that such a reading allows judges to wholly override the democratic process. Both Black and Stewart appeal to traditional notions of federalism and judicial restraint, arguing that the states are the protectors of individual rights and that using federal courts to "create" new rights like that of privacy to limit state legislative action runs counter to the founders' intentions, both in terms of respect for the legislative process, and also in terms of protection of state rights over federal power. Black argues against both substantive due process claims and the use of the Ninth Amendment to ground those claims in pre-existing rights:

> I have not yet adequately expressed the more than anxiety that I feel at the ever increasing scope given to the Fourteenth Amendment in cutting down what I believe to be the constitutional rights of the States. As the decisions now stand, I see hardly any limit but the sky to the invalidating of those rights if they happen to strike a majority of this Court as for any reason undesirable.[43]

Stewart dismisses Goldberg's argument even more forcefully: "But to say that the Ninth Amendment has anything to do with this case is to turn somersaults with history."[44]

Black's criticism of Goldberg's use of the Ninth Amendment in *Griswold*, whether legitimate or not in that case, would not have applied in *Buck*, since the right to have children is neither a new nor an invented right, but one taken for granted in common and civil law for centuries. While Black and Stewart argue that the Ninth Amendment primarily respects state's rights, a more convincing argument would be that the Ninth Amendment protects the rights of individuals recognized by the people as a whole, whether found in power wielded by the majorities within state legislatures or the rights of individuals apart from government. The most powerful application of the Ninth Amendment on this reading would be instances where state powers and individual rights overlap, as when the state legislature recognizes a long-standing traditional right that is not recognized in the federal Bill of Rights. Contra Justice Black, there is nothing in the Ninth Amendment that should allow a state legislature to overwhelm a long-standing foundational individual right, even if that right is not mentioned in the Bill of Rights. Family rights, particularly those involving freedom to reproduce (as distinguished from the less clear right *not* to reproduce), would fit squarely under the Ninth Amendment's protection of rights retained by the people.

Moreover, the right to have children is functionally different in terms of the applicability to the Ninth Amendment from the right not to have children. Although this paper does not address the validity of that latter right, it is important to note the difference between these two rights claims. The right to end a pregnancy had long been limited and controlled by English common law and American tradition. In particular, abortion could be limited after quickening, around the fourth month of pregnancy. Quickening was the first point at which a pregnancy could be understood to exist in a way that created an expectation of state protection of the unborn child. Limits on abortifacient drugs were understood to protect both the woman and the fetus, since such drugs often caused death of the woman as well.[45] Additionally, abortion was seen as sinful in the dominant religious views of the time and laws existed in many jurisdictions in the nineteenth and twentieth centuries limiting access to abortion and abortion-causing drugs.[46]

On the other hand, the right to have a child was consistently recognized by the state and coercive removal of children from unsuitable parents was almost always a family matter, one into which the state rarely entered.[47] In the 1850s, for example, most nations that recognized British common law were suspicious of even voluntary sterilization, with many such laws "stymied by arguments in favor of the liberty of the subject."[48] Thus, for at least a century, and really much longer, the assumption was that individuals have the right to bear and raise their own children, barring unique contexts like those involving enslaved persons (which, of course, represented a serious rights violation of its own). Because of this history, the right to have children is a traditional right, unlike the broader right to reproductive privacy cited in *Griswold* and rejected by Black.

The Ninth Amendment could have and should have served as a barrier against forced sterilization, as well as many of the other ways the state interferes with the family, from education to health care. The Fourteenth Amendment is less successful in this context, since its emphasis on due process protects life, liberty, and property, but does not provide substantive definitions for any of these rights, nor what constitutes due process of law. The Fourteenth Amendment, stripped of its historical context as the extension of life, liberty, and property to freed slaves, is indeed vague. But the content of due process protections can be amply supplied by the Ninth Amendment and the common law and natural rights protections it embodies.

The main difference between the efficacy of the Ninth and Fourteenth Amendments in protecting the right to reproduce is that the Fourteenth Amendment does not actually serve to define any of the rights to life, liberty, or property, but merely to protect people from having them taken away without due process. The Ninth Amendment, on the other hand, provides a path by which such rights could be identified and then protected based on their foundational nature and recognition in the mores and traditions of the people as Goldberg suggests. Due to their foundational nature, family rights, or the right to reproduction in particular, are much better understood as stemming from the Ninth Amendment protection of rights held by the people, rather than the protection of due process that ultimately failed to protect Carrie Buck from sterilization at the hands of the state. The Ninth Amendment should have forced the state to justify its intervention in areas of life traditionally protected from public scrutiny, particularly where fundamental rights were concerned.

The eugenics movement in the United States was cut short, not by wise jurisprudence and constitutional analysis, but by the recognition of the states themselves that this power was incredibly dangerous, particularly to minority rights, and that such laws probably would not withstand subsequent constitutional tests given the growth of Fourteenth Amendment jurisprudence. One important and overlooked lesson of the history of forced sterilization is that the Bill of Rights is ill-suited to protect familial rights precisely because the Bill of Rights deals primarily with those rights that were most likely to be abused by government: political rights and the rights of the criminally accused.

The failure to mention familial rights and reproductive rights does not indicate their relative unimportance, but instead demonstrates how foundational they were understood to be. Family rights were simply taken for granted because their centrality to human life was so obvious and because, traditionally, they had been little interfered with. Unfortunately, the way jurists read the Constitution now implies that any right not mentioned in the first eight sections of the Bill of Rights is an invented right and that state and local government officials can intervene in dramatic and dangerous ways in family decision–making without justification. While forced sterilization is no longer on the table, the forcible removal of children from their homes for minor parental offenses and non-offenses continues to grow.[49] A strong Ninth Amendment jurisprudence that takes into account the traditional autonomy of the family and the right to reproduction in common law would have offered a much more solid foundation for protection of the family against such assaults than the Fourteenth Amendment's limited protections alone can offer.

Of course, an emphasis on the limited protections of the Fourteenth Amendment, rather than a more thorough defense of limited government, is part and parcel of the nexus of progressive and conservative arguments that, whether intentionally or not, contributes to the erosion of family and reproductive rights. Progressives have little incentive to support robust parental rights that interfere with goals like universal compulsory education. Conservatives in turn use judicial restraint to support state laws that may violate female bodily autonomy by requiring invasive tests as limitations on abortions. The result is a scattershot approach to family rights that rejects a consistent and thorough defense of reproductive rights in favor of ideological goals. A Ninth Amendment protection of family rights, on the other hand, offers the possibility of a robust and consistent defense of reproductive rights as a foundational and private activity with nevertheless crucial implications for civil society. The Ninth Amendment, however, is the path not taken, one that takes into account the public nature of a fundamentally private act, respects the traditional and common law rights of a people, and recognizes the family as the foundation for all civil and political organization. That path, unfortunately, may very well now be permanently closed.

NOTES

1. See, for example, Christopher Wolfe's work *The Rise of Modern Judicial Review: From Constitutional Interpretation to Judge-Made Law* (Basic Books, 1986; *revised edition,* Rowman and Littlefield, 1994) and Rosenberg's *The Hollow Hope* (Chicago: University of Chicago Press, 1991) for discussions of the various traditions of judicial review, including judicial restraint and activist jurisprudence.

2. Estimates range between 60,000 and 70,000, with some arguing that even the latter number is a gross underestimation. See Edwin Black, *War Against the Weak: Eugenics and America's Campaign to Create a Master Race* (Dialog Press: 2012).

3. I discuss the differences between vaccination and sterilization in my later discussion of *Buck*, but for now the decisive difference is that vaccination is the enhancement of a natural ability that protects both the individual and society. Sterilization involves the destruction of a natural ability for the sake of public benefit. It therefore requires a much stronger justification for state coercion than vaccination alone. At the very least, the cases are not parallel and require different justifications.

4. Bashford, Alison and Philippa Levine, *Oxford Handbook of the History of Eugenics* (New York: Oxford University Press, 2010). See also Stephen Jay Gould "Carrie Buck's Daughter," *Natural History* (July 1984).

5. Stephen Jay Gould, "Carrie Bucks' Daughter." Also, as a characteristic and forceful example, see the letter from Teddy Roosevelt to Charles Davenport of the Eugenics Record Office (later Cold Spring Harbor laboratory) where Roosevelt says "I agree with you if you mean, as I suppose you do, that society has no business to permit degenerates to reproduce their kind." Accessed online at www.dnalc.org/view/11219-T-Roosevelt-letter-to-C-Davenport-about-degenerates-reproducing-.html.

6. "Eugenics' first objects is to check the birth rate of the unfit instead of allowing them to come into being. . . . The second object is the improvement of the race by furthering the productivity of the fit by early marriages and the healthful rearing of children." As quoted in Leonard, Thomas, "Eugenics and Economics in the Progressive Era," *Journal of Economic Perspectives*, 19 (Fall 2005): 208.

7. Ibid.

8. Leonard describes the progressive movement as being committed to four primary goals: "1) the explanatory power of scientific (especially statistical) social inquiry to get at the root causes of social and economic problems; 2) the legitimacy of social control, which derives from a holistic conception of society as prior to and greater than the sum of its constituent individuals; 3) the efficacy of social control via expert management of public administration; where 4) expertise is both sufficient and necessary for the task of wide public administration" (Leonard, 217).

9. Leuchtenburg, William. 1995. "Mr. Justice Holmes and Three Generations of Imbeciles." *The Supreme Court Reborn: The Constitutional Revolution in the Age of Roosevelt* (New York: Oxford University Press), 23.

10. Schwarz, Hunter. "Following reports of forced sterilization of female inmates, California passes ban." Washington Post, GovBeat Blog. September 26, 2014. Accessed 7/17/2015. "www.washingtonpost.com/blogs/govbeat/wp/2014/09/26/following-reports-of-forced-sterilization-of-female-prison-inmates-california-passes-ban/.

11. Leuchtenburg, 9.

12. *Buck* v. *Bell,* 274 U. S. 200 (1927).

13. Jules B. Gerard, "Capacity to Govern," *Harvard Journal of Law and Social Policy* 12 (1989), 107–10.

14. See Hoffheimer, Michael, *Justice Holmes and the Natural Law*, (Routledge, 2013).

15. Leuchtenburg.

16. Leuchtenburg, 25.

17. *Buck*.

18. Ibid.

19. *Henning Jacobson v Commonwealth of Massachusetts*. 197 U.S. 11 (1905).

20. *Pierce* v. *Society of Sisters,* 268 U. S. 510 (1925).

21. Leuchgtenburg, 14–15

22. While I don't have space to discuss it at length here, his dissent in Senn v. Tile Layers Protective Union, 301 U.S. 468 (1937) argues for "not merely freedom from bodily restraint but also the right of the individual to . . . establish a home and bring up children. Cited in Philip Thompson, "Silent Protest: A Catholic Justice Dissents in *Buck v. Bell,*" *Catholic Lawyer* 43 (139).

23. Thompson, "A Catholic Justice."

24. Leuchtenburg, 15.
25. *Oxford Handbook of the History of Eugenics* (105)
26. *Skinner* v. *Oklahoma ex rel. Williamson,* 316 U. S. 535 (1942)
27. Ibid.
28. Ibid.
29. Ibid.
30. Ibid.
31. Ibid, emphasis added.
32. As Leuchtenburg points out, there were already serious reservations on the scientific validity and societal efficacy of eugenics policies at the time (20–21).
33. *Buck*. The argument was, of course, made that she was exchanging sterility for freedom, which simply begs the question again of why her fundamental freedom could be violated in such a way as to make such a choice necessary.
34. Ryan Williams, "The One and Only Substantive Due Process Clause," *Yale Law Journal* 120 (2010).
35. See Christopher Wolfe, *The Rise of Modern Judicial Review*. New York: Basic Books, 1986, pages 148–56.
36. Leuchtenburg, 22.
37. Ibid, 23.
38. For a detailed discussion, see Lash, Kurt. "The Lost Jurisprudence of the Ninth Amendment," *Texas Law Review* 83:3 (2005).
39. *Griswold v. Connecticut*, 381 U.S. 497 (1965).
40. Ibid.
41. Ibid. Harlan actually quotes the decision in *Skinner*, arguing that "there is a 'realm of family life which the state cannot enter' without substantial justification," though he grounds this finding in a substantive due process reading of the Fourteenth Amendment rather than in the Ninth Amendment primarily.
42. Goldberg's dissent does, however, form the basis for a renewed scholarly interest in the Ninth Amendment, particularly the work of Randy Barnett. See his edited volume *The Rights Retained by the People: The History and Meaning of the Ninth Amendment* (Fairfax, VA: George Mason University Press, 1993) and also *Restoring the Lost Constitution* (Princeton: Princeton University Press, 2004). In both works, Barnett argues that the Ninth Amendment is best understood as protecting the "retained" natural rights of the people. While he does not discuss either *Buck* or *Skinner*, my argument here is to some degree an argument that reproduction is just such a retained natural right.
43. 381 U.S. 479 at 521n16 (Justice Black dissenting) quoting Justice Holmes' dissent in *Baldwin v. Missouri,* 281 U.S. 586 (1930).
44. 381 U.S. 479 at 529 (Justice Stewart, dissenting). See also Barnett's historical discussion of the Ninth Amendment that supports an individual reading of the Ninth Amendment over the states' rights argument made by both Black and Stewart in *Restoring the Lost Constitution*, 224–52.
45. Leslie Reagan, "Common Law and the Criminalization of Abortion," in *When Abortion Was a Crime* (Berkeley: University of California Press, 1998), 8–14.
46. Reagan, 10.
47. John Myers, "A Short History of Child Protection in America," *Family Law Quarterly* 449 (2008): 449–63.
48. *Oxford Handbook of Eugenics*, 106.
49. See, for example, Aviv, Rachel. "Where is your mother?" *New Yorker*, December 2, 2013.

Chapter Eight

Limited Government and the Family

Rival Jurisprudential Models

Mark A. Scully

Throughout the twentieth century the Supreme Court has heard disputes between families and state governments. Education policy is one of the main arenas for this conflict because it touches the nexus of human identity: private and public, family member and citizen, individual liberty and civic responsibility. This conflict is especially acute when we focus on one aspect of education in particular: civic education, broadly understood to mean educational regulations that intend to foster social cohesion and cultivate a shared civic identity. Many of today's debates in political theory, especially those pertaining to Rawlsian liberalism, wrestle with whether social cohesion, achieved through educative public reason, is a means to freedom, or whether individual freedom is itself a kind of civic education.[1] To what extent does the state's power over education—and particularly civic education—infringe upon the parents' control of their children's moral and ethical rearing? Or, alternatively, when does a parent's assertion of control interfere with a legitimate state interest in using education as a means to instill civic identity and social cohesion?

The Supreme Court recently addressed this theoretical question in the landmark case *Zelman v. Simmons-Harris*. Though this case did not explicitly address a program of civic education, the majority took the position of familial freedom while the dissenting justices emphasized social cohesion. The case involved an establishment clause objection to an Ohio program that provided cash vouchers to parents of children in Cleveland's failing school system, most of whom sent their children to Catholic schools. The five justice majority, upholding the vouchers, were quick to point out that money only made it to religious schools by parental choice. Thus, the state created a program that "generally . . . empowered [parents] to direct the aid to schools or institutions of their own choosing."[2] There were three different dissenting opinions, and all pointed to the potentially destabilizing social effect of enhanced parental choice. As Justice Breyer's described the stakes, Ohio invited religious conflict that could potentially tear at "the nation's social fabric."[3] The *Zelman* dispute invoked a fundamental conflict between parental liberty on one hand and civic harmony on the other hand.

The scholarship around *Zelman* quickly recognized that the case was "not about religion or religious truths," but instead "a debate about political principles—chiefly, what justice and equality require regarding schooling in a free society."[4] Some celebrated the Court's vindication of parental liberty. For instance, Joseph Viteritti argued that the *Zelman* opinion evinced "a growing body of Supreme Court jurisprudence that advance[ed] a pluralist vision of American democracy" that, in this case, "allow[ed] parents to align their children's education with their own values."[5] On the other hand, some scholars retorted that the Court's emphasis on parental choice neglected the state's interest in crucial civic identity. The Court, they argued, ratified a voucher program that diminished "the level of commitment to democratic values among future citizens, and thus on the stability of democracy,"[6] and, according to some, "condemned future generations to the stultifying beliefs and prejudices of their parents."[7] Some scholars who were less pessimistic wondered if the liberalization of vouchers actually provided a new means to exert social control over private institutions.[8] The fact that so many scholarly reactions concentrated on the family/society conflict rather than the decision's effect on educational outcomes reveals the vigor of this theoretical conflict in American society.

The *Zelman* debate raises a question: how American constitutional government has reconciled liberty—especially as it pertains to the freedom of families in education— to a communal interest in social cohesion, particularly when it comes to the power of states to form citizens through a shared educational environment. Based upon landmark cases, I contrast two different theories of the family and state power, as the Court has developed them in the twentieth century. In general, as the Court's conception of constitutionalism and limited government changed, so too did its understanding of the family, individual liberty and social duty. Thus, the first model—what I call the privacy model—emphasized limited government as limited powers, with a robust conception of unenumerated natural rights. From this notion of constitutionalism, the Court emphasized that familial relationships—especially parent-child relationships—enjoyed a degree of privacy operating in the lacuna of governmental power. The authority of parents to direct the education of their children is a crucial component of the natural familial relationship. It constitutes an essential part of the pursuit of human happiness, and as such, it is one of the freedoms reserved by the people. *Meyer v. Nebraska* and *Pierce v. Society of Sisters* typify this model.

But that does not mean that the Court saw no state interest in civic education. Indeed, the Court showed itself to be quite comfortable accommodating a relatively robust notion of state power to pursue civic ends in education policy. Accordingly, the Court said two things that pertain to the state's interest in civic education. First, family privacy notwithstanding, parents had a duty to facilitate the civic formation of their children. The Court never really develops this idea in detail, and perhaps meant it simply as an exhortation to parents. But the second is more concrete. Family privacy did not abrogate the limited state power to shape future citizens through education. This means that families could not stand in the way of reasonable and limited state efforts to instill civic-mindedness. Thus, the relationship between privacy and state power could be conceived as a balance of two distinct goods derived from specific relationships—familial relationships on one scale, and social and civil relationships on the other. The former were cultivated by privacy and the latter by limited state efforts at civic education.

The second model—the individualized liberty model—reflected an altered understanding of limited government that emerged over the course of the New Deal. Limited government came to signify the special protection of specific rights, meaning a jurisprudential preference for the personal and intellectual liberties having to do with the realm of free thought and opinion. These preferred liberties were understood to be exceptions to otherwise expanded governmental powers. But this focus on intellectual rights of individuals affected the notion of family freedom in two ways. First, the Court tended to downplay (and at times question outright) the unique educational authority of parent over child, and in so doing atomized the family into individual rights bearers. Second, as the Court focused on protecting intellectual individualism instead of any specific relationship—including civic relationships—it also turned away from the idea that civic and social duty might circumscribe intellectual autonomy. Thus, with respect to both the family and social responsibility to the community, this model emphasized individualism to a much greater degree than the privacy model. *West Virginia v. Barnette* is the case that demonstrated the Court's new approach to the family. And though the two models developed sequentially, it would be misleading to say that one model simply replaced the other. Instead, the two models represent distinct approaches to the relationship between the state and the family. Thus, I end the paper by showing how each theory contributed to a later landmark education case, *Wisconsin v. Yoder*. The majority opinion in that case possessed elements of both models, while the dissenting opinion from Justice Douglas expands upon elements of *Barnette* and the individualized approach.

PARENTAL LIBERTY, FAMILIAL PRIVACY, AND LIMITED GOVERNMENT

The Court's family privacy approach was epitomized by *Meyer v. Nebraska* (1923) and *Pierce v. Society of Sisters* (1925). Nebraska and Oregon (respectively) were troubled by their large ethnic German populations in the wake of World War I, and sought to promote cultural unity among their populations. In the first case, Nebraska banned any instruction in the German language until eighth grade. In the second case, Oregon outlawed all private schools, though it did so with a view toward the large parochial school system populated by ethnic Catholics. These laws regulated education in the state, but they aimed at the deeper goal of fostering social cohesion by stamping out the customs and practices of competing civic or national loyalties.

In both cases, the Court invalidated the state laws by appealing to the fourteenth amendment's promise that states will not deprive persons of liberty without due process. But interestingly the Court's opinion did not necessarily define a specific familial or parental right, and instead emphasized general limitations on government power. Thus, the *Meyer* opinion stated that "this Court has not attempted to define with exactness the liberty thus guaranteed" by the fourteenth amendment, but the "established doctrine is that this liberty may not be interfered with, under the guise of protecting the public interest, by legislative action which is arbitrary or without reasonable relation to some purpose within the competency of the State to effect."[9] The Court did not, therefore, articulate a specific and identifiable right, but instead a general limitation on state government's power to act without a legitimate purpose. The Court used the same jurisprudential means to invalidate Oregon's prohibition of private schools. The Court insisted that Constitutional rights "may not be abridged by legislation which has no reasonable relation to some purpose within the competency of the state."[10]

The Court's focus on the competency of state governments reflected their application of the *national* principle of limited constitutionalism to *state* governments. The Court implied that even though state powers were not enumerated like Congress's powers, state governments did not have indefinite residual powers either. The fourteenth amendment was the link connecting the logic of limited government from the federal system to state governments. As Randy Barnett has said, according to *Meyer* and *Pierce* even state governments need to show "that legislation infringing upon the liberties of the people really was a necessary exercise of the state's police power."[11] The Court said it would apply these constitutional principles when they invoked the "fundamental theory of liberty upon which all governments in this Union repose." Under that theory, the state had no legitimate purpose to "standardize its children by forcing them to accept instruction from public teachers only."[12] The family privacy model, therefore, rested upon a general theory of limited government.

Within this context of a generally limited government, the Court did not need to find a specific or discreet Constitutional right to parental control. Instead, they focused on the individual's residual liberties in general, and the fundamental relationship between family and the pursuit of happiness. *Meyer* asserted that the Fourteenth Amendment protected several fundamental rights, including "the right of the individual to . . . establish a home and bring up children." The Court uses "right" here in an indefinite way, referring generally to "those privileges long recognized at common law as essential to the orderly pursuit of happiness by free men."[13] What the Court was really protecting, therefore, was a natural relationship which required a degree of privacy. That meant that parent-child relationships were, by nature, exclusive relationships. To interpose state authority would undermine their fundamental character, weakening a relationship that is an essential component in the individual pursuit of happiness. The *Pierce* opinion similarly focused on the parental relationship, rather than a distinct right: "the liberty of parents and guardians to direct the upbringing and education of children under their control."[14] In both cases, limited government was understood to leave unperturbed the integrity of a variety of relationships and activities that are constitutive of our pursuit of happiness. The relationship between parent and child is one such relationship that fundamentally depends upon privacy—being left alone—to cultivate a direct, immediate, and intimate bond.

Though the Court clearly believed the family's privacy derived from limits on government power, the Court denied that family privacy or parental control was absolute. In fact, the majority in both cases went out of their way to contextualize family privacy in a larger framework of social responsibility. For instance, the Court in *Meyer* emphasized that the parent's "right of control" also went with the "natural duty of the parent to give his children education suitable to their station in life;" the state, acting with a view to this natural duty, can "enforce this obligation by compulsory laws."[15] Similarly, *Pierce* said that "those who nurture [the child] and direct his destiny have the right, coupled with the high duty, to recognize and prepare him for additional obligations."[16] Here the Court indicated that parents have a duty toward civic education that correlated with the privilege of privacy. These quotations, however, do not bring much clarity to the relationship between privacy and duty, other than the general expectation that proper parenthood would inculcate some notion of civic identity; the Court did not say whether failure to teach the latter would curtail parents' the family's privacy.

But the Court was clearer when it came to outlining legitimate state measures regarding civic education that did not unreasonably interfere with familial privacy. And here the Court suggested that privacy and duty were balanced against one another, rather than the idea that privacy is derived from fulfilling one's duty. The Court implied families were communities within a larger political community, and therefore privacy was not absolute, but correlative with certain civic obligations. Thus, part of parental duty meant abiding by limited and reasonable state measures to control children's education, familial privacy notwithstanding. In other words, the family is a private institution, but its members are also part of a larger civic community. Protecting the privacy of the former could not negate the duties owed to the latter.

The *Meyer* opinion developed this notion of limited privacy by making clear it objected only to the *comprehensive* ban on German language training, not the general presumption in favor of English language education. "Mere knowledge of the German language," the Court noted, "cannot reasonably be regarded as harmful."[17] Short of proscribing German entirely, the Court acknowledged the "salutary purpose of the statute" forbidding the teaching of foreign languages until eighth grade. The Court admitted the possibility of "baneful effects" from "permitting foreigners . . . to rear and educate their children in the language of their native land." Education which did not give priority to the English language created conditions that would be "inimical to our own safety" by teaching children that "they must always think in [their native] language, and, as a consequence, naturally inculcate in them . . . ideas and sentiments foreign to the best interests of this country." The Court went so far as to acknowledge that "the obvious purpose of the statute"—to ensure that English become "the mother tongue of all children reared in the state"—was a purpose that "[came] reasonably within the police power of the state."[18] This helps clarify that, in these cases, familial privacy was in a balance with the state interest in cultivating civic identity, and therefore a prudential judgment on the means chosen by the state was crucial to determining whether the state upset that balance.[19]

The privacy model, therefore, suggested that the Court recognized a complex relationship between family and civil society, and the fact that one person forms fundamental relationships within both communities. As such, the Court's approach tended to promote a balanced view of family as both a private good unto itself—a good preserved by protecting the integrity of its relationships—and as a transitional institution within a larger community. Or, to put it differently, the family was a distinct sphere, but also one that was concentric within the political community—its relationships distinct and dignified, but not entirely autonomous either. Thus, family privacy, viewed through the lens of responsible adulthood, was understood to be limited by legitimate and reasonable attempts to cultivate a shared civic identity through education.

INDIVIDUALIZING THE FAMILY

In *West Virginia v. Barnette* the Court considered whether West Virginia could require pupils to salute the flag and recite the pledge of allegiance, despite their religious objections. Like the controversies in *Meyer* and *Pierce*, the Supreme Court heard arguments against the state's power to foster and develop social cohesion; in this case, the state sought to instill in its young citizens social cohesion by developing in them the habits, through shared practice, of affection for and identity in the nation. Like *Meyer* and *Pierce*, moreover, the Supreme Court rejected the state law in question. Despite this similarity, *Barnette* built a very different jurisprudential model that emphasized the liberty of individual rights-bearers in a way that diminished the significance of parental relationships as well as any counter-balancing state interest in civic cohesion. But to understand the transformation in how the Court conceived of the family, we first must establish how it conceived of limited government.

The Court overturned West Virginia's flag salute and pledge of allegiance requirement by appealing to the first amendment's free speech protections, arguing that the state could not coerce an affirmation. Though this seems straightforward, the Court's decision to adjudicate on free speech grounds involved several significant departures from the jurisprudence of the privacy model. To begin with, the *Barnette* opinion was paradigmatic of the late New Deal Court's wariness toward substantive due process, and its tendency to expand the Court's application of judicial review. Instead, the *Barnette* Court preferred those named liberties in the Bill of Rights because they were apparently less subject to creative interpretation.[20] In this vein, *Barnette* asserted that rights grounded in the Fourteenth Amendment's due process clause, the very clause that *Meyer* and *Pierce* were built upon—would receive less protection than the "freedoms of speech and of press, of assembly, and of worship." The Court proclaimed that the latter could now only "be infringed . . . [in order] to prevent grave and immediate danger to interests which the state may lawfully protect."[21]

The Court's rejection of the Fourteenth Amendment and turn toward the Bill of Rights was actually about an altered conception of constitutionalism as a whole, not just substantive due process. The *Barnette* Court connected its preferred liberties approach to their attempt to save the concept of limited government from its eighteenth-century milieu. Thus, the Court rejected the anachronistic notion of liberty as "mere absence of governmental restraints," noting that such a "laissez-faire concept" had "withered." The preferred liberties approach allowed them to "translate" and "transplant" a limited government narrative into a new form of government that would achieve "social advancements" through the "closer integration of society and through expanded and strengthened governmental controls."[22] In other words, the

Bill of Rights approach allowed the Court to preserve some meaning of limited government, while simultaneously legitimizing the profound increase in the federal government's regulatory and redistributive activities through their sweeping interpretation of Congress's powers under the commerce clause. As opposed to the constitutionalism of the privacy model, which pointed to generally limited government based upon a natural rights philosophy, the individualized liberty approach began with rejecting any general limitation on government power. Instead, the Court posited that limited government referred to specific, enumerated, and fixed limitations based in the Bill of Rights.

Beyond a new idea of limited government, the Court's turn to the First Amendment also revealed a unique understanding of individualized, intellectual liberty. The privacy model was based upon protecting the integrity of natural familial relationship by essentially leaving that relationship alone, notwithstanding the ways in which privacy would be balanced against other social goods. But *Barnette*'s turn to the First Amendment indicated something new. To begin with, speech was not the most intuitive first amendment grounds to handle the dispute; free exercise was the more natural (and limited) first amendment basis to overturn the West Virginia law. The law punished *parents* of children who would not participate in the salute ceremony with fines and possible jail time. That meant that the law held parents responsible if they taught their children an anti-social religious doctrine. But the Court rejected the free exercise claim because it did not permit as far-reaching an outcome as they wanted. There may have been some who objected to the requirement on the basis of "opinion and political attitude" rather than religious conviction.[23] "Many citizens who do not share [the Barnettes'] religious views," the Court conjectured, still might object to the "compulsory rite [of the flag salute] to infringe constitutional liberty of the individual." [24] Free speech cast a wider net by seemingly protecting any form of intellectual objection to the salute and the pledge of allegiance. As such, the Court appeared more interested in expanding its power, despite its claim to turning to the Bill of Rights to limit its power. The Court essentially interpreted the First Amendment, as a whole, to suggest the autonomy of opinion in general, rather than a specific action like speech.

But the Court's turn away from free exercise toward free speech was revealing of their focus on autonomy in another way. At a basic level, the prevailing standard for speech was more flexible for the justices than the free exercise standard, since the latter required evidence of a discriminatory (that is, a non-generally applicable) law. Indeed, on the basis of the general applicability rule, the Court ruled 8–1 in *Minersville v. Gobitis* to uphold an identical law in Pennsylvania a mere three years before *Barnette*. But, under the prevailing free-speech standard, any attempt at censorship was unconstitutional unless there was a clear and present danger. What the state endeavored in this case—"involuntary affirmation"—was a more profound limitation on freedom than censorship and therefore, *a fortiori*, the case required at least as high a standard of review as censorship, if not higher. But since no one argued that there was even a clear and present danger, it was obvious that the requirement could not pass constitutional muster.[25]

But once again, the Court took an expansive constitutional interpretation in order to advance a notion of intellectual autonomy. That is because the Court's *a fortiori* argument spuriously equivocates between censorship and affirmation. The text of the Constitution only bans censorship, not involuntary affirmation: "Congress shall make no law . . . abridging the freedom of speech."[26] Of course, West Virginia did not abridge the Barnettes' speech, and so, strictly speaking, the requirement did not violate the Constitution. It did, however, compel a certain action that implied an interior conviction, and this was what the *Barnette* majority found unconstitutional. Thus, the Court asserted that "we are dealing with a compulsion of students to declare a belief;" or, again, "[i]t is also to be noted that the compulsory flag salute and pledge requires affirmation of a belief and an attitude of mind."[27] Ultimately, therefore, the Court interpreted the First Amendment to protect the unassailability of opinion itself—religious or not. The Court conceived of liberty in a highly individualistic and rationalistic way. Liberty meant the freedom to act on one's own opinions, and perhaps more importantly, to act *only* on one's own opinions, and not another's. Liberty meant the irreducibility of each single person to the opinions and convictions that they interiorly affirm, and any threat to that individual autonomy ran afoul of the newly expanded First Amendment.

This movement toward intellectual autonomy helps distinguish the individualized liberty from the privacy approach. The latter model emphasized the relational character of humanity. Thus, the family had liberty because of the dignity intrinsic to the parental relationship. But the person was not defined by one relationship, but by a complex array of relationships, and consequently no one relationship was accorded absolute protection. The privacy of the parental relationship must, therefore, be balanced against the need to properly dispose young citizens toward their civic relationships. The privacy model was therefore more flexible because it sought a prudential balance between the family as a private good existing in a context of other goods, including the state's interest in civic identity and cohesion. The individualized approach was, as its name suggests, far less relational, and as a consequence far less flexible when it came to balancing a state interest in civic identity. It was less relational because it spoke of human identity entirely as a matter of interior and intellectual affirmation, while our actions and communities proceed from a choice that reflected that interior autonomy. Consequently, any notion that identity can be formed by outside, relational influences—such as the shared experience of saluting the flag—contradicts the autonomy of interior opinion. There could be no legitimate effort by the community to show a preference or expectation for one kind of opinion as opposed to another. That did not mean the individualized approach rejects the need for social cohesion. Instead, *Barnette* argued (perhaps paradoxically) that cohesion would follow from protecting intellectual autonomy. That was because guaranteeing autonomy "diminished fear and jealousy of strong government" by "making us feel safe to live under it," thereby making us more likely to support that government.[28] The autonomy of opinion would, the argument implied, produce at least one thing in common: individuals would recognize in their self-determination the benefits of free institutions, and would also find themselves more attached to those institutions. In essence, pursuing private individualism would produce a spontaneous and harmonious civic devotion, though the Court does little to defend or explain why devotion, rather than disinterest, would settle among the people.

Finally, beyond diminishing the relation between person and civic community, intellectual autonomy also separated the child from the family. As I noted above, the Court's ruling completely ignored the family despite the fact that the law in question interposed itself between the relationship of child and parent. Legally and constitutionally, therefore, the law fundamentally threatened the rights of parents, especially their right to educate the child about religious doctrine. The identical *Minersville* case openly acknowledged this basic fact, even though it sided with the state and against the parents: "what the school authorities are really asserting is the right to awaken in the child's mind considerations as to the significance of the flag *contrary* to those implanted by the parent."[29] By focusing on the rights of children, the *Barnette* Court eschewed the privacy model, which had previously vindicated the rights of the young through the rights of parents, thereby granting legal and constitutional significance to the relational structure of the family. The individualized approach did not deny that structure, but implied that the Court was more interested in protecting children as individual rights bearers rather than in protecting unique familial relationships; if focused on all persons as intellectually autonomous from the state. Not only did this marginalize the family but it also tendered the possibility that children could seek the vindication of their intellectual rights over and against the authority of parents. This is the very issue that divided Justice Douglas from the majority opinion in the third case of this study, *Wisconsin v. Yoder*.

THE CONTINUING DEBATE: AMISH EDUCATION

Wisconsin v. Yoder (1972) involved Amish parents that were prosecuted for violating compulsory education laws. They kept their children out of secondary school and instead trained them in the Amish way of life at home. In a

6–1 decision (Justices Powell and Rehnquist recused themselves) the Court ruled in favor of the Yoders, arguing that the parents' free-exercise rights and their authority as parents trumped the state's interest compulsory education. Justice Douglas, however, objected to the majority's focus on the religious rights of *parents*, rather than the rights of the *children*. The latter, he argued, may have desired to continue their education rather than persist in the Amish way of life, and if so their right to education should be vindicated against the religious doctrine of their parents. Douglas's dissent, therefore, bears out a logical consequence of the individualized liberty approach in *Barnette*—that the Court's emphasis on the intellectual self-determination of children entails, at some point, an intellectual right against parental authority.

Before turning to Douglas's dissent, however, we begin with the *Yoder* majority opinion. The majority opinion does not simply fit into one model or the other. Instead, the opinion demonstrated elements of the privacy model, but with a relatively weak notion of civic community and responsibility. To begin with, the privacy approach is evident in the Court's affirmation of familial privileges in educational matters. Thus, despite the fact that the Court acknowledges that "[p]roviding public schools ranks at the very apex of the function of the state," the majority ultimately agreed that "even this paramount responsibility was, in *Pierce*, made to yield to the right of parents to provide an equivalent education in a privately operated system." That privacy reflected the importance of "parental direction of the religious upbringing and education of their children in their early and formative years," which is a function that has enjoyed "a high place in our society." Thus, the *Yoder* Court indicated that the "traditional interests of parents with respect to the religious upbringing of their children" would be respected, so long as the family understood their responsibility(quoting *Pierce*) to "'prepare [the children] for additional obligations.'"[30] Evidently, therefore, the Court reaffirmed the unique parental authority over education, so long as parents also recognized a social responsibility in education.

Much of the Court's opinion is dedicated to what it might mean for the Amish—whose children would grow up largely disconnected from society—to prepare their children for additional, social responsibilities. To begin, the Court rejected Wisconsin's claim, (based upon an extrapolation of the Court's ruling in *Prince v. Massachusetts*), that the parent's social responsibility required secondary school. *Prince* involved a legal guardian preaching on city streets, and using her child to sell religious pamphlets. The Court ruled against the parent in that case, arguing that parental authority could not violate the rights of a child. In the context of *Prince*, that meant protecting the child's safety and welfare from laboring on city streets. In *Yoder*, Wisconsin tried to argue that the Yoders similarly threatened their children's welfare by depriving them of an education and fostering ignorance—and by extension the parents were failing to prepare their children for "additional duties." But the Court rejected Wisconsin's *Prince* analogy by arguing that the Yoders were in fact living up to their duty to properly socialize their children. The Court said that "the Amish community has been a highly successful social unit within our society, even if apart from the conventional mainstream," and their "learning by doing" model of education outside the school system may very well "find ready markets in today's society" should they leave their religious community.[31] Though the Amish children may not ever be ordinary members of society, should they choose to leave their community, the Court concluded that their home-education would not hamper their entry into society.

Though the Court's affirmation of the privileged position of the parental relationship reflects a privacy approach to the family, the Court's correspondingly thin notion of social responsibility is actually closer to the individualized liberty approach. The *Yoder* Court's rejection of the *Prince* analogy depends upon the fact that the Amish would "find ready markets in today's society" should they leave their religious community.[32] But this reveals a narrowly economic conception of the individual's duty to the civic community. In essence, the Court's evidence that they are equipped for social productiveness amounts to the fact that "they reject public welfare in any of its usual modern forms."[33] In other words, *Meyer* and *Pierce* recognized that protecting familial privacy cannot come at the expense of instilling in children some sense of shared civic identity with the larger community. But the *Yoder* opinion did not see a state interest in civic education that must be balanced against parental authority; instead, the opinion seems to suggest the only legitimate state interest in education was to reduce its welfare obligations. Since Wisconsin cannot say that, as a result of the home-schooling, the Amish would likely become welfare dependents should they leave their community, they had no claim to balance against the parental authority. Thus, the *Yoder* opinion affirms parental privacy, but is far less willing than *Meyer* and *Pierce* to acknowledge a robust state interest in civic cohesion and in this sense leaned toward the individualized liberty approach.

While the majority opinion is a kind of hybrid of the two approaches to the family, Justice Douglas's dissenting opinion is wholly within the individualized liberty approach, and indeed made explicit the atomization of the family relationships that were implicit in *Barnette*. Douglas argued that the Court should consider that the free-exercise rights of the children might be impinged by the Court's ruling. If the Amish children reject their religious community's doctrine, the Court should see to it that they attend secondary school over their parents' objections. Douglas warned, therefore, that "the parents' notion of religious duty" was being imposed "upon their children." From this perspective, "the State may well be able to override the parents' religiously motivated objections" in order to vindicate the rights of children.[34] Just as was the case in *Barnette*, therefore, Douglas sought to make the children parties to the case; something the *Yoder* majority considered and rejected: "It is the parents who are subject to prosecution here . . . and it is their right of free exercise, not that of their children, that must determine Wisconsin's power to impose criminal penalties on the parent . . . The children are not parties to this litigation."[35] Douglas's dissent, therefore, amounted to the idea that neither state nor parent could deprive a child of their free exercise right. This was, in other words, a logical conclusion of the individualized liberty approach. That is, any action not arising from interior affirmation should be considered coercion. As such, parental authority itself could be considered coercive against intellectually self-determinant children—at least among children "mature enough to express potentially conflicting desires"[36]

Douglas welcomed the opportunity to clarify the competing models of family authority, saying that "[t]his issue has never been squarely presented before today." He looked back with skepticism at previous precedents (naming *Meyer* and *Pierce*), saying that "[o]ur opinions are full of talk about the power of parents over the child's education," but he preferred to highlight "recent cases" that emphasized "clearly . . . [that] the children themselves have constitutionally protectable interests." He then turned to *Barnette* as an authority to bolster his opinion, arguing that, in that case, the "vice of the regime was its interference with the child's free exercise of religion." Douglas believed that, in this case, the child should not be tethered to the religious heritage of his parents, and that each generation ought to be free to strike out on his own; that the intellectual autonomy of the individual was, in a practical sense, the right of the individual to define himself in any way he pleased. Thus, while Douglas acknowledged that "the parents . . . normally speak for the entire family," such a presumption would interfere with individual self-determination and autonomy; after all, the Amish child may prefer "to be a pianist or an astronaut or an oceanographer."[37] Accordingly, Douglas understood the family impeding the autonomy of the individual. Thus the individualized liberty approach differed from the privacy approach over a fundamental question about the human condition: are humans essentially relational, or is human dignity best achieved through unencumbered self-definition? If the former, then the family would be a privileged relationship, but only as a part of the complexity of human identity; if the latter, then the family is required perhaps for the necessities of life, but not to give meaning to life—and indeed, according to this account, perhaps meaning can only found by overcoming the family.

CONCLUSION

It should not be a surprise that one of the key differences between the two approaches to the family came from their different understandings of social responsibility, nor that the Court transitioned from one approach to another during the New Deal. The privacy model tended to see the family as a good unto itself—a natural structure that could not be subsumed by the state. But the privacy model also saw, in principle, the potential for complementarity between private and public. Consequently, social institutions like the family had both liberty and duty. The New Deal introduced a different perspective. Government's activism in social and economic regulation meant that it tended to compete with traditional social institutions like the family, churches, and civic associations to foster social goods. Thus, two things happened simultaneously with the New Deal. The national state diminished the idea that liberty meant social and economic self-determination (since that seemed to lead to widespread economic insecurity) and redefined limited government to refer to intellectual self-determination. At the same time, as the state came to replace the family's social responsibilities, the family's traditional authority over the ethical formation of its members seemed to conflict with the new-found idea that American liberty was intellectual autonomy. It made little sense to emphasize the privileges of the family when its social significance diminished, and its ethical authority positively threatened the American redefinition of liberty.

Despite the success of the New Deal and the rise of a national state though, the individualized approach has not vanquished the privacy approach to the family. We can see that in the *Zelman* debate, which witnesses an emphasis on the family and privacy in the majority opinion. Meanwhile the dissent did emphasize social cohesion, but through a kind of individualism that preferred private, individualized religious practice instead of highly institutionalized religious structures like a parochial school system. The majority, therefore, celebrated government *empowering* a social institution like the family, and did not hesitate to also empower a civic institution like a church. The *Zelman* dissent showed great trepidation about empowering a social institution like the church, but did not hesitate to weaken the family's freedom to take control over their children's education. The former understood freedom to come *through* civil society, while the latter understood freedom to be liberation *from* civil society. This debate shows us, therefore, that the way we conceive of liberty and limited government has profound consequences for how we conceive of the family, and the way we conceive of the family has profound consequences for how we conceive of governmental power.

NOTES

1. In the education context, Kevin Pybas's critique of Amy Gutman ("Civic Education and Social Diversity," *Ethics* 105 (1995): 557–79) and Stephen Macedo (*Diversity and Distrust: Civic Education in a Multicultural Democracy* [Cambridge, MA: Harvard University Press, 2000]) in a 2004 edition of *Perspectives on Political Science* 33 (2004): 18–29) is a good example of this debate. Pybas argues that Gutman and Macedo share a "unitary" approach to "civic education" because they "believe that, in the interest of social unity, the state's monopolization of education funds is necessary to ensure that most children are drawn into state schools so that they can receive the education on which liberal society supposedly depends" (19). Pybus instead emphasizes a "pluralist" approach to education which is founded upon the conviction that "in a free society views of the human good cannot properly be imposed by the state" (27). For instance, the unitary model "makes it difficult for many parents to pass on their beliefs and ways of life to their children—a point they applaud" (28). Meanwhile, the pluralist system of education would suggest that preserving and enhancing parental choice and freedom in education tends to encourage civic virtue while preserving individual liberty.

2. 536 U.S. 639, 649 (2002).

3. Ibid., 728–29.

4. Kevin Pybas, "Does the Establishment Clause Require Religion To Be Confined to the Private Sphere," *Valparaiso University Law Review* 40 (2005): 108.

5. Joseph P. Viteritti, "Reading Zelman: the triumph of pluralism and its effects on liberty, equality, and choice," *Southern California Law Review* 76 (2003): 1105–88, 1186. See also, Richard W. Garnett, School Choice and the Challenges that Remain: A Comment on Richard D. Komer's "School Choice and State Constitutions' Religion Clauses," *Journal of School Choice* 4 (2010): 94.

6. Moshe Cohen-Eliya, Yoau Hammer, "An Argument from Democracy against School Choice: A Critique of Zelman v. Simmons-Harris," *Loyola Law Rev* 49, no.4 (Wint 2003): 859–916, 889.

7. Klint Alexander, Kern Alexander, "Vouchers and the Privatization of American Education: Justifying Racial Resegregation from Brown to Zelman," *University of Illinois Law Review* (2004): 1153–54.

8. For example, Goodwin Liu and William L. Taylor, "School Choice to Achieve Desegregation," *Fordham Law Review* 74, no. 2 (2005): 791–823; Mark Tushnet, "Vouchers after Zelman," *The Supreme Court Review* Vol. 2002 (2002): 1–39.

9. 262 U.S. 390, 399–400 (1923).

10. 268 U.S. 510, 535 (1925).

11. Randy E. Barnette, *Restoring the Lost Constitution* (Princeton, Princeton University Press, 2004), 211

12. 268 U.S. 510, 535 (1925).

13. 262 U.S. 390, 399 (1923).

14. 268 U.S. 510, 535 (1925).

15. 262 U.S. 390, 399 (1923).

16. 268 U.S. 510, 535 (1925).

17. 262 U.S. 390, 400 (1923).

18. Ibid., 397–98.

19. Though I do not include it in the body of the text, the *Pierce* opinion reflected the same conception of parental duty as yielding to a legitimate state interest. Thus, the *Pierce* Court validated the state "concerning the power . . . to regulate all schools" including the power to ensure the "moral character and patriotic disposition" of teachers, who are responsible for ensuring that "certain studies plainly essential to good citizenship . . . be taught" 268 U.S. 510, 534 (1925).

20. This approach has generally been called the preferred liberties approach, and its most commonly traced back to Footnote Four from the 1938 case *U.S. v. Carolene Products*, 304 U.S. 144 (1938).

21. 319 U.S. 624, 639 (1943).

22. Ibid., 639–40.

23. Ibid., 636.
24. Ibid., 634–35.
25. Ibid., 633–34.
26. U.S. Constitution, Amendment I.
27. 319 U.S. 624, 631 and 633 (1943).
28. Ibid., 636.
29. 310 U.S. 586, 599 (1940) (emphasis added).
30. 406 U.S. 205, 213–14 (1972).
31. Ibid., 222–24.
32. Ibid.
33. Ibid., 222.
34. Ibid., 242–43.
35. Ibid., 230–31.
36. Ibid., 242.
37. Ibid., 244–45.

Chapter Nine

Liberalism, the Family, and the Right to Privacy

Griswold v. Connecticut *and Its Progeny*

Stephen A. Block

2015 marked the fiftieth anniversary of *Griswold v. Connecticut*, the case in which the Supreme Court first identified and provided protection for a constitutional right to privacy. Beginning with a seemingly narrow right to privacy in marriage that privileged and protected an institution deeply rooted in American and Western traditions, this right has been progressively expanded over the last half century. Given that liberalism has, since its origin, been built on the distinction between public and private, and given further that the Framers of the Constitution have for a long time been thought to have been steeped in the thought of Locke and other classical liberal thinkers and in one way or another attempted to institutionalize liberal principles, the right to privacy must seem on the surface at least to be an unobjectionable unfolding of the aspirations of liberal theory. Hence, the idea that the Constitution protects, even as it does not expressly mention, a right to privacy has become at least in some circles and perhaps even for most citizens a nearly unquestionable fact.

The apparently unexceptional expansion of individual freedom to pursue private fulfillment and happiness is nevertheless fraught with difficulties. The problems begin by reflecting on the putative origins of liberal society. Civil society and government can only seriously be understood by today's libertarians as based on a contract for the sake of the mutual accommodation of the rights and interests of each, as providing the conditions for the pursuit of individual ends and good. In spite of this fact, surprisingly little attention is paid to the problem that this view of the proper ends of government rests ultimately on a specific understanding of human nature. Most importantly, this understanding of human nature poses a concrete problem for civil association. Namely, even as human beings are not evil or cruel, they are ineradicably and *legitimately* self-interested. In general, this means that human beings are more concerned with preserving their own liberty than that of others. If they are not, moreover, the limited scope and ends of liberal government would make much less sense than it does. Without the discovery of rights in our deepest and strongest passions, there is little or no reason to limit the principal purposes of liberal government to the securing of those rights whose authority are rooted in our passions.

Given these presuppositions about human nature, which are indispensable to liberalism and its understanding of the foundation of rule and law, one must inevitably wonder how fundamentally self-interested individuals can be relied on to act justly, that is, to keep the promises and contracts that establish our obligations even when doing so is not in their interest. This difficulty was one with which the American Founders were deeply acquainted. Hence, the problem of liberal constitutionalism was for them the problem of how to establish a government strong enough to survive and perform the basic function of liberal government without being so strong and intrusive as to be a perpetual threat to the individualist goals that give rise to government in the first place.[1] In this important respect, even as the benefit of the private individual is the end of civil society and liberal government, that there should or must exist a realm of individual privacy free of governmental intrusion and regulation is by no means a given or necessary fact. In light of the liberal imprimatur on individualism and the pursuit of mundane self-interest, it must be greatly naïve to presume that individuals will willingly exercise their liberty in pursuit of their own happiness consistent with the liberty and interests of others. In all, although the securing of individual rights is a seemingly modest goal compared to the more extravagant goals of non-liberal regimes, liberal government cannot in practice be neutral on the practice of rights and individual liberty.

The foregoing is a very general sketch of the paradox at the core of liberal constitutional government. The American Founders concerned themselves deeply with the problem and brilliantly devoted all their efforts to managing this tension by establishing institutions devoted to remedying the problems of liberal association. At least in part, however, addressing these difficulties demanded certain prudent qualifications to the establishment of any purely or puritanically liberal theory. In this regard, at the heart of the American constitutional order is a tension between the theoretical presuppositions as to the origins and purposes of human association and civil government, which seem to privilege the individual above all, and the actual practices and institutions that make liberal government possible, including religion for example, but are nevertheless not fully reconcilable with the presuppositions of any theory of liberalism.

It is the argument of this essay that the right to privacy as a constitutional doctrine is a reflection of this tension, and that the doctrine arises in order to provide some respect and protection to the family, which is an institution necessary for any human association, but one that does not fit neatly with liberal theory. The difficulty, I suggest, is that there is no public understanding of the family as a liberal institution that can be provided without questioning the contractual basis of civil society and the state, on the one hand, or deforming the nature of the family, on the other hand. Aware that the family is nevertheless necessary to achieve the purposes of liberal government, the Court beginning in *Griswold* originated the right to privacy in order to immunize the family from public scrutiny. As such, the right to privacy had nothing to do with privacy as such, but rather with an immunity from giving any rational account of the activities or institutions now deemed as "private" but still accorded extraordinary shelter from state regulation. Without any precise account of the grounds for marriage or the family in a liberal constitutional order, however, the right to privacy was amorphous and had to expand into a right to engage in conduct that could be immunized from state control only because it was irrelevant or inconsequential, and did no harm or injury to another. But since there is no basis in reason or our legal or constitutional traditions for a right to inconsequential conduct to be elevated to the status needed to give it constitutional immunity from regulation, the Court had to hide the content of the right they were protecting behind various formulations as to what made some conduct or choices "private" and beyond regulatory control.

PRIVACY AND THE FAMILY

The problem of the Court's attempt to give an account of the family begins in *Pierce v. Society of Sisters*, where the Court attempted a rational explanation of family relationships. The case involved a Fourteenth Amendment challenge to an Oregon compulsory 1922 education law requiring all children, with a few exceptions, to attend a public school beginning in 1925. The Society of Sisters, a corporation devoted to religious and secular instruction of children, challenged the law on the grounds that the state deprived them of property without due process of law in violation of the Fourteenth Amendment. The Court ruled that the law did deprive the Sisters' property, but more significantly the Court held that the law was fatally flawed because its purpose as the standardization and uniformity of education ran counter to the "fundamental theory of liberty upon which all government of this Union repose," which precluded the standardization or homogenization of children.

As such, since the purpose of the law was inconsistent with the most basic notion of liberty underlying the Constitution, the deprivation of property was unrelated to any permissible state purpose. The Society of Sisters was therefore denied due process of law, and the Oregon statute was struck down as a violation of the Fourteenth Amendment.

Although *Pierce* would be continuously used by the Court as precedent for the next century (including, most significantly, in *Griswold*), the Court's reasoning in the case is problematically disjointed. In the climax of Justice McReynold's opinion of the Court in *Pierce*, he writes: "The child is not the mere creature of the State; those who nurture him and direct his destiny have the right, *coupled with the high duty,* to recognize and prepare him for additional obligations."[2] This crucial formulation speaks in terms quite familiar to liberalism—of rights and duties that can be traced back to express or tacit consent—but it nevertheless creates an insuperable paradox inasmuch as it attempts to combine rights and duties in parents. The exercise of rights is discretionary—the liberty to do or refrain from doing—while that of duties is certainly not. If parental authority is rooted in a duty to provide a proper upbringing for the child, the discretionary authority involved in the exercise of a right is by no means a given; and if, contrarily, parental authority is a right, the content of those duties are problematically vague.

It is nevertheless easy to see the problem faced by Justice McReynolds. There was a need to dignify parental authority, because the extent of authority in the parent recognized by the Court–an authority they are denying to the state–is extraordinary and makes little sense, if at least the right is merely a matter of personal interest or fulfillment of the parent. But inasmuch as parents have a "high duty" to raise and educate their children well in order "to prepare [them] for additional obligations," how does this duty not necessitate a means by which these duties can be enforced and obeyed, and thus invite the continual intrusion by the state in the parent-child relationship in the name of parental *duties*? This latter possibility can be avoided if and only if the relationship between parent and child can be formulated in such a way as to combine parental authority into a right, in order to demand a neutrality on the part of the state, and a duty to justify parental power in the first place. Such a combination is incoherent.

The confused reasoning in *Pierce* is but a manifestation of the fact that the family presents an acute problem for liberal constitutionalism. This confusion is not necessarily due to the fact that parents cannot be trusted with such power over children, but perhaps more so because they can. There has in reality been one overriding reason for according parental rights such respect in our tradition, immunizing decisions made within those relationships from state scrutiny, and for which reason *Pierce* has been more or less uncontroversial (although difficult to apply in particular circumstances). In the normal case, these relationships are governed not by the self-interest of different parties that motivates contracts but by love and affection, the ultimate concern for the well-being of the child or a common good.[3] This is to say that it must be presupposed that the high duties involved in parenting are self-enforcing, because human nature is such that the wellbeing of the child will be preferred over that of the parent. The ground of parental authority thus transcends all rights and duties, and as such, the family and the relationships within it cannot easily be understood as liberalism attempts to construe human relationships as contractual associations devoted to mutual benefits for the contracting parties. On the other hand, if this presumption were not made and the family was indeed contractual, there would be a continuing necessity for the state to regulate and set the terms of these relationships, as they do with economic contracts, for example. Any notion of the privacy of the family would thereby be undermined.

In this respect, the family is necessary in part to vindicate the possibility of a realm of human action free of perpetual government intrusion and oversight, because it is that realm of human relationships that is presumptively not governed by self-interested logic. The family operates as a liberal refuge, although this is so only because it can be presumed to be ordered in accordance with a rationality that is alien to liberalism, inasmuch as it presumes the authority and power of natural familial affection over the individual's mundane self-interest. The family and familial relations present a problem for liberal reason but also a solution to the problems inherent in its presuppositions. The family and its naturalness grounded in affection cannot really comport with liberalism, but liberalism must rely on the family for the support of its institutions, and particularly for providing a realm of privacy free of state oversight.

The Court originated the right to privacy specifically in *Griswold v. Connecticut*, which struck down a Connecticut law generally prohibiting the use of birth control, and the Court placed most precedential weight on the protection of parental rights in *Pierce.* While the Court did not, as is usually thought, actually declare a constitutional right to use birth control even within marriage and seemed to reserve the possibility of upholding a law that regulated distribution, the marital relationship was a constitutionally-protected realm of privacy and laws that swept so broadly as to have even an incidental effect on these constitutionally protected realms of privacy were unconstitutional. Justice Douglas writes, "Marriage is a coming together for better or for worse, hopefully enduring, and intimate to the degree of being sacred. It is an association that promotes a way of life, not causes; a harmony in living, not political faiths; a bilateral loyalty, not commercial or social projects. Yet it is an association for as noble a purpose as any involved in our prior decisions."[4] Although Douglas speaks here of the "noble purpose" of marriage, he never in fact explained what this noble purpose was or for that matter gave any indication of what it might be, except that it is distinct from economic and political ones. Indeed, he only vaguely explains how the law, which was not even enforced against married couples, in any way affected privacy within the marriage by referencing the revolting thought of searching the marital bedroom for signs of the contraband.

The most peculiar aspect of the Court's decision in *Griswold* is the fact that, unlike in most other cases in which a state law is found to impinge upon some liberty, especially some fundamental liberty, the Court does not even consider and evaluate the legislative purpose that would have justified the regulation of the marital relationship in this way. Douglas does not mention what the state claimed its purpose was, nor did he explain how it was unimportant or how the law did not advance the state's interest. Most importantly, it did not really explain what about the marital relationship the law in fact burdened. The Court therefore speaks of marital privacy as if it were an absolute right as well as a thoroughly indefinite right whose boundaries are obscure. Since no right, no matter how fundamental or important, has ever been accorded an absolute status and thus has always required the Court to balance the regulation of the right with the state's interest, this ultimately was not an accident. The only way to do such balancing is by in some way determining the impact of public regulation on the right and its exercise. This would have required an account of the content of that right and ultimately its purpose, in order to determine the outer limits of the right. In practice, this would have entailed explaining what marriage is and why a law that intrudes into the marital bedroom does "maximum detrimental impact" to the relationship itself. Which decisions made within a marriage are fundamental to it so that it can be clear what general across-the-board regulations that do not exempt married couples, like the Connecticut statute involved in the case, actually do violate or burden or abrogate the right to marital privacy?

The fact that a regulation prevents married individuals from making a decision they would like to make cannot of course be enough to invalidate a law. No one would think, for example, that prohibiting the use of narcotics would be an invasion of the privacy of the marital relationship, even if no exemption were made for married couples to choose to use narcotics together in the privacy of their bedroom in order to enhance their sexual experience. Such a prohibition would nevertheless be a regulation of some detail of marital intimacy, depriving them of the choice to engage in sexual conduct of their free choice. Even more, it would be necessary to ask why sexual decisions made by the married are more important than other marital decisions, economic ones for example, which unquestionably valid state regulations limit. The indefinite nature of the right to marital privacy as described by Justice Douglas is thus its most outstanding feature and it saves Douglas from giving a genuine account of marriage and its goods.

Justice Goldberg's concurring opinion in *Griswold* is instructive of the great difficulty in doing what Justice Douglas refrains from doing in the

Court's opinion. Unlike the majority opinion, Goldberg does attempt to apply a balancing test to determine if the state's interests are weighty enough to regulate this activity by married couples. Goldberg begins this analysis from traditional distinction between the legal prohibition of non-marital sexual conduct, which is unquestionably conduct the state has a right to forbid, and marital sexual intimacy, because "the intimacy of husband and wife is necessarily an essential and accepted feature of the institution of marriage, an institution which the State not only must allow, but which, *always and in every age,* it has fostered and protected."[5]

While this distinction articulated by Goldberg is undoubtedly true, Connecticut did not of course impose a sexual regimen on married couples merely by prohibiting the use of contraceptives. Hence, the problem in Goldberg's analysis is that he attempts to take refuge in a traditional presumption that specifically marital intimacy, as opposed to non-marital intimacy involving the same conduct, is of great importance. Goldberg cannot reasonably presume that reproductive control is a necessary predicate of marital intimacy as Western or American practice understood it, for otherwise marital intimacy would not have existed before the availability of effective birth control. If the protection of marital intimacy is rooted in the long-standing traditions of the legal promotion and protection of the marital relationship, the connection between reproductive control and marital intimacy is tenuous at best. Goldberg does nothing to explain how this regulation in any way affects marital intimacy as it has been fostered "always and in every age." Accordingly, even as Goldberg attempts to be more precise than Douglas, he nevertheless is forced to take refuge in vague generalizations, and ultimately irrelevant traditional and historical distinctions, as to the purposes of marriage and the privacy right related to marriage that justify elevating this institution.[6] In spite of the fact that all nine Justices, including the dissenters, in *Griswold* were unanimous in their disapprobation of the Connecticut statute, not one of them gives any explanation of the nature of marital intimacy or what goods it serves and promotes that are so thoroughly harmed by the law.

Douglas' spiritualization of the marital relationship had the effect of shielding the actions within marriage from public scrutiny. It may of course be that because the Court was articulating a right to render marriages infertile and thus dissolving any necessary connection to an objective common good shared by the couple, it was losing any way of speaking about marriage or its object and thus turning it, for legal purposes, into an institution that is completely idiosyncratic and self-defining. But the Court did not in fact claim any such right of the married in the case, and by at least indicating that a law regulating distribution and sale of contraceptives would not have intruded upon marital privacy, such a law would probably have been even more effective in depriving marital couples of access to contraceptives.[7] Hence, the Court putatively did not strike down the law because it actually prevented the use of birth control, and thus did not break the connection entirely between marriage and children. Rather, one might ask what Douglas could have said about marriage and the family that would have been comprehensible in light of liberal rationality and thus would have justified affording this specific relationship the protection the Court sought to give it. What, after all, could possibly be considered an individual's rationale for marriage and childbearing at all, for taking on burdens, limits, and barriers to personal liberty that those relationships traditionally entail? Because liberal contractual reason offers little place for love and affection, or the nobility of self-sacrifice, as essential to the health of the human soul or to human happiness, it is entirely unclear what account of the marriage as rooted in these virtues and goods could be comprehensible to the logic of liberal individualism, except by radically questioning the imprimatur of individualism that is the ground of liberalism.

The right to privacy begins in *Griswold* in part in response to the need to shield noble actions and perhaps even those necessary from a reductionist contractual rationality, but this meant more than anything else establishing a realm of human action that could be freed from giving any rational public account of itself. The Court, as the principal expositor of that kind of rationality in being *the* voice of liberal constitutionalism, had to invent the right to privacy–the immunization of a realm of action or decision-making that could be free from rational public scrutiny, that never was required to give an account of its rationality and thus left it to its own self-definition, rather than the Court's. The right to privacy began therefore as the ever-strange combination of judicial activism and judicial restraint, an activism necessary to free the Court of the responsibility of giving a public, constitutional understanding of marriage and the family, its purposes, and its grounds in order to protect it from excessive state intrusion.

CONSEQUENCES, AUTONOMY, AND THE EXPANSION OF THE PRIVACY RIGHT

The Court's answer to the difficulty of articulating precisely what it was about the institution of marriage that privileged it above all other political or economic associations was to be vague and indefinite about the purposes that defined and limited the institution of marriage. In this, they might have been prudent, for it is not at all clear that the institution of marriage, like that of parental rights, can adequately be articulated in terms consistent with liberal principles. Inasmuch as privacy became the realm of action that was private only inasmuch as it did not need to explain itself publicly, however, the right to privacy inevitably devolved into a right to be unimpeded in actions that are fundamentally inconsequential. The Court today speaks of the privacy right very much as the freedom to do as one wishes so long as the action does not harm the interests of another or the state.[8] The Court nevertheless could not initially formulate the right in this way, for if it did, it would have had to explain from the beginning why such a right to what must be viewed as insignificant conduct in order to require neutrality by the state and itself to its individual exercise is important enough to justify the Court developing an entirely new constitutional right for its protection. Why should the Court or the state or anybody else care to vindicate trivial action that the individual has no intent or ability to explain, that is defensible only because it is purportedly benign? The Court attempted to avoid answering this basic question in two slightly different waves of the development of the privacy right, the first by focusing entirely on the consequences of purportedly inconsequential action as falling within the right to privacy and the second by attempting to explain how inconsequential action is in fact consequential by introducing "autonomy" as the "heart of liberty."

Following the Court's ruling in *Griswold,* the Massachusetts legislature revised its own birth control regulations to prohibit only the distribution and sale of birth control devices to the unmarried, which would therefore in no way sweep so broadly as to affect sexual intimacy within the marital relationship. The law was nevertheless challenged in 1972 in *Eisenstadt v. Baird.* In part, because the Court in *Griswold* had done nothing at all to define the limits of the marital relationship, the Court was given the opportunity to expand the privacy right well outside of the marriage. The generality of the prohibition of contraceptives was the constitutional problem with the Connecticut statute in *Griswold,* inasmuch as the law swept so broadly as to impede a constitutionally protected relationship of greater importance than any other relationship. By contrast, the Massachusetts law was challenged for precisely the opposite reason under the Equal Protection Clause, for creating an impermissible legal distinction between married and unmarried individuals. Whereas the Court in *Griswold* could leave the foundation of marital privacy indeterminate, as soon as any legal distinction was made on these grounds, it was necessary to provide some account of the distinctive features of the marital relationship as opposed to any other relationship in order to decide such a case. Authoring the opinion of the Court in *Eisenstadt*, Justice Brennan significantly found no special importance to the marital relationship, asserting without argument that "the marital couple is not an independent entity, with a mind and heart of its own, but an association of two individuals, each with a separate intellectual and emotional makeup." With this assertion in hand, it became necessary too that "if the right to privacy means anything, it is the right of the individual, married or single, to be free from unwarranted governmental intrusion into matters so fundamentally affecting a person as the decision whether to bear or beget a child."[9] Inasmuch as Brennan's formulation is accurate, there is no ground at all for elevating marriage above any other contractual association involving "two individuals, each with a separate intellectual and emotional makeup."

Massachusetts justified its ban on distribution of contraceptives to the unmarried principally on the grounds that the ban would deter illicit sexual conduct—fornication. Given that Justice Brennan in one fell swoop dissolved any relevant distinction between the married and unmarried by reducing the marital relationship to the same level as any other relationship involving separate individuals, it might have followed that a fornication prohibition that necessarily rests on the distinction between married and unmarried couples would be invalid under the Equal Protection Clause. Brennan strangely declines to take this course, and instead attacked the law's rationality by presuming that the law was a mere reflection of irrational public animus to contraceptives and was thus not related at all to its fornication ban.[10] Brennan claimed, in sum, that the state itself did not genuinely forbid fornication or that the law was not in any way related to the enforcement of its fornication ban. This conclusion he inferred from the fact that the state did not forbid the unmarried from procuring devices for the prevention of sexually-transmitted diseases (hence Massachusetts *de facto* permitted sexual conduct by not requiring that fornicators risk disease to engage in it) and because the penalty for distribution of birth control was significantly harsher than the penalty for the fornication aided by such devices. Once it was found that the purpose of the law was unrelated to the prohibition on fornication or enforcing that prohibition by adding a disincentive to illicit sexual conduct, the distinction between married and unmarried individuals made by the law was undoubtedly irrational. If Massachusetts permitted the unmarried alongside the married to engage in sexual conduct of their choice, the law could not be a reasonable regulation if it imposed a necessity that legally permitted fornication result in an unwanted pregnancy for one and not the other.

Brennan's inference that Massachusetts did not genuinely forbid fornication was hardly a fair reading of the factual record, as there was no reason to doubt that the unavailability of birth control to the unmarried would be effective in deterring fornication. Why then does Brennan choose more or less to manipulate the factual record rather than simply declare the law forbidding fornication itself invalid? At first glance, it seems that such a ruling would have followed with perfect logic from his reductionist definition of the marital relationship to a mere association of separate individuals.

I want to suggest that there is a deeper ambivalence to Brennan's reasoning about marriage than it seems at first. In sum, even as reducing the marital relationship to an association among individuals could very well have resulted in the striking down of state fornication prohibitions, the logic could have led to very opposite conclusion. The dissolution of the relevance of the distinction between the married and unmarried, a distinction upon which *Griswold* principally relied, could equally erode the basis for any constitutional immunity from state regulation of sexual conduct whether for the married or unmarried. However much Brennan wished to establish an individual constitutional right to engage in consensual sexual activity, the pertinent question that he undoubtedly was not prepared to answer was why, absent its connection to a constitutionally protected institution, sex should be constitutionally privileged activity. Why, for example, is sexual liberty of greater significance and consequence to the individual or to society than economic liberty, such that state commercial and economic regulations are perfectly permissible while those regulating sexual conduct would be an invalid governmental intrusion at all? Lacking any basis in deeply-rooted traditions of the nation, it would have been incumbent on Brennan to answer such questions.

The Court in *Eisenstadt* simply had no way to make any such argument. Instead the Court provided the first general formulation of the right to privacy in order to avoid answering the question at all. This formulation, which would govern much of the Court's privacy jurisprudence for the next twenty years was that "those decisions so fundamentally affecting a person as the decision whether to bear or beget a child" are private and receive heightened protection from state intrusion. The Court does not say that sexual conduct itself is a decision "fundamentally affecting" the individual. Instead, it hid behind the very significant product of sexual conduct—childbearing. The reality is of course that the Court was protecting from state intrusion a decision to ensure that those decisions we make do not ever "fundamentally affect" us by ensuring that individuals have the ability make their sexual conduct infertile—that individuals, married or unmarried, can engage in voluntary sexual activity without consequence. Under this formulation of the right to privacy, therefore, the Court simply obscured what in fact was being protected under the right, thereby getting what it wanted all along without ever arguing for it.

The extension of the right to privacy to cover the abortion decision as but another means to prevent sexual choices from being consequential was very simple, because underlying the right to privacy thus formulated was essentially the right to act without state presumption of the consent to the necessary consequences of the decision one freely makes. Hence, in *Roe v. Wade,* when weighing the separate interests of the woman's freedom against the state's claim to be protecting maternal health and human life, it made no difference at all to Justice Blackmun that most pregnancies are the result of voluntary sexual conduct and are not simply foisted on women seeking an abortion. Rather the consequences of an unwanted pregnancy were so terrible as to justify expanding the right to privacy to cover the abortion decision:

> The detriment that the State would *impose* upon the pregnant woman by denying this choice [to terminate her pregnancy] altogether is apparent. Specific

> and direct harm medically diagnosable even in early pregnancy may be involved. Maternity, or additional offspring, may force upon the woman a distressful life and future. Psychological harm may be imminent. Mental and physical health may be taxed by child care. There is also the distress, for all concerned, associated with the unwanted child, and there is the problem of bringing a child into a family already unable, psychologically and otherwise, to care for it. In other cases, as in this one, the additional difficulties and continuing stigma of unwed motherhood may be involved.[11]

Because an unwanted pregnancy "fundamentally affects" the woman in these ways, it necessarily falls under the right to privacy. Of course, it is also the case that the State imposes all kinds of detriments on human beings, by criminalizing certain kinds of choices that allow us to remedy the unwanted consequences of choices we have already made. The only grounds for distinguishing the two circumstances is to assume that the individual took upon himself or herself certain risks, consenting to the foreseeable results, wanted or unwanted, of the action. The unspoken presumption of the Blackmun opinion, then, is that it is invalid for the state to take into consideration the voluntariness of the sexual conduct that caused the pregnancy in the first place. Blackmun does so only by reiterating the difficulties of an unwanted pregnancy, under the pretense that individuals have a right only to suffer what they want irrespective of one's voluntary action. The right to abortion is but an extension of the core of the right, which is most fundamentally the right to engage in inconsequential conduct in the first place, and thus arises the need, now formulated as a constitutional right, to render it perpetually inconsequential.

Justice Blackmun will proceed from his description of how difficult pregnancy is to deciding the case by balancing the right to privacy against the state's interests, finding the limit of this right in the state's compelling interest in fetal life after the fetus reaches viability. Blackmun provides almost no account of why viability is of any constitutional importance at all to the state, and for this reason, the logic of his line-drawing at viability has been criticized as arbitrary.[12] But the apparent arbitrariness of viability masks the deeper although unspoken rationale of the Court's line-drawing at viability. The logic of viability follows from the principle that human beings have a fundamental right to remain *infinitely* un-obliged for their sexual conduct, irrespective of whether it is voluntary or involuntary—that at no point should the individual be required to make a sexual decision that limits their freedom and independence in the future. Hence, the capacity of the fetus for physical "independence" from the mother at viability is relevant only because it is the point at which the fetus can be theoretically (although not practically) disowned by the mother without the necessary (but nevertheless likely) death of the child. Viability was not, therefore, even the point at which a pregnant woman could finally by the state be understood to have consented to the care of her child. If it were, there would be no principled reason not to push that point back even to the origin of pregnancy. As such, it would threaten to unravel the veiled core of the right to privacy—the right to inconsequential sexual conduct. Since the Court had done nothing to show how or why such conduct is so highly important to the individual or society as to require its liberation from almost all legal constraints, the actual right had to be hidden under a more reasonable right that decisions fundamentally affecting the individual are in some sense of utmost importance to the individual.

The pre-viability abortion right subsumed under the right to privacy is but the continuation of the right not ever to have consented to one's pregnancy, and the abortion right is therefore but a way to secure this realm of sexual liberty as a realm infinitely free of consequence. It follows naturally then that what legitimates the state's interest in the fetus's life has nothing to do with the status of the fetus itself, but entirely with the capacity of the woman to remain perpetually un-obliged and unencumbered, independent of her prior choices and actions. The state's interests in prenatal life are dependent entirely on this fact and are shaped entirely by this new, and ultimately unarticulated, understanding of human freedom.

Unlike in *Griswold*, where Justice Douglas' opinion of the Court studiously avoided rooting marital privacy at all in the Due Process Clause, the Court took the crucial step in *Roe* of establishing the right to privacy as a substantive protection of liberty under the Due Process Clause. In so doing, it immediately raised the objection that the right to privacy thus understood was simply a new version of the discredited liberty of contract jurisprudence during the *Lochner* era, in which the Court used the Fourteenth Amendment to strike down economic regulations limiting the liberty of contract.[13] While this objection to the right to privacy has ever since been the standard critique of the Court's privacy jurisprudence, the actual substance of liberty under these two versions of substantive due process is quite different. The liberty of contract as it was defended by the Court was essentially the freedom to make oneself responsible and to freely take on legally-enforceable obligations. The right to privacy, by contrast, is a freedom to act and be free not only of legally-contracted obligations but any and all consequences that will limit one's future freedom of action. It is the right to act without consenting to anything at all, and thus more generally required the severing of individual freedom from responsibility.

The understanding of freedom that informs this right to privacy has its roots in a romantic understanding that liberty consists in a spontaneity freed from rational constraints, as an escape from the utilitarian logic that necessarily governs liberal contractual reasoning.[14] The common ground of marital privacy and the privacy right articulated in *Eisenstadt* and expanded in *Roe* is thus clear enough. Just as marriage and the family cannot really be explained in terms of a rational contract without distorting the nature of those relationships, so also this understanding of freedom is essentially anti-contractual and frees the individual from ever tacitly making them. If one were to attempt to provide any rational explanation of its importance, purposes, or consequences, the liberty being protected would be dissolved immediately, for it would be subject to purposes higher than the liberty itself.

The paradox of the right to privacy is that the right has been developed by the Court only by progressively diminishing in importance and significance what it is purportedly protecting from governmental intrusion. Thus the privacy right must be presumed to be of great importance, but not a single reason ever has or for that matter could be offered for this crucial presuppositions needed to make any of the Court's reasoning coherent. It is for this reason that the Court attempted at least initially to hide what liberty it was really protecting–a completely and literally unaccountable understanding of human freedom–behind a formulation of the privacy right concerned with immunizing those decisions "fundamentally affecting" the individual.

It was thus necessary that the Court develop the theory of privacy as "autonomy" in order to redeem this inconsequential liberty and demonstrate why meaningless conduct from the perspective of the public can be so meaningful and consequential so as to justify the Court's solicitousness in protecting the right. If and only if the meaning of a choice and action, irrespective of its content or truth, is thoroughly subjectified and, therewith, meaning-giving itself put forward as the core of human dignity, can the right to privacy be redeemed by attempting to ennoble a pure subjectivism. The Court was afforded the opportunity to do this in *Planned Parenthood v. Casey*, in which the Court had to justify its upholding of *Roe* by explaining how it was a logical extension of the other, less controversial, areas of human activity deemed to be constitutionally private. After noting that "our law affords constitutional protection to personal decisions relating to marriage, procreation, contraception, family relationships, child rearing, and education," the Joint Opinion famously declares:

> These matters, involving the most intimate and personal choices a person may make in a lifetime, choices central to personal dignity and autonomy, are central to the liberty protected by the Fourteenth Amendment. At the heart of liberty is the right to define one's own concept of existence, of meaning, of the universe, and of the mystery of human life. Beliefs about these matters could not define the attributes of personhood were they formed under compulsion of the State.[15]

The most striking part of this now famous formulation of liberty is its absoluteness, and in this absoluteness, its grand and un-defended departure from all other understandings of human liberty. The traditional view of human freedom was that there is a fundamental distinction between liberty and license, and that human beings can be free and fully retain their dignity as human beings and still live under the rule of law. This was so only because some acts and decisions were simply not relevant to human dignity and freedom. There was therefore always an inherent limit on the freedom to do as we list. And in accordance with distinction between liberty and license, there was nothing at all that required licentiousness to be understood merely as harmful or injurious to others or the state.

Oddly enough, this view has been at the core of the Court's privileging certain rights over others, rather than articulating a general liberty right to do as one pleases. But articulating a view of this kind about the human being would require a consideration of the human being himself that would necessarily constrain the free-wheeling defining of all things that the Court thinks should be accorded such dignity and ultimately would constrain privacy, because the Court would be called upon necessarily to give an account of the human being rather than an ever-redefining "person."

In spite of the broad decisional autonomy articulated in the Joint Opinion had would render invalid any distinction between liberty and license, the Court ultimately could not avoid making such a distinction. The Court had no intention of establishing a general decisional privacy right, even as the autonomy principle articulated would surely mandate it. This formulation of the "heart of liberty" is invoked, however, to justify and explain the Court's prior privacy right rulings, which had relied on distinguishing "personal choices" that fall under the right to privacy from other kinds of decisions that are apparently not personal enough to merit such consideration. But after this assertion as to how liberty protected by the Due Process Clause should be understood, there cannot genuinely be any measure at all as to what choices are "central to personal dignity and autonomy," for to do so requires the Court to provide a necessary limit on personal and autonomous defining of all things. By distinguishing choices, the Court is attempting to have its cake and eat it too.

Sensing the inadequacy and ultimately the irrelevance of the principle they articulated to decide this case, the Joint Opinion had to resort to its old logic that these decisions, including the abortion decision, "fundamentally affects" the woman:

> Though abortion is conduct, it does not follow that the State is entitled to proscribe it in all instances. That is because the liberty of the woman is at stake in a sense unique to the human condition and so unique to the law. The mother who carries a child to full term is subject to anxieties, to physical constraints, to pain that only she must bear. That these sacrifices have from the beginning of the human race been endured by woman with a pride that ennobles her in the eyes of others and gives to the infant a bond of love cannot alone be grounds for the State to insist she make the sacrifice. Her suffering is too intimate and personal for the State to insist, without more, upon its own vision of the woman's role, however dominant that vision has been in the course of

> our history and our culture. The destiny of the woman must be shaped to a large extent on her own conception of her spiritual imperatives and her place in society.[16]

Ultimately, to perpetuate the privacy right and its otherwise arbitrary privileging of some kinds of conduct that originate in the freedom of conscience (disjoined from any genuine religious dictates) over others, the right to privacy had to be explained, and this was the only explanation available to the Court. It was therefore the one that comported entirely with the primacy, authority, and legitimacy of selfishness that governs all liberal public reasoning. The objective nobility of motherhood and of relationships within the family can be nothing more than a hangover from a bygone past, a viewpoint that can in no way be manifested in the law or foisted on a woman. It was precisely to avoid this conclusion that the Court first articulated a right to privacy to provide an island within liberal society, a refuge from liberal reason, in order to protect the family from such logic.

The principle invoked by the Court to arrive at its conclusion that the abortion decision is one in which the pregnant woman is to be privileged is thus a strange one, above all because it ignores the tensions between liberal theory and liberal practice. The woman's decision is privileged over all other judgments as to the status of the being she is going to destroy, because of the fact that she herself bears the lion's share of the consequences. More generally, this means that it is because the woman is the *most* interested party she has the ultimate right to decide the case. This seems to comport quite well with the self-interest governing liberal principles, for who else is better equipped to look after personal interests and thus judge what is in their interest than the individual himself or herself? Individual rights to judge one's own good are an affirmation of the authority of human selfishness in our polity. But all of this would forget that this liberal imprimatur on self-interest contains a fundamental quandary that the Court simply fails to address, which is that personal interest is also the cause of the corruption of judgment and fairness. There was nothing more self-evident to the great liberal thinkers than that disinterested judgment, in which the subject judging is able to treat that which is to be evaluated as an "object," is superior to interested judgment. Judging in one's own case is the cause of the corruption of judgment, for the private passions and desires are necessarily involved and they distort judgment and usually render it unjust.[17]

One might say all American political institutions and the great efforts of the Framers were devoted to managing this political problem, which included their careful construction of the institutional features of the federal courts that were designed to render federal judges independent and induce a disinterestedness needed to decide cases under law. Both of these principles—self-interest and disinterestedness—are outgrowths of the same primacy of mundane self-interest that lies at the core of liberalism, for being just and thus dealing justly with different parties could not be presumed, precisely because one must presumptively prefer oneself rather than the fair or just resolution of a controversy. Only the judge whose interests are not implicated can really judge fairly. For the same reason, the family cannot be explained in terms of this liberal presumption, for this is not true of the family. This contradiction between the privileging of interested judgment and disinterested judgment in turn is but one formulation of the insufficiency of the principles of liberalism–that even as minimal as liberal justice is (fulfilling one's promises and contracts), it is not easy to establish because of liberal individualism.

This contradiction can be transcended if and only if there is a fundamental connection between one's own good and that of others, such that the good of others is not an obstacle to one's own happiness even when the interests of the parties are different and distinct. Our liberal constitutional order has thus always quietly rested on natural affection to transcend the difficulties its own principles generate.

CONCLUSION

The incongruity of the Court's privacy jurisprudence arises above all from the fact that the Court ultimately is attempting to use it to bring about an ever purer liberalism that privileges the individual and perpetually expands it into every association, including the family, even as the right to privacy as rooted in the family began in *Griswold* in the ultimately failed attempt to preserve liberalism from itself by freeing the family from serving any definite state purposes. It remains to be seen how the transformation of the right to privacy into autonomy as sublimated selfishness in which, irrespective of the choices an individual freely and willingly makes, a person has a right to remain perpetually free of obligation and the consequences of individual decisions will have on these institutions. It nevertheless seems likely that its effect will be to erode the only ground upon which the family has any constitutional or legal significance, and in so doing also erode the practical ground for liberty and privacy itself. It was in those bygone ages when it was presumed and *expected* that a parent, due to the natural affection for child and family, would willingly put the child's interests above their own that there could be any constitutional relevance to the institution of the family as more sacred or nobler than any other human association. Inasmuch as this expectation must be discarded in a rush to elevate a dogma of liberty invoking the authority of the "spiritual imperatives" of the individual, imperatives at odds with the good of the family and its members, the ground for parental authority and ultimately any special immunity to the family or marriage from state oversight is dramatically weakened. The strangest fact in all of this is that the

Court has as of yet found no contradiction at all in including parental rights as one set of these rights of autonomy.

NOTES

1. See especially James Madison, *Federalist* No. 39, in *The Federalist Papers*, ed. Clinton Rossiter (New York: New American Library, 1961), 228.

2. *Pierce v. Society of Sisters*, 268 U.S. 510 (1925), at 535. The incoherence of *Pierce* is evident in other ways as well, above all in the rather significant differences in the reasoning from that of *Meyer v. Nebraska*, which was decided two years earlier and for which Justice McReynolds also authored the Court's opinion, and usually stands alongside *Pierce* as establishing a Fourteenth Amendment parental right to direct the upbringing of child. In that case, the Court struck down as a violation of the Fourteenth Amendment a law that prohibited foreign language instruction as an infringement on the parental right to direct the education of their children, but it does so following a very different logic than that of *Pierce*: "The desire of the legislature to foster a homogeneous people with American ideals prepared readily to understand current discussions of civic matters is easy to appreciate. . . . But the means adopted, we think, exceed the limitations upon the power of the State and conflict with rights assured to plaintiff in error," *Meyer v. Nebraska*, 262 U.S. 390 (1923), at 402. In *Meyer*, the state goal of fostering homogeneity was not what invalidated the law, but rather that the state never showed that prohibiting foreign language instruction was sufficiently related to a valid state purpose, for experience showed that foreign language instruction was not injurious to children. In *Pierce*, by contrast, the very purpose of the law to foster a homogenous people through the standardization of children was itself what invalidated the law under the Due Process Clause for it deprived the Society of Sisters of property without any valid state interest to justify it.

3. See especially *Troxel v. Granville*, 530 U.S. 57 (2000), at 68.

4. *Griswold v. Connecticut,* 383 U.S. 479 (1965), at 486.

5. *Griswold v. Connecticut*, 383 U.S. 479 (1965), concurring at 499.

6. When Justice Goldberg comes to his discussion of the irrationality of the policy means, moreover, Goldberg will claim that the law is unconstitutional, because it is both over-inclusive and under-inclusive. It is under-inclusive, Goldberg says, because the state did not forbid disease-preventing devices, and such devices were legally permitted to both married and unmarried individuals. Goldberg does not say explicitly why this fact is significant, although presumably he means that Connecticut law, in allowing for the general availability of disease-prevention, was an ineffective deterrent of promiscuous sexual conduct. If the law was attempting to discourage illicit sexual activity, a more general and inclusive regulatory scheme of all such devices would have been necessary. But its claim as to the law's under-inclusiveness in not deterring conduct that it legitimately prohibits belies his claim that it is over-inclusive, because the contraceptive prohibition specifically did impinge upon the married couple's constitutionally-protected intimacy. In sum, Goldberg argues that the law had no effect at all inasmuch as it was too permissive and that it had a targeted effect on marital intimacy. Surely, these are not consistent inferences to make about a general prohibition and Justice Goldberg cannot really have it both ways.

7. "The present case . . . concerns a law which, in forbidding the use of contraceptives, *rather than regulating their manufacture or sale,* seeks to achieve its goals by means having a maximum destructive impact upon that relationship," *Griswold v. Connecticut,* 383 U.S. 479, 485 (1965).

8. See Justice Kennedy's bald assertion in *Lawrence v. Texas*: "As a general rule . . . [the] State, or a court, [should not] define the meaning of [an intimate sexual] relationship or . . . set its boundaries absent injury to a person or abuse of an institution the law protects," *Lawrence v. Texas,* 539 U.S. 558 (2003), at 567.

9. *Eisenstadt v. Baird,* 405 U.S. 438 (1972), at 453.

10. *Eisenstadt v. Baird,* 405 U.S. 438 (1972), at 452.

11. *Roe v. Wade*, 410 U.S. 113 (1973), at 153.

12. Since no argument, historical, textual, or rational, is provided by Justice Blackmun to demonstrate why viability is relevant except that it is the point at which the fetus is capable of "meaningful life" outside the womb, John Hart Ely notes that "The Court's defense [of the constitutional relevance of viability] mistakes a definition for a syllogism" ("The Wages of Crying Wolf: A Note on *Roe v. Wade*," *The Yale Law Journal* 82 (5): 924.

13. As Justice Rehnquist wrote: "As in *Lochner* and similar cases applying substantive due process standards to economic and social welfare legislation, the adoption of the compelling state interest standard will inevitably require this Court to examine the legislative policies and pass on the wisdom of these policies in the very process of deciding whether a particular state interest put forward may or may not be 'compelling,'" *Roe v. Wade*, 410 U.S. 113 (1973) (dissenting at 174).

14. In his famous dissent in *Olmstead v. United States*, Justice Brandeis first formulated the right to privacy as follows:

> The makers of our Constitution undertook to secure conditions favorable to the pursuit of happiness. They recognized the significance of man's spiritual nature, of his feelings, and of his intellect. They knew that only a part of the pain, pleasure and satisfactions of life are to be found in material things. They sought to protect Americans in their beliefs, their thoughts, their emotions and their sensations. They conferred, as against the Government, the right to be let alone—the most comprehensive of rights, and the right most valued by civilized men. (*Olmstead v. United States*, 277 U.S. 438 (1928), at 478.

Whatever one makes of Brandeis' reading of the purpose of the Fourth and Fifth Amendments here, his "right to be let alone" stands in stark contrast to what the Court has done with regard to the privacy jurisprudence. The privacy jurisprudence since the 1960's has been devoted to striking down the regulation of conduct under the privacy right, not the governmental intrusion into a private sphere. Even under Brandeis's dissent, therefore, there was no doubt that the federal government had the authority to prohibit the conduct for which Olmstead was convicted. Whatever right to privacy Olmstead had, it had no bearing whatsoever on the question of whether the regulation and criminalization of his conduct was constitutional. Put more simply, Brandeis' right to privacy retains its character as private, while the privacy jurisprudence from the 1970's on has no necessary connection to privacy save the name. For a critique of Brandeis' privacy argument, as well as an excellent explanation of its differences from contemporary privacy doctrine, see Grant B. Mindle, "Liberalism, Privacy, and Autonomy," *The Journal of Politics* 51 (1989): 575–598.

15. *Planned Parenthood of Southeastern Pennsylvania v. Casey,* 505 U.S. 833 (1992), at 851.

16. Ibid., at 852

17. See Thomas Hobbes, *Leviathan* (Indianapolis: Hackett Publishing, 1994), 98, 111; and James Madison, *Federalist* No.10, in *The Federalist Papers*, ed. Clinton Rossiter (New York: New American Library, 1961), 77.

Chapter Ten

Obergefell v. Hodges and the Privacy Doctrine

Liberty, Autonomy, and the Family

Patrick N. Cain

When the U.S. Supreme Court first identified the family as a source of a fundamental right to privacy in *Griswold v. Connecticut*, it seemed to promise a newfound defense of the traditional or natural family. Subsequent cases, however, used privacy rights to expand the legal meaning of the family, thereby allowing for a far broader definition of acceptable family life than was present at the conception of America's constitutional order. Needless to say, this broadening of the family's legal definition has given greater access to the legal family to those who were excluded from its original boundaries, leaving American citizens with a greater freedom to claim its legal framework than ever before. And with this expansion of boundaries came a kind of narrowing as well, at least in the sense that certain conceptions and purposes—sexual (or gender) diversity, procreation, and the rearing of shared biological children—became increasingly excluded from what is recognized as legally essential or important to marital and familial life.[1] Of course, since no one is excluded from participating in these more traditional practices in their own family, the overall thrust of this movement can be claimed as a general increase in the liberty of American citizens, if liberty can be understood as having a multiplicity of equally good options, and if the changes in marriage and family law provide such a reality. If the options for marriage are equally good, then it is only right that the Court's privacy jurisprudence developed in such a way as to prioritize individual autonomy over any set social or political purpose for the family.[2]

In light of the broadening of the family's legal definition, and given that marriage is a legal and public affirmation of a relationship shared by a couple, it may seem fitting that in *Obergefell v. Hodges* the Court employed the language of liberty rather than privacy when it argued that same sex couples have a fundamental right to be married by the state and to receive the associated legal benefits. After all, it would have seemed strange to our ears if the Court had answered the plea for a right to same-sex marriage with the rejoinder that marriage is a private act not to be interfered with by the state.

Yet privacy was not simply absent from the Court's decision, for even as it spoke in the language of liberty, the Court invoked its privacy jurisprudence, suggesting that, "like choices concerning contraception, family relationships, procreation, and childrearing, all of which are protected by the Constitution, decisions concerning marriage are among the most intimate that an individual can make."[3] And the word "privacy" does make one[4] brief appearance when, quoting *Zablocki*, the Court argues that it would be "contradictory 'to recognize a right of privacy with respect to other matters of family life and not with respect to the decision to enter the relationship that is the foundation of the family in our society.'"[5] Although the Court relies on the language of liberty, privacy is the foundation for the fundamental right to marry. But what exactly is the connection between liberty rights and privacy rights, and how might they be understood so as to require the state to provide a marriage license?

Taking these questions as my starting point, this essay traces out the connection between liberty and privacy rights, beginning with Brandeis's and Warren's famous 1890 article advocating that the Court adopt a legally protected right to privacy. I examine the Court's acceptance of this privacy argument in *Griswold v. Connecticut,* showing why that doctrine makes liberty its primary subject in subsequent cases. Doing so, I argue that although the right to privacy as adopted by the Court is founded in and depends upon a notion of personal ownership and freedom that is fully separate from governmental interference and public purposes, its claims ultimately require and culminate in an appeal for public and governmental affirmation of the very thing or activity being held as private.[6] Understood in these terms, the Court's declaration of the right to privacy is not simply the recognition of a fundamental liberty guaranteed by the constitution; the right to privacy doctrine is rather the source from which fundamental rights are derived, including the right to marry someone of the same sex, which the Court announces in *Obergefell v. Hodges*.

THE RIGHT TO PRIVACY

In their famous *Harvard Law Review* article "The Right to Privacy," Brandeis and Warren claim to have discovered a legally protected, but unidentified, right to privacy alongside the common law conception of property.[7] They argue that within past legal decisions resides a right to privacy that extends beyond material goods, protecting (to varying degrees) an individual's thoughts, emotions, sensations, life, habits, and acts.[8] Brandeis and Warren articulate this right with the object of protecting "the privacy of private life" by securing privacy protections, which end (somewhat tautologically) only at the point at which "a man's life [ceases] to be private."[9]

To illustrate this right to privacy, Brandeis and Warren identify a number of cases that made illegal the violation of another's privacy for material gain, including two in which photographers were prohibited from selling copies of clients' photographs.[10] What was fundamentally at stake in these cases, they argue, was not who owned the physical photographs or negatives, but rather who possessed rightful control over the publication of the affairs of private life. Thus, contra the courts who heard the cases, Brandeis and Warren argue that the clients had the right to keep these photographs private not primarily because releasing them would violate any implied contract, but rather because their publication would infringe upon the clients' privacy. In other words, what the privacy right claims is not private property in the usual sense, but rather a kind of property right in the "widest sense, including all possession, including all rights and privileges, and hence embracing the right to an inviolate personality."[11] In fact, Brandeis and Warren suggest that that this broader conception of property is really a claim of absolute self-ownership, since the principle protecting privacy is not really "the principle of private property, but that of an inviolate personality."[12] The right to privacy, they argue, affords the "basis upon which the protection which the individual demands can be rested."[13]

Understood in this way, the right to inviolable personality (or privacy) would seem to involve both a right to keep things private (another party cannot publish one's photograph without consent), and a right to publicity (one is able to immediately turn around and publicize the same image, even by selling the same photograph oneself).[14] What is fundamentally entailed in claim of "inviolate personality," is the absolute right of the individual to control her identity, since it wholly belongs to her. And since one's personality is inviolable, the individual can carry it with herself, even as she enters the public square. Inviolable personality includes one's entire identity, including all of one's rights, an identity that is not separable from the individual whether in private or public. In other words, what is fundamentally claimed by the right to privacy doctrine is not simply the "right to be let alone,"[15] in the sense of having the right to keep things or information hidden away, out out of the public square, or secret from the government.[16] Rather, the right to privacy as "the right to be let alone" is much broader, since one's whole self must be let alone even in public; one's self definition must be protected in public as well as private.[17] Indeed, as Brandeis will later say when sitting on the Supreme Court, the "right to be let alone" is "the most comprehensive of rights."[18]

PRIVACY AND THE SUPREME COURT

The reasoning supporting Brandeis's and Warren's argument for a right to privacy necessarily entails the need to secure public affirmation for that claim, and it is fitting that the Supreme Court's adoption of this right to privacy doctrine takes place in *Griswold v. Connecticut*. Therein, the Supreme Court struck down a Connecticut law that prohibited, not the private use of contraceptives, but their public sale. The grounds the Court used for doing so was not that Connecticut's law involved intrusion into the home or bedroom or doctor's office (i.e., into a particular sphere of human life), but rather that it affected a set of activities that the Court deemed legitimately private, due to their relationship to familial life.

Because the Court's declaration of a constitutional right to privacy in this case depended on this seeming confusion between what is private and public, critics of the Court's reasoning have argued that its reasoning in the privacy cases is incoherent. Richard Posner, for instance, argues that the Court makes this error because it equates "privacy with the purposes for which people want privacy."[19] What I want to suggest is that this supposed incoherency of the privacy doctrine contains a deeper consistency—one that does not deny Posner's description of the relationship between privacy and purposes, but accepts and even depends upon that relationship so described. The right to privacy argument does not *incoherently* equate privacy with the purposes for which people want privacy, it *consciously* requires the equation of privacy with the purposes for which people want privacy. Consistent with the reasoning of Brandeis and Warren, the right to privacy cannot be separated from purposes; if personality is inviolable, then insofar as that personality requires certain actions, those actions must too be protected. It is on this understanding that the Court grounds the right to sell birth control upon the right to use it. The public affirmation of a private right is in this sense coeval with the public affirmation of a particular way of life; if the right to use birth control is a matter of privacy then the right to publically purchase it must likewise be affirmed.

To claim the right to use birth control as a private matter worthy of protection involves having birth control recognized as a legitimate choice by the Court (private cocaine usage does not currently receive the same recognition). Right to privacy claims thus do not ultimately aim at the preservation of a sphere outside of public control; instead, right to privacy claims entail an attempt to receive public approval for particular behaviors. And this recognition in turn seems to require affirmation that the activity in question flows from one's inviolable personality. Human action must be understood as inseparable from, and in some ways as almost identical to, individual personality or personhood. Adopting the premises of Brandeis and Warren, the Court's implementation of the right to privacy is therefore primarily concerned with protecting self-definition, and with receiving public affirmation of one's inviolable personality.[20] The right to privacy as a constitutional right involves the right to define oneself by what has been deemed by the government to be legitimately private.[21]

It is worth noting that in *Griswold's* governing opinions, the foregoing articulation of privacy rights lies hidden on the surface, with the Court presenting privacy as an outgrowth of the family, or at least of marriage. The right to privacy incudes the use of contraceptives in marriage, argues the Court, because in dealing with the family, "we deal with a right of privacy older than the Bill of Rights—older than our political parties, older than our school system. Marriage is a coming together for better or for worse, hopefully enduring, and intimate to the degree of being sacred."[22] Although here the Court's language seems to suggest that the family forms a kind of inviolable sphere distinct from the individualistic norms that Brandeis and Warren suggested ought to govern privacy claims,[23] when one considers that the sacredness (or privacy) that is at stake in the *Griswold* ruling especially includes the sexual intimacy of married life, it is easier to see how result of the decision works to enshrine the logic of modern privacy rights as described. After all, the right to privacy as protected by *Griswold* in the form of a right to birth control ensures that the evidence of sexual intimacy (including the deeds produced by it) remain within the compete control of the married couple. Children make public what a couple might otherwise want to keep private. Or more precisely, children are a result of a private activity whose public character must, by necessity of the child's own individual character, fall outside the complete proprietary control of the parents. As all parents know, children violate the right to control one's publicity. To retain the proprietary control of sexual intimacy—to have an inviolable self—therefore requires the right to privacy in the form of birth control.

Marriage, of course, is not necessary to privacy thus understood. It is not surprising then, that the Court soon makes explicit the individualistic roots of its decision in *Eisenstadt v. Baird*. There the Court argues that "if the right of privacy means anything, it is the right of the individual, married or single, to be free from unwarranted governmental intrusion into matters so fundamentally affecting a person as the decision whether to bear or beget a child."[24] This means that a decision to engage in sexual practices outside of marriage must be identified as co-equal with the previously described sacred right of marriage. In *Eisenstadt*, as in *Griswold*, privacy is be understood as inseparable from the purposes for which people want privacy; the recognition of the right to privacy identifies and affirms the excellence of sexual practices, and that they form part of one's inviolable identity.

Following this same logic, the modern right to privacy must ultimately include the right to procure an abortion, a fact recognized by the Court in *Roe v. Wade*.[25] This right allowed for even more protection for the privacy of sexual relations and abortion, with those activities and their results now placed under the control of the individual, and made public only as chosen by her. Thus, in *Planned Parenthood v. Casey*, the Court famously writes: "at the heart of liberty is the right to define one's own concept of existence, of meaning, of the universe, and of the mystery of human life."[26] Roundly dismissing this formulation as an absurdity,[27] many conservative opponents of abortion did not fully grasp the ways in which the Court's statement articulates the internal consistency that undergirds the privacy doctrine: one is free to privately define one's identity; that identity is inviolable; that identity involves actions; and that identity must be affirmed by the public.[28] One has the right to live out their identity publically if so chosen. It is therefore fitting that, in *Casey*, the Court claims to be "reaffirming the central holding of *Roe*."[29] Rather then abandoning the appeal to the right to privacy, *Casey*'s famous liberty statement lays bare the reasoning hidden within it. The general right to privacy argument is revealed as being the right to the public affirmation of one's self-definition.[30] On *Casey*'s understanding, affirming and securing the self-definition that is liberty is the purpose of the American constitution.

OBERGEFELL V. HODGES

In contrast to those who have mocked the Court's *Obergefell* reasoning as illogical on its face,[31] I have attempted to show that there is ample ground for understanding it as wholly consistent with Brandeis's and Warren's privacy doctrine as it has be adopted by the Court. As I noted at the outset, the *Obergefell* Court legitimizes same sex marriage on the grounds that marriage is the fulfillment of some of the deepest and most personal desires of the human being.[32] Indeed, it says that it is the individual's *private decision* to enter into marriage that confers the fundamental liberty that is the right to marriage.[33] This is so because this choice "shapes an individual's destiny," and because it is a decision that "is among life's most momentous acts of self-definition."[34] Indeed, "there is dignity in the bond between two men or two women who seek to marry and in their autonomy to make such profound choices."[35] Consistent with the Court's earlier privacy cases, for the *Oberge-*

fell Court, individual self-definition is a necessary part of autonomy or self-ownership. And this self-definition is inviolable, for it is the Petitioner's "immutable nature" that "dictates that same-sex marriage is the only real path to the profound commitment [of marriage]."[36] The individual, understood in terms of self-ownership, or as an inviolable self, or as having dignity, is wholly free to define the meaning of her freedom, and has the right to exercise it accordingly, without any obligations to others or to the political community. Absolute privacy is the source of such absolute liberty, and cannot be achieved without it.

As we have seen, for such an absolute liberty to become law, the Court must codify the right, or remove the limits or obligations the law places on citizens. But since the Court cannot codify absolute liberty, it must decide which choices are worthy of its protection. By conferring the right to marry the Court "dignifies couples who 'wish to define themselves by their commitment to each other.'"[37] Dignity must be asked for, but it is up to the Court to provide it.[38] In *Obergefell v. Hodges* the legal implementation of the right to privacy argument requires the public and governmental definition of the very thing being held as private.

NOTES

1. Elsewhere in this volume James Stoner argues that in the case of the latter of these three, the Court has made some moves in the other direction.

2. The Court's move toward personal autonomy has struck some as Lockean (see, for instance, Peter Augustine Lawler's remarks about Locke in this volume), although scholars are divided on Locke's view of the family (see Thomas G. West, "On Nature and Happiness in John Locke," *Claremont Review of Books*, 2004, www.claremont.org/crb/article/nature-and-happiness-in-locke, accessed October 21, 2014). Perhaps the closest Locke comes to affirming the family as natural occurs in his *First Treatise*, when he notes that humans, like beasts, have a natural inclination to sacrifice themselves for their family (§.56). However, this description of the natural parental instinct is in tension with Locke's endorsement of reasoned self-preservation, as Locke implies when he follows his account of the natural family with a story of Peruvians who begot and fattened children in order to eat them (§.57). He then contrasts reason with beastly instinct (including, presumably, the willingness to die for one's child), writing: "Thus far can the busy mind of man carry him to a brutality below the level of beasts, when he quits his reason, which places him almost equal to angels" (§.58).

3. U.S. Supreme Court. *Obergefell v. Hodges*, 576 U.S.___(2015), at 12.

4. In contrast, the word "liberty" is used twenty-five times by Kennedy in the *Obergefell* opinion.

5. *Obergefell v. Hodges* at 13. Quoting *Zablocki*, at 386.

6. By adopting a right-to-privacy doctrine that tends to make the private public, the Court follows the path laid out by the political thought of John Locke, which famously holds that government is founded with the purpose of protecting private property. While this argument seems to conceive the public as being in service of the private, Locke admits that its implementation requires that public recognition and affirmation of what was originally private and conceived in private (compare Locke, *Second Treatise*, §. 28 with §. 87 and 151). On Lockean grounds, privacy is not fully compatible with civil society, if it is compatible at all.

7. There is some reason to think that the article was written primarily by Brandeis. See Dorothy J. Glancy, "The Invention of the Right to Privacy," *Arizona Law Review* 21 (1979): 6.

8. Warren and Brandeis, "The Right to Privacy," *Harvard Law Review* 5 (1890), 194, 206, 216.

9. "The Right to Privacy," 215.

10. *Tuck v. Priester*, 19 Q.B.D. 639 (1887) and *Pollard v. Photographic Co.*, 40 Ch. D. 345, 349–352 (1888).

11. "The Right to Privacy," 211.

12. Ibid., 205.

13. Ibid., 211.

14. Violations of privacy might "forestall the profits that the individual himself might secure by giving the matter a publicity obnoxious to him, or to gain an advantage at the expense of his mental pain and suffering." Ibid., 205.

15. Ibid.,193.

16. Which Posner assumes in his critique of privacy in "The Uncertain Protection of Privacy by the Supreme Court," *The Supreme Court Review* 173 (1979): 173–216.

17. Thus Richard Posner suggests in his influential critique of privacy that the right to privacy first takes form as the right to publicity. "The Uncertain Protection of Privacy by the Supreme Court,"177. See also, Melville B. Nimmer, "The Right of Publicity," *Law and Contemporary Problems* 2 (1954): 203–223.

18. *Olmstead v. United States*, 277 U.S. 438 (1928), Brandeis dissenting at 478.

19. "The Uncertain Protection of Privacy by the Supreme Court," 193.

20. This would help to explain Brandeis's somewhat tautological definition of privacy, which resists giving any definite account of which matters are by nature private. Privacy is in this way left free to be determined by the individual under the Court's supervision.

21. This mixture of a private conception of rights that must also be validated by the government has also become the norm in search and seizure cases. This trend can be traced back *U.S. v. Katz* 389 U.S. 347 (1967), when the Court formalized a broader approach to privacy in search and seizure cases than provide by a literal reading of the Fourth Amendment (which limits privacy to specific places and things). From that case the Court adopted Justice Harlan's reasonable expectation of privacy test, which designed the following two part test to determine when a governmental search has violated the 4th Amendment: "first that a person have exhibited an actual (subjective) expectation of privacy and, second, that the expectation be one that society is prepared to recognize as "reasonable" (*U.S. v. Katz,* at 361). The first part of the test involves self-definition, and the second, the legitimizing of that definition by the public.

22. *Griswold v. Connecticut,* 381 U. S. 479 (1965).

23. The Court forgoes attempting to show how the sacredness of marriage depends upon access to birth control.

24. *Eisenstadt. v. Baird,* 405 U. S. 438 (1972).

25. *Roe v. Wade*, 410 U. S. 113 (1973).

26. U.S. Supreme Court, *Planned Parenthood v. Casey*, 505 U. S. 833 (1992), at 851. The Court repeats the phrase when ruling against Texas's anti-sodomy law. *Lawrence v. Texas,* 539 U. S. 538 (2003).

27. Hadley Arkes called them fatuous. Robert George said the Court was not describing anything. It was just inventing a rationale to justify the right it had invented in *Roe v. Wade.*" Hadley Arkes and Robert P. George, "The Supreme Court 1997: A Symposium," *First Things*, October, 1997.

28. Apart from the fact it appears in an abortion case, *Casey*'s famous liberty statement might seem innocuous, especially since critics of it might, under different circumstances (e.g. in defending freedom of religion) themselves assert their own right to choose their "own concept of existence, of meaning, of the universe, and of the mystery of human life." What then is at the heart of their objection? One suspects that it is the Court's articulation of the privacy dotrine; its claim that one's freedom depends upon the *defining* these things for oneself (and the concomitant right to act in accordance with those definitions).

29. *Planned Parenthood v. Casey*, at 853. Ronald Dworkin, Thomas Nagel, Robert Nozick, John Rawls, T. M. Scanlon, and Judith Jarvis Thomson argue that the reasoning of *Casey* is consistent with its famous liberty passage: "The analysis in *Casey* compels the conclusion that the patient-plaintiffs have a liberty interest in this case that a state cannot burden with a blanket

prohibition. Like a woman's decision whether to have an abortion, a decision to die involves one's very "destiny" and inevitably will be "shaped to a large extent on [one's] own conception of [one's] spiritual imperatives and [one's] place in society." "Assisted Suicide: The Philosophers' Brief," in *New York Review of Books*, 44:5, March 27, 1997. The "philosophers" are arguing for the permissibility of suicide. Locke reaches a similar conclusion in regards to suicide (see Michael Zuckert, *Launching Liberalism*, Kansas: University of Kansas Press, 2002, 192.)

30. This is precisely how Ginsberg puts it in her review of the Court's decision: "There was a time, not so long ago, when women were regarded as the center of home and family life. . . . Those views, this Court made clear in *Casey*, are no longer consistent with our understanding of the family, the individual, or the Constitution 505 U. S., at 897. Women, it is now acknowledged, have the talent, capacity, and right to participate equally in the economic and social life of the Nation. *Id*., at 856. Their ability to realize their full potential, the Court recognized, is intimately connected to their ability to control their reproductive lives. *Ibid*. Thus, legal challenges to undue restrictions on abortion procedures do not seek to vindicate some generalized notion of privacy; rather, they center on a woman's autonomy to determine her life's course." *Gonzales v. Carhart*, 550 U. S. 124 (2007). Quoting Casey, she adds: "'[t]he destiny of the woman must be shaped . . . on her own conception of her spiritual imperatives and her place in society.' *Casey*, 505 U. S., at 852." There is some reason think Ginsberg is right that the Court's approach is proves particularly problematic for the traditional natural family, not only because the family requires a sphere apart from public regulation, but also because its character and deeds proceed from its understanding that the human person is not inviolable. Indeed, it is this understanding that has made the family supportive of political (but not tyrannical) rule.

31. Scalia is highly critical of the majority opinion: "the opinion's showy profundities are often profoundly incoherent. 'The nature of marriage is that, through its enduring bond, two persons together can find other freedoms, such as expression, intimacy, and spirituality.'(Really? Who ever thought that intimacy and spirituality [whatever that means] were freedoms? And if intimacy is, one would think Freedom of Intimacy is abridged rather than expanded by marriage. . . . What possible 'essence' does substantive due process 'capture' in an 'accurate and comprehensive way'? It stands for nothing whatever, except those freedoms and entitlements that this Court really likes." *Obergefell v. Hodges*, Scalia, J., dissenting at 7-8. In a note to this passage, Scalia adds: "If . . . I ever joined an opinion for the Court that began: 'The Constitution promises liberty to all within its reach, a liberty that includes certain specific rights that allow persons, within a lawful realm, to define and express their identity,' I would hide my head in a bag."

32. *Obergefell v. Hodges*, at 3.

33. Ibid, at 12.

34. Ibid, at 13, quoting *Goodridge*, 440 Mass., at 322, 798 N. E. 2d, at 955.

35. Kennedy's use of the term dignity has led some to worry about its implications. For instance Jonathan Turley (a supporter of the *Obergefell* ruling) writes: "Dignity is a rather elusive and malleable concept compared with more concrete qualities such as race and sex. Which relationships are sufficiently dignified to warrant protection? What about couples who do not wish to marry but cohabitate? What about polyamorous families, who are less accepted by public opinion but are perhaps no less exemplary? . . . The justice does not specify. It certainly appears as if *Obergefell* extends this protection because same-sex unions are now deemed acceptable by the majority." "The Trouble with the Dignity of Same Sex Marriage," Washington Post, July 2, 2015, www.washingtonpost.com/opinions/the-trouble-with-the-dignity-of-same-sex-marriage/2015/07/02/43bd8f70-1f4e-11e5-aeb9-a411a84c9d55_story.html. Accessed, November 15, 2015. For a similar critique, see Susan McWilliams's chapter in this volume.

36. *Obergefell v. Hodges*, at 4.

37. *Obergefell v. Hodges*, at 14, quoting *United States v. Windsor*, 570 U.S. ___ (2013), at 14. The Court is of course equally willing to dignify those who wish to leave their marriage.

38. *Obergefell v. Hodges*, at 26.

Chapter Eleven

Democracy in Justice Kennedy's America

Reading Obergefell *with Tocqueville*

Susan McWilliams

Writing the majority opinion in *Obergefell v. Hodges*, Justice Anthony Kennedy turns—as so many Americans have done, in so many situations—to the authority of Alexis de Tocqueville's *Democracy in America.* Tocqueville, Kennedy writes, recognized "that marriage is a keystone of our social order." Kennedy quotes Tocqueville as follows:

> There is certainly no country in the world where the tie of marriage is so much respected as in America . . . [W]hen the American retires from the turmoil of public life to the bosom of his family, he finds in it the image of order and of peace. . . . [H]e afterwards carries [that image] with him into public affairs. [1]

In Kennedy's telling, Tocqueville recognizes what the Supreme Court would come to echo in 1888, in *Maynard v. Hill*, that "marriage is 'the foundation of the family and society, without which there would be neither civilization nor progress.'"[2]

Even a glance at the way Kennedy cites Tocqueville, though—with all its brackets and ellipses—suggests that there are things being left out in the retelling. Indeed, that is the case; although Tocqueville did not say much about marriage in the United States, he says much more than Kennedy allows us to see. Looking at what Kennedy leaves out of his quotation of Tocqueville, in fact, indicates some of the broader cultural and historic erasures that are present in the *Obergefell* decision (and in the Supreme Court's latter-day treatment of marriage and the family in general). As is often the case, the silences are more powerful than the notes.

There is a further irony, too, to Kennedy's citation of Tocqueville, which is that in some of the same sections of *Democracy in America* in which Tocqueville talks about marriage and the family, he also speaks about broader cultural and political forces that help to explain why the Supreme Court's recent opinions on matters of marriage and family look the way they do.[3] That is to say, Kennedy's use of Tocqueville illustrates broader phenomena of cultural confusion and concealment in Supreme Court jurisprudence on matters of marriage and family—but at the same time, Tocqueville's fully considered thoughts on marriage help to illuminate why those phenomena have occurred. If the Court's majority opinion in *Obergefell v. Hodges* involves acts of intellectual masking or shrouding, Tocqueville gives us ways to see that decision that are enlightening.

While I do not pretend this essay to be an exhaustive evaluation of the *Obergefell* decision or a weighing in on its constitutional merits, I do think that standing *Obergefell* next to Tocqueville yields some suggestive possibilities for evaluating the evolution of recent Supreme Court jurisprudence—and recent American political thought, more generally speaking—on questions of marriage and family.

Specifically, I think that reading *Obergefell* with Tocqueville reveals the intellectual and political *weakness* of the contemporary Supreme Court. The Tocquevillian analysis reveals a Court which may make decisions (like *Obergefell*) that have great and far-reaching effects, not the least of which is the centralizing of administrative power. Paradoxically, though, this Court renders those decisions from a position of intellectual insecurity and political deference. Reading through the eyes of Tocqueville, it is hard not to conclude that the prevalent and popular buzzwords that fly around this Court—that it is "activist," or that it has a coherent vision of a "living Constitution," and so on—almost all overstate the Court's intellectual independence.[4] Reading through the eyes of Tocqueville, it is hard not to conclude that most thinking about the contemporary Supreme Court needs to be rethought.

STABILITY, SOCIALITY, AND THE STATE

We may begin getting to a bigger picture by considering in full the section of *Democracy in America* that Kennedy quotes in *Obergefell*, even though the section is a lengthy one. Tocqueville's words read as follows:

> There is certainly no country in the world where the tie of marriage is more respected than in America, or where conjugal happiness is more highly or worthily appreciated. In Europe, almost all the disturbances of society arise from the irregularities of domestic life. To despise the natural bonds and

> legitimate pleasures of home, is to contract a taste for excesses, a restlessness of heart, and fluctuating desires. Agitated by the tumultuous passions which frequently disturb his dwelling, the European is galled by the obedience which the legislative powers of the state exact. But when the American retires from the turmoil of public life to the bosom of his family, he finds in it the image of order and of peace. There his pleasures are simple and natural, his joys are innocent and calm; and as he finds that an orderly life is the surest path to happiness, he accustoms himself easily to moderate his opinions as well as his tastes. Whilst the European endeavors to forget his domestic troubles by agitating society, the American derives from his own home that love of order which he afterwards carries with him into public affairs. [5]

Kennedy's more selective quotation gets the spirit of Tocqueville's argument right, then, in the general sense that the old Frenchman thought that marriage occupied a place of distinct importance in American life. Tocqueville clearly thought that marriage is a central institution for Americans, both in terms of their private associations and their public lives. That much is without dispute.

And Tocqueville does relate, as Kennedy suggests, the institution of marriage to "the Nation's social order."[6] But past that general relating of marriage to social order, Tocqueville's story importantly diverges from Kennedy's account of things. As the full selection from *Democracy in America* reveals, Tocqueville saw marriage in America as productive of a broader political order, and thus productive of political stability. Domesticity, Tocqueville argues, has political utility in America largely because it results in public docility. People who are happily married and who have genial lives at home are less likely to be upsetters and agitators; thus, that Americans respect and seem to enjoy the institution of marriage means that the country as a whole enjoys relative political stability. The national interest in marriage, by this account, is an interest in political stability, in the stability of public culture at large.

The word "stability" does appear a number of times in Kennedy's opinion in *Obergefell*, and to that extent one might think that he echoes Tocqueville's thinking on this matter. But tellingly, Kennedy always uses the word and concept of stability in terms of private individuals and never in terms of the body politic as a whole. He says, for instance, that marriage "affords the permanency and stability important to children's best interests" and that under the status quo "same-sex couples are consigned to an instability many opposite-sex couples would deem intolerable in their own lives."[7] The stability value of marriage, in this account, accrues mostly if not only to those individuals who are immediately involved in it: the spouses and their children, if there are children in the picture. Even as Kennedy makes a single gesture to the concept of a broader "social order," nowhere does he explain or emphasize the connection between marriage and stability on a social level, properly speaking. What gets downplayed if not outright obscured in Kennedy's majority opinion is the idea so central to Tocqueville's account of marriage in America: that the stability that marriage provides is not *merely* private and personal, but that it is also, and perhaps more importantly, public and political.

Kennedy's narrative, even as his words echo Tocqueville's on the surface, thus provides a different basis for asserting that the government has an interest in marriage in the first place. Tocqueville's justification for that interest would be relatively straightforward: Married people, especially happily married people, tend to be more docile and orderly citizens. The state has an evident interest in the stability that comes from having a more docile and orderly citizenry, and thus the state has an interest in marriage. Kennedy's justification, by contrast, looks something like this: Marriage is a stabilizing institution for the people in it, as well as for any children that might be attached to that marriage. That kind of stability allows individuals to flourish and be happy in ways they might otherwise not. The state has an interest in individuals flourishing and being happy, because that is likely conducive to social order, and thus the state has an interest in marriage.

Comparatively, I think it is fair to say, Kennedy's argument lacks intellectual clarity—or at least has a muddier, more indistinct political vision than it might. More than twenty years after Mary Ann Glendon argued, in *Rights Talk*, that an increasing focus on the individual and a privileging of individual rights in American political speech were leading to a debasement of civic discourse marked by a "missing language of sociality," Kennedy's logic reads like a case study for her argument.[8] Although Kennedy indicates that he wants to tie the institution of marriage to "social order," he seems not to have the language to be able to do it in a direct or entirely convincing way.

The comparison to Tocqueville's argument sets into relief how awkward the Court's current logic is when it comes to asserting that a state has even a minimal interest in regulating marriage. After all, it is not hard to start with Kennedy's logic in *Obergefell* and conclude that, if marriage is something that is primarily experienced and valued by individuals in private relationships, people should be allowed to choose the terms of their marriages—much like they choose the terms of their friendships—without any interference or encouragement or recognition from the state at all. (Tellingly, it's effortless to apply this part of the *Obergefell* reasoning about marriage to the category of friendship: Friendships, too, confer stability and even dignity to the lives of individuals, and we might even say that people have a "right" to friendship and to the choice of which friends they have, and yet so far nobody seems to think that legislators should weigh in on the question of who can and should be friends with whom.) Even if Kennedy is right that marriage distinctively provides stability and dignity and even transcendence for individuals (a matter that at least some "happy single" people have called into question), it is not necessarily clear that he or others on the Court know how to argue that there is a clear or distinct state interest in regulating marriage.[9]

To explore it from a different angle, the *Obergefell* decision shows how the intellectual turn toward seeing and articulating things in terms of individual or private rights actually, almost paradoxically, often serves to justify a substantial expansion of state power. (That idea shouldn't be a surprise to anyone who has studied Hobbes's *Leviathan*, but it is a truth that rarely gets articulated in terms of contemporary jurisprudence.) Despite this Court's focus on individual rights in terms of "freedom," a word that gets used liberally in *Obergefell v. Hodges*, nobody doubts that the Court's decision maintains and even extends national power. The expansion of the idea of any given individual right goes hand in hand with the expansion of the state. Determined to make a case in terms of private relationships and individual rights, the Court contributes to an "accumulation of power" at the state level that goes beyond even that which Chief Justice Roberts worries about in his dissent from the majority opinion.[10] As in other recent cases, here, the Court seems to be ushering in a massive expansion of state power without intending to do so. In this regard, it's hard not to regard the Court's political thinking as dangerously thin: the Court points toward despotism in searching, earnestly, for freedom.

Here again, the comparison to Tocqueville is illuminating. Although Tocqueville arguably provides a firmer justification than does Kennedy for articulating a state interest in marriage, he also did not see marriage as an institution first governed or determined by state order. Rather, as I elaborate below, he described marriage as a kind of social institution that "directs the manners of the community, and, by regulating domestic life, . . . regulates the state."[11] Tocqueville's view of political power and public relationships, rooted outside the concept of individual right, makes room for a whole host of diverse social relationships and dynamics that are absent in the Court's account in *Obergefell.*

Historians of family jurisprudence in America have often told a story in which "individual happiness" has come to take precedence over "stability" as a value associated with marriage.[12] The majority's opinion in *Obergefell* tells us that this story is not quite right; rather, the notion of stability has endured, but it has been somewhat incoherently collapsed into the category of individual happiness and private right. Tellingly, Tocqueville could have predicted this phenomenon; in the United States, he wrote, where "the laws and customs make no condition permanent," people will demonstrate a particular "restlessness of temper" which leads them, even when they think they desire stability, instead to seek the "the shortest cut to happiness." Add into the mix the "individualism"—roughly, the focus on private rather than public goods—that Tocqueville thought was the basis for much "erroneous judgment" in democratic nations (particularly a kind of "erroneous judgment" that leads toward the soft despotism of power that Tocqueville most feared), and it's not hard to see how the Court got to the logic at work in *Obergefell*.[13] Consider Kennedy's statement about same-sex couples: that "without the recognition, stability and predictability marriage offers, their children suffer the stigma of knowing their families are somehow lesser."[14] Although he seems to suggest in the first half of the sentence that marriage offers stability that the Court wants to promote, the second half of the sentence reveals that he considers the Court's real interests to lie in the stigma felt by the children of parents who are unable to marry. It is their happiness, in which we are meant to understand stability plays some important but undefined role, that is the real interest here.

THE ROLE AND RULE OF RELIGION

Tocqueville's own logic, in considering marriage, was rooted in a comparative analysis between American and European societies. And notably, that comparison is absent in Kennedy's selective quotation of Tocqueville. So what does Tocqueville gain by that comparison, and what might Kennedy lose by obscuring it? Why is it, we must ask, that Tocqueville thought marriage so much more important to Americans than to Europeans?

Tocqueville provides two answers to that question. The first, which is worth discussing at some length, is that Tocqueville identifies Christianity as much more powerful in the United States than it is in the countries of Europe. Tocqueville is very clear on this, writing that the veneration of marriage that he saw in America is interesting most notably because it illustrates Christianity's powerful hold on the nation. In fact, the section of *Democracy in America* from which Kennedy quotes Tocqueville in *Obergefell* is titled "Indirect Influence of Religious Opinions Upon Political Society in the United States," and in that section Tocqueville clearly situates the American respect for marriage as a testament to the nation's pervasive Christianity. For Tocqueville, it would be impossible to tell the story of marriage in America, to situate it culturally and historically, without at least mentioning that the institution was rooted in, and has evolved along with, Christian—largely Protestant—modes of understanding. "There is no country in the world where the Christian religion retains a greater influence over the souls of men than in America," he writes, "and there can be no greater proof of its utility, and of its conformity to human nature, than that its influence is powerfully felt over the most enlightened and free nation of the earth."[15]

The easy thing to say here is that Tocqueville would surely join those commentators who have argued that in ignoring the particularly Christian foundations of marriage in the United States, the majority's opinion in *Obergefell* is willfully blind, merely as a matter of national history and cultural origin. Given that the decision purports, at least at moments, to review the history and precedents attending marriage in the United States, it is undoubtedly odd that in it, no mention is made of Christianity at all, and religion as an abstract category of belief makes only a couple of cameo appearances.[16]

But Tocqueville's way of thinking about marriage points us to an even deeper level of analysis, a level that goes beyond the particular power that Christianity had and/or has in the United States. That is because for Tocqueville, the fact that American marriage has predominately religious roots is important because it means that marriage is primarily located in the social rather than the legal order.[17] Indeed, he situates his claim about the American respect for marriage in terms of a broader claim about the relationship between religion and the laws in American life. "In the United States," he writes, "religion exercises but little influence upon the laws, and upon the details of public opinion; but it directs the manners of the community, and, by regulating domestic life, it regulates the state."[18] In other words, Tocqueville thought that key to understanding marriage in America was to understand its Christian origin—*not* for the purpose of making the claim that Christian views of marriage should result in consciously Christian or religious acts of lawmaking, as some contemporary pundits have argued, but more fundamentally, for locating marriage as one of what the sociologist Robert Nisbet would call, evoking Tocqueville, the "mediating institutions" of associational life.[19] In the Tocquevillian account, marriage should not be considered as primarily a political institution, the bounds of which are properly defined and determined by the state. Rather, marriage is primarily a religious institution, the bounds of which are properly defined within local, social, and cultural groups. Because Tocqueville regarded marriage as part of the constellation of social institutions and associations that are predominately religious in their nature and resonance, he located them upstream from state action. His idea is that the practice of marriage—along with the practice of religion, by and large—influences the community and the manners of a place, and those in turn help to shape the character and nature of the laws. Even as Tocqueville found ways to articulate a state interest in marriage, as argued above, he did not argue that the state should be the primary mover in establishing the guidelines for marriage as an institution.

In fact, as any student of Tocqueville knows, he thought it critical that social institutions like marriage be preserved as such, since their existence as local and associational centers of gravity served important political functions. In his account, local associations and social institutions serve the positive function of preserving the vibrancy and diversity of communities that provide energy to democratic life. They also serve to diffuse power in a mass state, helping to guard against the kind of administrative centralization that prefigures or marks a turn toward despotic rule. Similarly, they help to mitigate the tyranny of the majority—the habitual deference to and even worship of mass opinion—that constantly threatens modern democratic states. Harvey Mansfield and Delba Winthrop have even noted that for Tocqueville, the American family itself placed a "keenly felt limit on the desire to extend public power," since it is in the family that people are able to enjoy love and companionship that far exceed the "abstract compassion" of the public sphere and that help to "focus and deploy their energies" in life.[20]

With that in mind, the implications of the Court's removal of religion from its account of the history attending American marriage in *Obergefell* begin to seem more profound. For by removing religion from the story—even merely as a historical or precedential matter—the majority obscures the surest ground for understanding marriage as a predominately associational, rather than political or legal, institution. By playing down the religious foundation of marriage in America, then, Kennedy is playing down the degree to which marriage in America was historically founded in associational life outside the formal stricture of law. And that erasure thus makes it easy for the Court to take the reins in defining and delimiting the institution of marriage in the United States: to transform it into a primarily political and legal relationship. In doing so, the Court contributes to a strengthening of administrative centralization and a lessening of the restraints on the operations of the tyranny of the majority in American life.

To be fair, we might not want to give Justice Kennedy and the contemporary Court too much credit on this count. Even the most casual observer of American politics knows that there has been a broad and consistent trend toward administrative centralization for well over a century in the United States. This Supreme Court cannot be held responsible, blamed or praised, for moving American marriage from the primarily social to the primarily political realm. In *Obergefell*, the Court is not confronting a country in which marriage is treated or understood primarily as a social institution; it has long been subsumed within legal and political orders. Marriage has long been codified in the laws of the American states, and those states, as Kennedy relates, have made marriage "the basis for an expanding list of governmental rights, benefits, and responsibilities" that include:

> taxation; inheritance and property rights; rules of intestate succession; spousal privilege in the law of evidence; hospital access; medical decisionmaking [sic] authority; adoption rights; the rights and benefits of survivors; birth and death certificates; professional ethics rules; campaign finance restrictions; workers' compensation benefits; health insurance; and child custody, support, and visitation rules.[21]

By the time the Court was asked to render a decision in *Obergefell v. Hodges*, in other words, it is unquestionable that marriage in America had long ceased to be a primarily social or religious institution, grounded in local or associational life. The word "expanding" in Kennedy's decision is telling;

the clear movement of popular opinion and legislation in the United States over time was—long before the year 2015—toward making marriage a more and more weighty category of political recognition. The Court's opinion, in that regard, does not represent a major rupture from well-entrenched practices and understandings.

Also to be fair, the Court's decision in *Obergefell* does suggest that American understandings of marriage have had a social basis across time. But in the Court's telling, the key driver of American conceptions of marriage is popular opinion—what Kennedy in this decision calls "societal understanding" and in other cases he calls the "emerging awareness" of the population.[22] Key to the decision in *Obergefell* is the notion that popular opinion about marriage has changed in the United States over time, and those changes in opinion have to be recognized by the Court and in the laws. Implicit in the Court's decision in *Obergefell*, voiced powerfully and all but silently, is that the social authority in the nation has moved over time from the pulpit to the populace. The key engine of belief and faith in American society, to which the Court acknowledges it defers here, is popular opinion.

Note that although Kennedy claims that "it is of no moment whether advocates of same-sex marriage now enjoy or lack momentum in the democratic process," he then immediately turns to the precedent of *Lawrence v. Texas*, a decision Kennedy also wrote—and in which, notoriously, he rested much of his argument on the claim that there is "emerging awareness that liberty gives substantial protection to adult persons in deciding how to conduct their private lives in matters pertaining to sex."[23] It is hard to imagine an argument based more explicitly in public opinion (or the Court's perception of that public opinion). Thus even in the *Obergefell* decision where Kennedy resists the idea that the Court is deferring to some idea of popular opinion, he is backing up into that very kind of deference.[24]

Tocqueville could have seen this coming. He writes quite explicitly that in any democratic state, over time popular opinion would become the pervasive "moral authority" of the nation. In America, he writes, "The power of the majority in America [is] not only preponderant, but irresistible," rooted as it is in the "theory of equality" that "there is more intelligence and wisdom in a number of men united than in a single individual." Central to Tocqueville's well-known idea of the tyranny of the majority is the understanding that, over time, and especially in conditions of weakened associational life, Americans will have a more and more difficult time resisting the logic that ascribes moral authority to conventional wisdom and public opinion—or, to be even more precise, to what any given person perceives to be conventional wisdom and public opinion.[25]

More specifically, Tocqueville predicts that over time popular opinion in America will overtake religion as the primary source of faith in society and would triumph in any clash of beliefs between the two—"for as public opinion grows to be more and more evidently the first and most irresistible of existing powers," he writes, "the religious principle has no external support strong enough to enable it long to resist its attacks." He continues, "In ages of equality, kings may often command obedience, but the majority always commands belief."[26] Even as Tocqueville understood religion to be foundationally, historically and culturally important in American life, he also understood that there would be an inevitable move in the nation, over time, toward the location of moral authority and faith in the realm of public opinion.

The Court's decision in *Obergefell* thus corresponds to Tocqueville's prediction both in principle and on paper. It shows that in the United States, even the judiciary branch, with its distinct "nonmajoritarian" power cannot entirely resist the song of the tyranny of the majority that is the siren of modern democratic life (even despite Tocqueville's hopes that lawyers and courts could mount such resistance).[27]

LOVE AND LIBERTY

Let us return, though, to the other reason that Tocqueville argues that marriage is more venerated in the United States than in Europe. "In aristocratic countries the object of marriage is rather to unite property than persons," he writes:

> It cannot be wondered at if the conjugal tie which holds the fortunes of the pair united allows their hearts to rove; this is the natural result of the nature of the contract. When, on the contrary, a man always chooses a wife for himself, without any external coercion or even guidance, it is generally a conformity of tastes and opinions which brings a man and a woman together, and this same conformity keeps and fixes them in close habits of intimacy.[28]

Tocqueville goes on to make a strong argument that, essentially, democracies are more conducive than aristocracies to what he calls "love-matches" because the culture of democracy schools people throughout their lives in making their own choices.[29] (Central to this story, for Tocqueville, is his observation that Americans in particular avail their daughters of a serious education that schools them to be comfortable with freedom and choice, which they eventually exercise in making the choice whether to marry, knowing full well how hard marriage is for women in particular.)[30]

In other words, American life accustoms Americans to being able to choose things for themselves, and that comes to include the idea of choosing a spouse. Marriage in America, in Tocqueville's telling, has always been powerful because it is tied up with "that spirit of individual independence" that animates American energies, both for good and for ill.[31]

Considered in light of the argument about popular opinion above, the importance of this claim cannot be understated. Tocqueville's argument about the power of marriage in America suggests that over time, Americans are inevitably going to accustom themselves to the idea that individuals should be independently allowed to choose a spouse. Over time, that opinion becomes an article of national faith, rooted as it is in the experience and belief of the majority. And, despite the truth of the protests of Justice Roberts in his *Obergefell* dissent—the argument that "the traditional definition of marriage" has always involved a relationship of one man and one woman—the underlying and trumping idea is that of the "spirit of individual independence."[32] In the Tocquevillian account of American culture and history, the respect accorded marriage in the United States, rooted so strongly in the creed of individual choice and independence, seems almost inevitably to point to a conclusion like that in *Obergefell.*

Tocqueville thought that, underlying all other political dynamics and forces in the United States was "the gradual development of the principle of Equality."[33] While emerging from various political and religious traditions of thought, that principle of equality was, in Tocqueville's telling, bound to take on a life of its own. In so doing, the self-enchanting and self-propelling logic of equality would come to have trumping power over all sorts of other social, cultural, political, legal, and intellectual forces. It would become the prevailing creed and the determinant of all articles of faith. As Americans became ever more committed to the principle of the equality of conditions, Tocqueville prophesied, they would harness their convictions to that belief with ever greater fervor, distancing themselves increasingly from those forces that might serve to mitigate against the worst excesses of egalitarianism.

Even love, Tocqueville thought, was susceptible to the workings of the equality of conditions:

> The tumultuous and constantly harassed life which equality makes men lead, not only distracts them from the passion of love, by denying them time to indulge in it, but it diverts them from it by another more secret but more certain road. All men who live in democratic ages more or less contract the ways of thinking of the manufacturing and trading classes; their minds take a serious, deliberate, and positive turn; they are apt to relinquish the ideal, in order to pursue some visible and proximate object, which appears to be the natural and necessary aim of their desires. Thus the principle of equality does not destroy the imagination, but lowers its flight to the level of the earth.[34]

Notably, Tocqueville's account helps to explain part of the workings of the phenomenon described above, that Americans have increasingly treated marriage as a political and legal category important for the conferral of certain distinct, measurable benefits. And why the Court in *Obergefell*, beholden even beyond its own telling to public understanding, treats it in much the same terms.

By Tocqueville's account, then, the logic of the decision in *Obergefell* is in part a testament to the American conviction that, by the nation's long-standing logic of individual independence, each individual should be free to marry the person whom he or she loves. It is also a testament to the fact that over time, Americans have come to enshrine the category of marriage in the law in terms of calculable, material benefits that accrue to individuals. Over time, seeing marriage in those terms has eviscerated the social and religious origins of marriage. The nation has been following that trajectory for most of its history. Understanding that, what is remarkable about the Court's opinion in *Obergefell v. Hodges* is how unremarkable it is; its logic represents a continuance of, rather than a break from, a cultural machinery that has been in operation, by Tocqueville's telling, since the founding.

CONCLUSION

At first glance, Alexis de Tocqueville might have been surprised by the majority's opinion in *Obergefell v. Hodges*, especially because he is cited as an authority in it. After all, Tocqueville imagined that the judiciary could serve as a restraining or mitigating force to the logics of individualism and tyranny of the majority that, to his mind, most threatened the political health and dynamism of modern, mass democratic life. "The more we reflect upon all that occurs in the United States," he writes, "the more shall we be persuaded that the lawyers, as a body, form the most powerful, if not the only, counterpoise to the democratic element." He calls lawyers the "American aristocracy," imagining that the judicial class would be the one to stand against, rather than to enable, the kind of privatist thinking and deference to the majority that are likely to run rampant in modern democratic states.[35]

And yet lying in Tocqueville's own analysis of marriage and democracy in America are virtually all the building blocks you need to construct an explanation of the Court's decision in the *Obergefell* case, and in other recent cases on matters of marriage and the family. Essentially, what we can see in the recent Court jurisprudence is an increase in the forces of: 1) individualism, which predisposes Americans to see almost everything in individual and private rather than public and political terms; and 2) the tyranny of the majority, which becomes stronger and stronger as the mediating ties of associational life become weaker, and which disposes all Americans to defer to the perceived forces of public opinion. These contribute to 3) administrative centralization, which Tocqueville thought would become increasingly attractive to Americans, who would be "naturally fond of central power," especially when "it happens that this same power faithfully represents their own interests."[36] The story here is that those three great forces, the specters that haunt Tocqueville's account of modern democracy, are growing, as he worried they might, ever more powerful. They are so powerful that even the highest judicial body in the land defers and contributes to their reign.

Now, because the Court itself is a central political body, and thus its authorization of administrative centralization pulls powers inward, it is tempting to treat this Court—as have so many of its critics—as a power-grabbing body that is actively seeking to enrich and expand its provenance. But I think the Tocquevillian analysis suggests that this puts the emphasis in the wrong place. For although the Court's opinion in *Obergefell* effectively asserts the position of the Court to decide, it does so by a kind of abnegation of intellectual and political independence. Rather, the Court holds itself, or is held, in thrall to privatist logic and mass opinion. Kennedy's opinion in *Obergefell* is not an opinion that comes from a self-understood position of judicial strength; it comes from a position of self-understood judicial weakness or deference. In other words, although the Court seems to be asserting its own power to decide, its argument defers to long-term shifts in legislation and cultural history, and to shorter-term shifts in public opinion. And the majority in this case suggests that it is proper for a judiciary body to so defer.

Tocqueville would certainly be worried about that fact, but he again might not have been taken aback by it. For even as Tocqueville saw the judiciary as a kind of counterbalancing institution in American life, he never portrayed the judiciary as particularly strong or independent. Rather, he described a federal judiciary that was not as strong as others imagined it. "Federal judges are conscious of the relative weakness of the power in whose name they act," he writes, thinking mostly of federal power *vis-à-vis* the states, but suggesting more broadly that there were limits to the ways in which the Supreme Court—or any judiciary body in a modern democratic state—would be able to maintain a forceful, independent, counterbalancing position to counter the logics of individualism and majoritarianism (and the administrative centralization toward which those two primary forces conspire).[37]

Reading *Obergefell* with Tocqueville, then, suggests that those critics of the decision who call it the work of an "activist" Court, or who see this as evidence of disproportionate strength in the judicial branch, are wrong. I think it is perhaps more appropriate to see the majority opinion in *Obergefell* as the work of a *weak* Court. It is a Court that lacks a strong public language and political understanding, having been hampered by the prevailing logic of individual and private right. It is a Court that has acceded in many ways—and in no small part out of necessity—to the logic of the tyranny of the majority. And while this decision surely contributes to administrative centralization, it does so from a backed-into-a-corner kind of reasoning. Reading *Obergefell* with Tocqueville reveals that these days, the United States has a

Supreme Court which may make decisions (like *Obergefell*) that have great and far-reaching effects, not the least of which is the general centralizing of administrative power. Paradoxically, though, this Court renders those decisions from a position of intellectual and political insecurity. From the position that Tocqueville allows us to inhabit, it seems that Alexander Bickel was very wrong by being partly right: the contemporary Court may well be the "least dangerous branch," but in a way that makes it the most dangerous branch.[38]

At the very least, reading *Obergefell* with Tocqueville reminds us that to understand the place of *Obergefell* in American jurisprudence and political thought, it is not merely enough to look to the legal precedence dating back to *Griswold v. Connecticut*. And it is certainly not enough to look at the partisan affiliations or personal histories or religious convictions of particular justices, or the body-by-body makeup of the contemporary court. Rather, it is necessary to consider far more foundational dynamics in American politics. Among other things, reading *Obergefell* with Tocqueville suggests that recent Supreme Court decisions on matters of marriage and family cannot be attributed merely to momentary whims or passing fads (except to the extent that part of what marks the tyranny of the majority is susceptibility to faith in passing fads). It suggests that this most recent spate of decisions is bound up in forces that go far beyond the jurisprudential precedence that members of the Court claim as their anchor. The weights are heavier, and go far deeper, than that.

NOTES

1. U.S. Supreme Court. *Obergefell v. Hodges*, 576 U.S. ___ (2015), at 16.
2. Ibid.
3. By "recent," I mostly have in mind decisions that the Court has made in the fifty-year period between 1965 and 2015. I follow the lead of other scholars who see the Court's decision in *Griswold v. Connecticut,* 381 U.S. 479 (1965) as a watershed, especially in terms of articulating the idea of marriage as a fundamental right, and that right in turn as tied to a certain kind of right to privacy. See, for instance: Marvin B. Sussman, et al., eds., *Handbook of Marriage and the Family Volume I,* second edition (New York: Plenum Press, 1999), 555.
4. See, for instance, Christopher Wolfe, *Judicial Activism* (New York: Oxford University Press, 1997). See also David A. Strauss, *The Living Constitution* (New York: Oxford University Press, 2010).
5. Alexis de Tocqueville, *Democracy in America: Volume I,* trans. Henry Reeve (Cambridge: Sever and Francis, 1863), 389. Though I do not consider Reeve's translation to be the best available English translation of Tocqueville, I refer to it in this essay because it is the translation that Kennedy references in the *Obergefell* decision.
6. *Obergefell v. Hodges*, at 16. This phrase is also emphasized in the syllabus to the decision (at 4).
7. Ibid., at 15, 17.
8. Mary Ann Glendon, *Rights Talk* (New York: Free Press, 1993).
9. "Being single doesn't mean that the world is empty and awful," writes Michael Cobb, in response to the *Obergefell* decision in "The Supreme Court's Lonely Hearts Club," *The New*

York Times, June 30, 2015, www.nytimes.com/2015/06/30/opinion/the-supreme-courts-lonely-hearts-club.html.

10. *Obergefell v. Hodges*, at 26 (Roberts, C. J., dissenting).

11. Tocqueville. *Democracy in America: Volume I*, 388.

12. See, for instance: Robert L. Griswold, "Law, Sex, Cruelty, and Divorce in Victorian America, 1840-1900," in *Family & Society in American History*, ed. Joseph M. Hawes and Elizabeth I. Nybakken (Champaign, IL: University of Illinois Press, 2001), 152.

13. Alexis de Tocqueville, *Democracy in America: Volume 2*, trans. Henry Reeve (London: Longman, Green, Longman, and Roberts, 1862), 162-163; 118.

14. *Obergefell v. Hodges*, at 1.

15. Tocqueville, *Democracy in America: Volume I*, 387-388.

16. Kennedy's mentions of religions include lines like: "Marriage is sacred to those who live by their religions," and "There are untold references to the beauty of marriage in religious and philosophical texts" (*Obergefell v. Hodges*, at 3). The only mention of Christianity that appears anywhere in the *Obergefell* decision is in Justice Antonin Scalia's dissent, and there Scalia only mentions Christianity to point out that the religious backgrounds of the justices on the Supreme Court—not a one is Protestant, and not a one is an evangelical Christian—are wildly unrepresentative of the population of the United States as a whole (*Obergefell v. Hodges,* at 6 [Scalia, J., dissenting]).

17. William Mathie notes correctly that Tocqueville is ambiguous about how strong religion must be to perform these kinds of roles; Tocqueville seems to portray religion in America more as a social "habit" that grounds mores rather than as a matter of deep conviction. See "God, Woman, and Morality: The Democratic Family in the New Political Science of Alexis de Tocqueville." *The Review of Politics* 57.1 (1995): 17. Pierre Manent's work on this topic is also noteworthy. See *Tocqueville and the Nature of Democracy*, trans. John Waggoner (Lanham, MD: Rowman & Littlefield, 1996), 88.

18. Tocqueville, *Democracy in America: Volume I*, 388.

19. Robert Nisbet, *The Quest for Community: A Study in the Ethics of Order and Freedom* (Wilmington, DE: ISI Books, 2010).

20. Harvey Mansfield and Delba Winthrop, editors' introduction to *Democracy in America*, by Alexis de Tocqueville (Chicago: The University of Chicago Press, 2000), lxxx.

21. *Obergefell v. Hodges*, at 5.

22. Ibid., at 16–17; 21. *Lawrence v. Texas*, 539 U.S. 558 (2003), at 559.

23. Ibid., at 25. *Lawrence v. Texas*, at 572.

24. For this reason alone, I am not unsympathetic to—though I do not entirely believe—the idea that Justice Kennedy carefully plotted the precedential path to his decision in *Obergefell.*

25. Tocqueville, *Democracy in America: Volume I,* 325.

26. Tocqueville, *Democracy in America: Volume II*, 30.

27. Mark Graber, "The Nonmajoritarian Difficulty: Legislative Deference to the Judiciary." *Studies in American Political Development* 35 (1993): 35–73.

28. Tocqueville, *Democracy in America: Volume II,* 245.

29. Ibid.

30. He writes:

> When the time for choosing a husband is arrived, that cold and stern reasoning power which has been educated and invigorated by the free observation of the world, teaches an American woman that a spirit of levity and independence in the bonds of marriage is a constant subject of annoyance, not of pleasure; it tells her that the amusements of the girl cannot become the recreations of the wife, and that the sources of a married woman's happiness are in the home of her husband. As she clearly discerns beforehand the only road which can lead to domestic happiness, she enters upon it a once, and follows it to the end without seeking to turn back. Ibid., 241–42.

31. Notably, given the preceding analysis, Tocqueville regards "that spirit of individual independence" as the "most dangerous antagonist" of religious authority in a democratic state. Ibid., 32.
32. *Obergefell v. Hodges*, at 9 (Roberts, C. J., dissenting).
33. Tocqueville, *Democracy in America: Volume I*, xv.
34. Tocqueville, *Democracy in America: Volume II*, 248.
35. Tocqueville, *Democracy in America: Volume I*, 355.
36. Tocqueville, *Democracy in America: Volume II*, 361.
37. Tocqueville, *Democracy in America: Volume II*, 181.
38. Alexander Bickel, *The Least Dangerous Branch: The Supreme Court at the Bar of Politics* (Indianapolis, IN: Bobbs-Merrill, 1962).

Chapter Twelve

Parenthood and Procreation

Scott Yenor

It seems increasingly necessary to think of marriage and family life in terms of traditional views and revisionist views. On the traditional view, family solidarity and a communal living between two spouses superseded individual identities and even determined them. Sexual relations between the man and woman were, under the best of circumstances, exclusive and their relation was enduring, to be broken, if at all, only for serious reasons. Communal living of the couple was structured around procreation and raising children.[1]

Laws throughout the Western world and specifically American law acknowledged the centrality of these institutional arrangements, presumably because, as studies show, children, in the main, fare better when their biological parents are their parents. Such holdings sometimes prevented the state from intruding into the inner workings of families, but they always acknowledge the dependence of political society for the inner workings of the family. In *Meyer v. Nebraska* (1923), the Supreme Court vindicated the constitutional rights of parents to have their children taught in a foreign language; the court was protecting parental rights to direct the education of their children but also the rights "to marry, establish a home and bring up children."[2] *Skinner v. Oklahoma* (1942), where the Court struck down a statute imposing sterilization on certain felons, stands for the idea that "marriage and procreation are fundamental to the very existence of society."[3] In *Loving v. Virginia* (1967), the court struck down an anti-miscegenation statute, holding that marriage is "fundamental to our very existence and survival" because marriage supports couples as they propagate society.[4] Citations could be piled up (and have been piled up[5]) where the same complex of opinions governed in American law. This idea can be traced back to the American Founding and to the political philosophy of John Locke.[6] In any event, biology or sexual reproduction seems to give rise to parental obligations and societal expectations that a vast majority of parents take seriously. Courts have been most interested in protecting this "mechanism" from state interference in these decisions so that parents could assume their duties and discharge them as they saw fit (within minimal limits).

Yet this link between having children and caring for them has been revised in late modern times. Modern reproductive technologies such as artificial insemination, modern legal concepts such as adoption and surrogacy, and modern social developments such as the rise of single-parent families point toward the same phenomenon—the severance of biological reproduction (i.e., the father and mother coming together to provide genetic materials out of which a new life forms) from the education and care of the child.

Coinciding with this has been a great change in the legal conception of the family, culminating in the Supreme Court's *U.S. v. Windsor* (2013) and *Obergefell v. Hodges* (2015) decisions that national and state laws defining marriage as a union between a man and a woman violate the Constitution. These decisions further erode the "procreative prejudice" at the heart of the institution. Marriage concerns first and foremost the interests of adults in these decisions. Having the right to marry allows same-sex couples, according to *Windsor*, to "enhance their own liberty," achieve "protection," while conferring "dignity" and "a status of immense import" for making "personhood." Same-sex marriage also allows the law to acknowledge the "intimate relationship between two people."[7] When the court deigns to mention children, it is in the context of discussing how children of same-sex couples will live in concord with, and gain dignity from, their communities when the right to marry is granted to the same-sex couple with whom they live.[8] *Obergefell* builds on the same adult-centered vision of marriage, in that it sees marriage based "in the concept of individual autonomy," reflecting "a two-person union unlike any other in its importance to the committed individuals," and allows for the public recognition and stability for children who somehow come along to same-sex couples. All of this affirms, in the *Obergefell* Court's eyes, that "marriage is the keystone of our social order" and that "marriage is foundation of the family and of society."[9] If children had been the justification for the idea that society depends on the family in the previous era, what is the basis for that contention according to the *Obergefell* court, since children for the most part fall outside the purpose of *Obergefell's* adult-centered marriage?

The pre-1980 line of cases depended on a kind of reality—marriage and family life or the household in general—involving the needs and limits that the body places on human relationships. The *Obergefell* decision the children seem to come out of nowhere, since, obviously, same-sex couples of themselves cannot reproduce. Controversies about birth certificates, where same-sex marriage advocates would like to be listed as parents instead of the natural parents, involve the same kind of forgetting of the bodily reality of human life.[10]

Contemporary marriage law and opinion raise the question of why those who "have" children should parent or educate (and be responsible for) them, since having and parenting or educating of children appears to lie outside the purpose of marriage in this revised, adult-centered view.

Yet characteristics of our law and experience also assume that biological parentage and legal guardianship for purposes of care and education are and remain linked. As procreation has ceased to be a purpose of marriage, the idea that the education of children could serve as an organizing purpose of a marital union has also withered. This suggests that the two notions are connected. Perhaps the most notable recognition of this link is that, even after a half a century or more of family decline, in a clear majority of cases, biological parents raise their children throughout their nonage.[11] Children whose "daddy's name is donor," tend to feel, studies show, abandoned, isolated from their families and confused about their identity.[12] The link between procreation and parenting is seen in other areas, in what we do and in what we leave undone. The most spectacular and somewhat anachronistic recognition of this link is that men may have to pay child support when a sexual liaison leads to a child. (Why is a sperm donor different from a man who, from a one-night stand, impregnates a woman? Why must the latter pay child support for years or live under community disapprobation as a "deadbeat dad" while the former is applauded and walks away without any assumption of paternity, though he is biologically the father?) There is also the common assumption that those who give birth to children will also care for them—and exceptions to this norm (such as adoption and surrogacy) sit at the margins of our experience and undergo heightened state scrutiny; those "deadbeats" who shirk their duty subject to one of the last commonly accepted signs of moral disapprobation. In all or nearly all states and nations, birth parents commit a crime of abandonment if they simply leave the hospital without their child, never to return.

These inconsistent observations—questioning whether procreation and education are linked while assuming that they are connected for the purposes of common life—force us to think about the fundamentals of family life on the procreation and education of children. How do we account for the public's presumption that (legal and biological) parents are responsible for their children? Why might legal parenthood be related to biological parenthood? Should biological and legal parenthood continue to be related? What does the recognition of this relationship imply about marriage, family life, and the public's interest in those institutions? Should the public resolve its inconsistency in this matter? If so, in which direction should it head?

THE REVELATION IN PHILOSOPHIC ALTERNATIVES

These questions cannot be ignored: children need some kind of intense personalized care to survive and thrive. While some developments point toward divorcing biological parenthood from parenting (e.g., the procedures most states use to become an adoptive parent may resemble licensing and surrogacy and sperm donations may morph into selling babies for a price), those developments remain on the periphery and, to different degrees, need not call into question our basic assumptions about the relationship between procreating and parenting. That we accept such arrangements on the periphery may be a function of our commitment to limited government or our worry of what government would have to do to prohibit such actions as it would be a genuine endorsement of them. That we accept such arrangements is further evidence of Aristotle's wise admonition that we cannot expect political or ethical science to yield demonstrable truths.[13] Some variations and exceptions from the norm are bound to happen in human affairs. Mistakes occur when we see variations and exceptions as subversive of the norm or as indications that some norm does not or cannot exist.

Minding these qualifications, we mostly assume that the birth-mother is the mother and will be the mother and that she will identify the birth-father, who will be the father; birth-mothers are responsible for mothering or parenting and birth-fathers are responsible for fathering or parenting. Whether this amounts to a reliance on nature or the closest thing to nature or whether it is deeply inbred in human beings through a combination of laws, love and nature need not detain us now. This is a primordial fact of law and life in nearly every society that has ever existed: biological parenthood is related to child-rearing, absent some compelling reason to separate the two. That a fact *is* does not tell us why a fact *is good* or why a particular relationship is valuable and worth maintaining, however. The connection between making babies and raising babies is perhaps the least bad way to bring children (up) into the world; it might be even better than that.

Let us try to approach the question of why this arrangement might be good through the back door. Why have civilizations rejected alternatives to the birth parent-parenting connection? Who should be tasked with educating and raising and paying expenses for newborn children until they can shift for themselves? Few are proposing that society distribute children randomly or on the basis of parental merit (as determined by a parental test, perhaps) or as a piece of valuable property to be sold to the highest bidder. We as a people or civilization, out of respect for individual liberty, are not prepared to join a particular man to a particular woman at the public's behest as the best parents for a particular child. Neither does the public yet entertain ideas of having parents licensed. No society has successfully embraced or executed the chiliastic vision of human cloning followed up by purely public education, articulated with the greatest clarity in Aldous Huxley's *Brave New World*. Nor is the idea that children should be raised in common, as in Plato's *Republic* or Engels' post-revolutionary world, on the public agenda.

Consider for a moment the idea that children should be allocated to parents on the basis of merit and raised toward their proper destiny. On this proposal, we might make judgments about adult parenting abilities and match parents with the children who would thrive under those parents. Let us assume, for the sake of argument, that we had good measure of each of parenting abilities and a child's proclivities. Plato seems to have just such an arrangement in mind in his *Republic*, where the just city in speech abolishes the family (at some level) and replaces it with a system of allocating children to the circle of the city corresponding to the metal in their soul.[14] Mothers and fathers tend to see gold in their children, even though many have only bronze or, perhaps, even, fool's gold. This overestimation leads to a misallocation of time and energy; lesser parents may not be suited to bring out the best in their greater child.

While such an arrangement may indeed do justice in the abstract to each particular child, Aristotle (perhaps on Platonic grounds) objects to the communal raising of children.[15] Aristotle considers the Platonic suggestion to be holding children in common because the community must interpose between the child and his "parents" in allocating children to proper parents and because no particular parents will be taking charge of any particular children: golds will raise golds; silvers silvers and so on. "What belongs in common to most people," Aristotle writes, "is accorded the least care."[16] Broadly communal child-rearing institutions fail to bring out what is distinctive and excellent about each child: they fail as educational institutions. They fail because the connection between a birth mother and her child cannot be reproduced with communal institutions, where care and attention are diluted and where there is no particular, durable, responsible connection between the child and caregiver. Plato's arrangements may also fail to produce children, in that women and their mates may not be interested in bearing children if they cannot also raise them.

There may indeed be other ways of getting the "right" parents together with the "right" children than the way Plato intimates in the *Republic.* To argue that communal arrangements are inferior to arrangements where a particular set of adults care for children does not tell us *what* the particular arrangement should look like or *how* children should be allocated to them. What we have done need not be what we do. Perhaps children could be bought and sold in a market. Semen or eggs could be bought. Surrogates could rent out their wombs. Perhaps more widespread adoption could allow an objective third party to evaluate the parental capacity of all (or most) who would enter into the adventures in parenthood and to allocate children accordingly. Perhaps society could adopt a parental licensing scheme or perhaps we could engage in an ever-greater trimming of parental responsibilities and a transfer of that which is trimmed to state institutions (though this would raise the problem of communal institutions).

These proposals promise to sever the link between biology and parenthood because the link is sub-rational and unnecessary. Advocates seem to promise a more egalitarian, rational, scientific parenthood.[17] They promise to free parenting from the taint of biological determinism, to make parenthood much more consistent with individual choice, and to define "father," for instance, in terms of actual investment in or suitability for rearing the child as opposed to siring the child or merely providing the semen from which a child's genetic constitution comes. They promise to define mothering in terms of contributions to nurturing and caring for the child as opposed to breeding the child consequent to a sex act or implantation. What is it, after all, about copulating or gestating that qualifies one to provide proper care for a child? "What father in a thousand, when he begets a child, thinks farther than the satisfying of his present appetite?" John Locke asks.[18] The question answers itself, posed in this fashion: nothing exclusively animal or biological qualifies one to raise a child. Again, there seems to be a kernel of truth in the effort to sever procreation from education: parenting a child is a moral quality that comes from, or is at least assisted by, desiring to parent, and desiring to parent is analytically distinct from having sex.

Men and women make *sine qua non* contributions in reproducing children, in that a mother's egg and a father's sperm make the child and without either a child cannot form. The education of a child is a much less necessary development, sometimes successfully completed by one parent, sometimes unsatisfactorily completed by two, and sometimes completed by non-biological parents. The unique contribution to education made by each parent is less apparent and more subject to individual variety and parental choice. Certainly copulation can be separated from breeding—both in that one can pretty successfully prevent breeding through various birth control methods and in that human beings have the ability to reproduce (now) without first having sex. Sex is, or can be, optional. This provides another reason to sever links between procreation and education. Copulation, breeding, and procreation seem to be analytically distinct moments, separate from one another and from parenting and the desire to parent.

BINDING PARENTHOOD AND PROCREATION

Those who do not believe that reproduction and education should be (or are) connected wish to hear compelling reasons for its continued existence. Their demands provide a picture of the child brought into the world independent and without strings attached, without any prior personal identity. They see the mother and father as detached and willing to ask—earnestly, perhaps, and in the best interest of their children—how children should be allocated according to the principles of justice and public reason. Love of one's own gives way, on their reading, to what might be seen as a higher love, a love for what is in the best interest of the child (even if that means that the child be raised to someone else). There will be no special concern for keeping one's own as one's own if that would improve the child's life. Stripped of "selfishness" and jealousy, parenthood would become objective, rational and scientific. This vision of independence for the children is, perhaps, the best case to be made for the de-institutionalized view.

Against this view, I submit human beings do not and could not allocate child-rearing responsibilities or justify them on the basis of contractual reasoning; rather, we *acknowledge* them as goods and realities antecedent to government. No test in the world can "properly allocate" children, and we should be glad that none could. Mothers desire to take care of their own children and are well equipped, physically and psychologically, to do so; their love of their own is indispensable for the job before them. Fathers, while not as connected as mothers, invest in their children too as their own. This love of one's own provides the most important parenting attribute. Connections among these goods are related to our bodily natures and human identity. Let us not get too far ahead of ourselves with such considerations.

The pertinent question for our purposes is whether the three functions (sex, procreation, and parenting) are best linked. The connection between biological parenthood (a unity of sex and procreation) and parenting are at the center of this controversy. Parenting involves the total care of the child, from meeting the child's basic immediate physical and psychological needs to the education of a child. Education of the child centers on the cultivation of distinctive faculties, pointing a child toward proper conduct and character, aiding a child in relating to others, helping to assure that the child gains knowledge of the important things in life and, ultimately, pointing a child toward a happy, prospering life. Parenting at its best aims at the "best being" of the child.[19]

The idea behind linking biological parenthood (mere being) and parenting aimed toward best being is this: Parenting requires an open-ended and unpredictable commitment to the best being of the child; and marriage is the commitment that prepares parents for and resembles the open-ended commitment that is necessary for the upbringing of the child. Sexual relations, mutual pursuit of a common good, and intense personal relations in a series of unpredictable circumstances—the concomitants of self-giving love—cement the commitment between husbands and wives and thereby prepare the way for committing each adult to provide the best being of their child. Marriage is a school for parenthood. Neither relation is completely explicable in terms of contract. Neither can be defined perfectly beforehand. Each calls forth a covering love to make all the rest possible. Perhaps that love is "sacrificial" or "self-denying" but it is a concept of those words that includes self-fulfilling or self-discovery.

Parents see children as their own or as belonging to them in several senses. Children belong to parents in that they come from the bodies of mothers with the sexual contribution of fathers; children are flesh of their parents' flesh. The mother especially knows the child as hers and often feels a spontaneous joy in the presence of her infant and less often in the presence of her teenager. As the child matures, such a love becomes a personal love for a unique creature. Parents may see children as continuations of themselves and, perhaps, examples of their immortality. Children are also, under the best of circumstances, embodied examples of the love husbands and wives have for one another. As such, parents are much more likely to sacrifice for each other and for their common progeny. The intense, personal love of husband for wife and vice versa prepares each to provide intense, personal attention to children. Responsible to each other, husband and wife take responsibility for their children. This is a framework of commitment in which both the man and the woman see a child as their own, accept responsibility for the child's nurturing and education, and will not quit responsibilities when the going gets tough.

Not much prepares one to become a father or a mother, just as not much prepares one to be a husband or a wife. Yet much prepares one for these tasks—preparation comes from living in a family and being a son or daughter and preparation for parenting comes in part from marriage. Marital and parental life is filled with unpredictable revolutions, unexpected joys and sorrows, and unchosen responsibilities. Those situations call for a commitment to one's promise and one's duty. Rational control is an antithesis of love, in this decisive sense. Such a love is strongest on multiple fronts, when it is shared and part of something larger than itself. Perhaps it is strongest when it is part of a providential order, but consideration of this possibility would take us beyond the limits of reason alone.

When this framework misfires, we get confirmation of how these goods are connected. Sex without commitment—that is, without a commitment like marriage—ends up, in the main, worse for attaching both parents to the child and such children receive a measurably worse education than children raised with the commitment of two parents. Children of divorce are less well parented—to judge by results—than children of intact families.[20] Step-fathers, who do not see children as flesh of their flesh, are usually less committed to a child's wellbeing than a "natural" father, as much social science evidence confirms.[21] The public requires that adoptive parents go through a serious set of inquiries and "home studies" in order to test their commitment to the children, in part acknowledging that the state is right to be more suspicious of relationships not based on the pairing of biological and actual parenting. We see a commitment to connecting sex, procreation, and parenthood in the difference between how a one-night stand that yields pregnancy and a sperm donor are treated in our law and opinion. The "dead-beat" dad pays child support, which means that the sex act, which led to procreation, creates parental obligations of support. The sperm donor, whose biological contribution to the child is indistinguishable from the "dead beat's," has no such obligation.

Parental overestimation of a child is a most useful, intractable delusion benefiting all of society and benefiting each child. Love of one's own leads to care for one's own and sacrificing (joyfully) on behalf of one's own child. Parenting does not involve counting the costs. The link between biology and parenthood seems to be part of our humanity. There are chemical and hormonal links between a mother and child that cannot be easily ignored or changed with alternative hormonal therapies. The body, it seems, has a logic all its own, where the connections grounded in the body take on an importance all their own. A land where the claims of biological parenthood are negligible will be a land with few children. A land that does not depend on the link between biological parenthood and nurturing parenthood denies a central reality of human life. A land that does not acknowledge that link subverts the lifeline to its own existence.

POPULATION DECLINE, THE "BIRTH DEARTH," AND MODERN EDUCATION

The health of family life depends on its employment, which, in turn, depends on the distinction between the private and the public. There is a mysterious point at which families and the state share important duties. Parents and the state share educational responsibilities—the most enduring private and the most conspicuous public "institutions" have overlapping jurisdiction over the shape of the future. Parents have seemingly exclusive control over children, especially in their early years. Having participated in authoring the children, parents participate in shaping them. Parents have and raise children for independent lives on their own, yet they do so with the aim of participating in a particular society with particular mores. Parents teach children the language and norms of a wider community as part of their preparation for future life as citizens and for their best being. The health of the wider community depends in part on the quality and quantity of citizens it receives from private families.

This means that the wider community, when it minds the distinction between private and public, depends on something that is beyond its direct capacity to produce and control. The state generally, and the modern Progressive state in particular, is not content to receive its future citizens "ready-made" by private entities such as families. As the child matures, the (Progressive) state takes an increasing role in supervising, regulating, providing for, and, indeed, displacing parents through educational policies broadly conceived. Done partly in the name of mitigating parental bias, such educational policies aim to perfect the "socialization process" and mold citizens toward important public values. The state is not always patient in taking what it gets from private families, and there is a tendency for the state to become increasingly "paternalistic" in the sense of coopting to itself the educational tasks formerly completed by parents. Certain thinkers envision the withering of the family and especially of fatherhood while the state assumes more functions.[22]

Thus "the war between the state and the family" takes shape—a war as old as the political community itself[23] and as new as modern welfare states and compulsory public education policies.[24] The political community wants the family or parent(s) to act in a particular way and is willing to trim the responsibilities of the family and parents to achieve its way; the state acts as a provider and caretaker of some things. The family provides the personal attention due to one's own—also acting as a provider and caretaker on other things. These "dual sovereigns" share spheres. Families have been willing, over the course of modern times, to allow more penetration from the state into their sphere—perhaps due to the decline in the place of family in the human heart and perhaps due to the sheer expense of raising children.

Those in the "loss of function" school of sociology chart the shrinking of the family's sphere of sovereignty, though it is crucial to see it from two angles. Sociologists have been at the forefront of the "loss of function" thesis and the "decline of the family" thesis.[25] The family forfeits some tasks to the state in order to better consolidate its power over a smaller territory (the loss of function), while, on the other hand, the state's ability to perform the tasks formerly completed by or centered in the family is compromised by the "decline of the family." The loss of function thesis holds that as the family loses sovereignty over economic production and then education, it comes to have a constricted role in providing emotional support. The decline of the family thesis holds that as less formal alternatives to the nuclear family such as divorce and cohabitation and parentless children become more prevalent, social ills such as crime, poor education outcomes, and unemployment are more likely to follow. If the loss of function and the decline of the nuclear family are related, it seems that as the state assumes more functions, it becomes difficult for the state to accomplish the functions it assumes.

No area of public policy reveals the links—and the attempts to sever the links—between family and the state more clearly than education. Intact, interested two-parent families are a chief determinant of educational success in the American context—the private underlays the public.[26] The kind of environment in the home—the extent and variety of parental supervision, the living examples, the artistic and religious culture of the home—tells much about the educational prospects for children. At the same time, spending on public education demonstrates a pronounced aspiration for the state to assume the educational function that (some) families cannot or will not perform—here the public eclipses the private without recognizing its continued reliance on the private. Very few educational programs have been discovered in the American context to compensate for the cultural shortfall of those born outside two-parent families. Since economic success is increasingly related to educational credentials and attainment, the family divide in America has become a class or chaste divide—separating the haves (who disproportionately come from two-parent families) from have nots (who are less likely to come from two-parent families).[27]

State involvement follows the principle of the division of labor, where parents focus on the heart while the state focuses on the head. Many families are willing to transfer their educational functions to the state for several reasons: technical education exceeds the capacities of many parents; the expense of private education makes it appear prohibitive; parents would have to forgo terrific opportunity costs in the workplace to school their children themselves; education through an objective third party provides a suitable corrective to the sometimes excessive partisanship of parents on behalf of their own children. Yet, the "objective third party" still depends on the cooperation of the child and the parents for the success of educational endeavors; intact families are disproportionately likely to provide that cooperation—the head does not operate well without the heart.

Education is only one example of how diverse policies relieve families and parents of the financial burdens of parenting. But education also allows us to see how the state still silently relies on the family for the accomplishment of its function. There is another, even more spectacular example of this state reliance on the private: fertility. Fertility is, for now, at least, a private decision reflective of sexual acts. Yet fertility itself determines whether a society will or can continue—so in this decisive sense states are dependent upon private decisions for their future. Fertility rates are declining throughout the modern world and they have been for centuries. We have a dangerous "birth dearth" within a long-term population decline. In fact, total fertility rates are below replacement in many countries: Singapore's is 1.1. Those of Japan and Poland are 1.3, and those of Germany, Austria and Italy 1.4. In Russia the rate stands at 1.6, in France 2.08, and the United States 1.9 (all are approximations).[28] What is more, declining fertility rates seem to defy easy categorization. China's women submit to China's "One Child Policy," while many women in America and much of Europe choose to have one child. No particular explanation for the phenomenon suffices if all nations are caught up in the same tide; we must search for a general explanation if tyrannical control (China) and free choice (the U.S. and the West, generally) yield approximately the same results.

Most scholars and commentators embrace a very general explanation: the spirit of modernity. This is both revealing and not revealing. It is revealing in that it suggests the temporal element connected with powerful, regime-level ideas surrounding individual autonomy, a more self-centered meaning of human happiness, and the human urge to control the forces of nature. It is also revealing in that it suggests that there are limits to what human beings can do to reverse this broader, irresistible tide. Modernity as explanation is not revealing, however, in that it does not tell us what is missing or what it is about human beings that has changed their "calculus" of having children.

The spirit of modernity manifests itself in different guises in different locales. What causes this birth dearth? Demographic-policy wonks focus, for instance, on the ways in which educating children has become increasingly expensive as a factor in driving down the willingness of parents to procreate. Each child costs over a million dollars in modern America, for instance—costs figuring in the provision of necessities and contributions to "best being" and in the opportunity costs of parents' foregone wages. Social Security is a big drag on fertility, diverting costs from child-rearing to retirement programs. So, too, is the cost of homes, and especially bigger homes suitable for bigger families. The cost of education (broadly conceived) holds down procreation. Lower the price of children and people will be more likely to have more children. Imagine how far fertility would tumble if parents were denied public provision for K-12 education or child tax credits or other benefits. Imagine how much higher we could move fertility if we provided parents with more. Or so the reasoning goes.

Worried about demographic collapse, most countries have unsuccessfully tried to move the needle on fertility through financial incentives. Whether it is through attempts to curb the costs of birthing a child or to provide pay to stay home with children under two or to provide state sponsored or assisted child care (in addition to the provision of public school and, in many countries, government provided health care) the best that can be said is that "subsidies produce returns mostly at the margins."[29] Advertising campaigns promoting love-making and the famous Putin love benches (which slant toward the center as an encouragement to physical contact) have failed to staunch declines in fertility.

Why have such efforts failed? Perhaps one reason such efforts have not measurably moved the fertility needle is that the subsidies or financial enticements have not been large enough. We could pay women enough to make them genuine breeders and then turn those children into wards of the state, for purposes of education. It stands to reason that sufficient wages (whether $100,000 or $1 million) will, eventually, attract sufficient laborers to give birth to the children we otherwise would not have. How would we analyze such an incentive structure as a matter of principle? In conceiving of such labor as outside the bonds of marriage, such a proposal severs the link between procreation and marriage in a most decisive way. In removing the norm that parents should have an active role in educating their children, the proposal severs the link between biological parenthood and parenting. In making labor a matter of wages, it removes any expectation that love, sacrifice and responsibility move people to have children or that there be enduring, exclusive relations between husband and wife; it assumes mercenary motives for biological parenting, as opposed to motives of love and responsibility.

This leads to the following conclusion: we have not proposed such large subsidies because they subvert the moral universe of marriage and family life and they contradict what we think of as providing for the "best being" for a human being. These proposals point to a post-human future. No matter how much our courts, our laws, or our public opinion seek to deny the connections between biology and parenthood or between marriage and parenthood, we continue to depend on them as a civilization and assume them to be controlling in a vast majority of cases.

Biological parenting is connected to parenting as such, through the human love of one's own and through the virtues of love and responsibility. That evidence for this connection approaches universal support suggests that the connection may very well be natural. Fertility has fallen and the family has contracted as the family's share of the sphere of provision and education—as the sphere of parenting, that is—contracts. Take public schooling as the paradigmatic case to illustrate this argument. According to the "cost of parenting leads to the birth dearth" argument, one would have expected birth rates to rise with the advent of public provision of education because it decreases parental cost and it makes working outside the home more imaginable for both parents; public provision in this area lowers the cost of parenting. In fact, however, fertility fell apace with the introduction of public schooling and fell more as public provision expanded through twelfth grade. Removing "burdens" from parents does not seem to encourage them to have more children.

In fact, the nearly universal failure of "incentive structures" suggests that things may work in the opposite direction. Modernity, it is said, consists partly in the transferring or "loss of functions" from the family to the state. "Loss of function" is another phrase for "removing burdens." Famous exponents of the "loss of function" thesis, Emile Durkheim and Anthony Downs, see the family reduced to its irreducible core in later modernity: to producing children, cultivating emotional closeness, and restraining sexual desire among spouses. If this is all that marriage and family life are about, perhaps we should ask a fundamental question, "Why bother?" As children cease, in several respects, to be one's own and as the state takes over responsibility for education and provision, parents are less interested in having children and there are fewer reasons to marry. Parents may have children because they would like to raise them and care for them, provide for them, and love them. As the state makes parenting easier by performing its main tasks, it cultivates an attenuated sense of responsibility among parents for the future and it shrinks the sphere of love and concern. Perhaps the growth of the state leads to the birth dearth. As the state and the wider community crowds out the job of parents and hence the virtues associated with parenthood, perhaps fewer people have children.

I am not arguing that transferring functions or costs to the family will cause another baby boom. I am making a broader cultural contention. Love and responsibility are the virtues or "social capital" from which parenthood springs. As the state assumes parenting functions (i.e., education, provision, etc.) it fosters virtues or a way of life that emphasizes self-centeredness and autonomy, as well as a way of thinking that emphasizes the present; marriage and family life are bound to be less central to one's life, less fecund, less fulfilling, and more and more counter-cultural. Building capacity in families involves, above all, ensuring that married couples and families generally have a significant job to do. Only then do they reproduce in greater numbers and embrace their responsibilities as crucial to their own being. Underemployment in the family leads to its decline.

PROCREATION, EDUCATION, AND BEING HUMAN

No one can give a completely rational account of the connections at the heart of marriage and family life, at least not on the grounds of the modern scientific understanding of the rational. Human beings did not make these connections; they are preexisting, grounded in the particular and peculiar character of the human body, almost universal and hence have a strong claim to be natural. Claiming that these connections are "natural" does not *ipso facto* mean that they are entitled to respect. That they are related to the human in some deep, fundamental way, however, suggests that destroying those connections will indeed make us into something other than human; destroying those connections points us toward a post-human future.

Let us consider these connections starting from the connection between sex or the physical act of love and procreation.[30] Sexual reproduction reflects the importance of our being male and female. The sexes relate to one another or are complementary for the purposes of reproduction. They complement one another for the purposes of sex (where they have genitalia suited to the physical act of sex) and procreation (where their genitalia convey the genetic stuff out of which new life forms). From the perspective of the parents, the procreative act completes the sexual act and conveys essential truths about the nature of human being. The sexual act reflects a desire to become one with another or of transcending our alone-ness or separateness, yet the fact that individuals have separate bodies means that they cannot overcome that separateness through the act of sex. Sexual passion relents and exhausts itself without reaching the completion for which it aims. The procreative act, in contrast, does complete this desire to become one with another in the children born of the sexual act. Only through children do human beings overcome the separateness and become one with another. The high act of creation does not stand without the low sexual passion.

Let us connect these connections between sex and procreation to the educative mission of parents. This relation is also an important lesson in human limits. Remember Locke's less than exalted view of sexual relations: "What father in a thousand, when he begets a child," Locke asks, "thinks farther then (sic) the satisfying of his present appetite?" Those of a more personalist philosophy entertain a more exalted view of sex, holding that one can seek the good of the other in the act of sex but not to use the other as a means of self-satisfaction. Regardless of which view holds, neither sees human beings intending to participate in the creation of children through sex; children come through indirection as a result of the invisible hand of nature. This is an important parenting lesson. Children are not products of our intentions or wills; they come to us despite our contrary wills; they are gifts and even surprises. Nature's indirection provides the proper clue to the attitude parents entertain as they educate their children.

It is impossible to say at what point the disruption of the connection between procreation and education makes us something other than human or at what point this disruption threatens the future of self-government. Some think that "discarding the traditional family" with these connections "would change the whole character of human existence."[31] How can we entertain such thoughts? They seem to take leave from the realm of reason to the realm of prophecy or imagination. How would "humanity" look on the other side of the traditional family? How would our social institutions work? Can we even think as if these institutions are entirely malleable to the human will?

Defenders of marriage and family life recognize ways that participation in marriage and family life teaches human limits, grounds abstract plans. Marriage and the family are standing reproaches to assertions of human autonomy or the technological view of the world. Intense focused love, sacrificial love, the sufferings and untold joys associated with the stuff of living, the highs and lows, the love of one's own—all of these, I say, are central to the human experience. Learning to deal with them magnanimously or philosophically or charitably is central to a life of character and wisdom. Marriage and family life bring with them tensions that constitute "the pain of living"[32] and hence also the joys of living. In Huxley's *Brave New World*, the elimination of the traditional family and its connections produces (mostly) a breed of happy animals, easily controlled by state power, unable to love other human beings, unable to appreciate the past, undisturbed by suffering due to heavy doses of medication. Does the "end of marriage" and family life point to the elimination of human depth?

Movements toward this post-familial world are in evidence. Sex without consequences is more easily practiced; fewer people are having children the old-fashioned way and it is more possible to have children with the aid of technological innovations. Does this portend an erasing of human depth? Does it portend a better or worse way of dealing with our psychological landscape?

One would expect that a decline of the traditional family would bring with it a decline in human responsibility, in our effectiveness for self-government, a relative lack of concern about the future, a purely physical, pleasurable understanding of the goals of sex, a wider acceptance of psychotropic drugs, a rise in loneliness, and other things. Yet since human nature cannot be conquered, we would also expect that different outlets might arise to register the restlessness of human nature: gangs or forms of fanaticism might replace families as a source of belonging, for instance. Allegiance to political ideas or politics itself might replace a concern with the more humble private realm.

No matter how much our contemporary views wish away the links between procreation and education, those links persist and will persist. These links reveal that the public depends on the private since both procreation and education are the result of "private" decisions. No alternative means of making these moments public is available, and if one were available it should not be embraced. Efforts to separate having children and raising them are indeed ill-founded. Laws and mores should be grounded in the biological and personal realities of human life. Anything less is uncivilized.

NOTES

I would like to thank Ralph Hancock, James Stoner, Arthur Milikh, and David Azerrad and my editors for their encouraging comments on this work and for their suggestions to improve it. All mistakes are mine alone.

1. Mary Ann Glendon, *The Transformation of Family Law: State, Law, and Family in the United States and Western Europe* (Chicago: The University of Chicago Press, 1989), 291–94 and Max Rheinstein, *Marriage, Stability, Divorce and the Law* (Chicago: The University of Chicago Press, 1972).

2. 262 U.S. 390, at 399.

3. 316 U.S. 535, at 541.

4. 388 U.S. 1, at 12.

5. See Helene Alvare, "Same-Sex Marriage and the 'Reconceiving' of Children," 64.3 *Case Western Reserve Law Review* (2014), 831–33.

6. Scott Yenor, "The True Origin of the Family: The Founders and the Family," First Principles Series Report # 48 at www.heritage.org/research/reports/2013/10/the-true-origin-of-society-the-founders-on-the-family; John Locke, *The Second Treatise of Government*, para. 78-

81; and Yenor, *Family Politics: The Idea of Marriage in Modern Political Thought* (Waco: Baylor University Press, 2011), chapter 2.

7. 133 S. Ct. at 2695, 2690, 2692, 2696, 2692.

8. 133 S. Ct. 294.

9. 576 U.S. 12-16 (slip opinion).

10. See Adam J. MacLeod, "Birth Certificates, Fatherhood, and Same-Sex Marriage: Sotomayor v. Sotomayor," *The Public Discourse* (5 November 2015) www.thepublicdiscourse.com/2015/11/15945/.

11. By my calculations, in 2012, 59.9 percent of children lived with two married biological parents, 3.5 percent lived with two unmarried biological parents, and 32.7 percent lived with one biological parent (either re-married with another or cohabiting with another), though these numbers include adoption numbers. 3.9% are living with no biological parents, though this number includes grandparents. Parsing out adoptions yields a total of 2.3 percent of children are adopted. Making the most conservative estimate possible, namely that grandparents are not biological and that there is no overlap between the 3.9 percent and 2.3 percent numbers yields 6.2 percent of children are living with no biological parents. Cf. "America's Families and Living Arrangements," at www.census.gov/prod/2013pubs/p20-570.pdf with "America's Children and Stepchildren," www.census.gov/prod/2014pubs/p20-572.pdf. These numbers are steady across time and culture, see Rose Kreider, US Census Bureau, "Adopted Children and Stepchildren: 2000" (2003), 14.

12. See "My Daddy's Name is Donor," http://americanvalues.org/catalog/pdfs/Donor_FINAL.pdf

13. Aristotle, *Nicomachean Ethics*, trans. Robert C. Bartlett and Susan D. Collins (Chicago: The University of Chicago Press, 2011), 1094b13–1095a12.

14. Plato, *The Republic*, trans. Allan Bloom (New York: Basic Books, 1968), 457dff.

15. Aristotle, *Politics*, 2nd Edition, trans. Carnes Lord (Chicago: The University of Chicago Press, 2013), 1262a25–1262b35.

16. *Politics*, 1261b32.

17. Susan Muller Okin, *Justice, Gender and the Family* (New York: Basic Books, 1987), 171, who envisions a society in which "childbearing would be so conceptually separate from child rearing and other family responsibilities that it would be a cause for surprise, and no little concern, if men and women were not equally responsible for domestic life or if children were to spend more time with one parent than the other."

18. Locke, *First Treatise on Government*, Para 54.

19. Hans Jonas, *The Imperative of Responsibility* (Chicago: The University of Chicago Press, 1984), 101.

20. See, for example, Judith Wallerstein, et. al., *The Unexpected Legacy of Divorce* (New York: Hyperion, 2000) and Elizabeth Marquardt, *Between Two Worlds: The Inner Lives of Children of Divorce* (New York: Three Rivers Press, 2006).

21. David Popenoe, *The War over the Family* (New Brunswick: Transaction Publishers, 2005), 93–94.

22. Bertrand Russell, *Marriage and Morality* (New York: Horace Liveright, 1929), 204–20 and Yenor, *Family Politics,* 168–71.

23. See Fustel de Coulanges, *The Ancient City* (Baltimore: The Johns Hopkins University Press, 1980), cf. Book 2, Chapters 8–10 with Book 3.

24. Patricia Morgan, *The War between the State and the Family: How Government Divides and Impoverishes* (New Brunswick: Transaction Press, 2008).

25. See the treatments of Emile Durkheim and modern sociologists in Yenor, *Family Politics*, chapters 5 and 10.

26. See Mitch Pearlstein, *From Family Collapse to America's Decline* (Lanham: Rowman & Littlefield, 2011) and *Broken Bonds* (Lanham: Rowman & Littlefield, 2014).

27. See Charles Murray, *Coming Apart* (New York: Crown Forum, 2012) and Andrew Cherlin, *Labor's Love Lost: The Rise and Fall of the Working-Class Family in America* (New York: Russell Sage Foundation, 2014).

28. Jonathan V. Last, *What to Expect When No One is Expecting* (New York: Encounter Books, 2013), 148.

29. Last, *What to Expect*, 161.

30. Contraception, *in vitro* fertilization, surrogate motherhood, and, finally, perhaps, human cloning undermine the connection between these two experiences, though in different ways.

31. Jacob Joshua Ross, *The Virtues of the Family* (New York: The Free Press, 1994), 258.

32. Tocqueville, *Democracy in America*, trans. Harvey C. Mansfield and Delba Winthrop (Chicago: The University of Chicago, 2000), 4.4.6.

Chapter Thirteen

Does the Law and the Constitution of the Family Have to Change?

James R. Stoner, Jr.

Does the law and the constitution of the family have to change? Many people in our society have for some years ardently insisted that it must, and they have now won a mandate from the Supreme Court of the United States ordering that their view become the law of the land. Since the Supreme Court of the state of Hawaii opened the question whether the restriction of marriage to a man and a woman was a violation of the constitutional guarantee of equal protection of the laws in 1993, the argument was widely made that the law of the family has to change to allow same-sex unions in order not to offend the Constitution.[1] An initiative in Hawaii reaffirmed traditional marriage in 1998, but the following year the Vermont Supreme Court struck that state's marriage law and insisted that the material benefits of marriage be extended to same-sex couples, which the Court allowed the legislature to do by permitting legally recognized civil unions.[2] That approach was soon rejected by the gay community, however, on the ground that providing all the legal benefits of marriage without the name cast a stigma on same-sex couples, so in 2003 and 2004 the Massachusetts Supreme Judicial Court, appealing to an equality clause in the state's 1780 constitution written by John Adams, required that marriage in the state be available to two otherwise eligible adults regardless of their sex.[3] Meanwhile, voters in many states passed amendments putting into their constitutions what had always before been taken for granted, that marriage could exist only between a man and a woman, but by the end of the decade courts in several states began to follow Massachusetts' lead and require state recognition of same-sex marriage, state legislators for the first time passed statutes requiring the same, and in the 2012 elections three states established same-sex marriage by popular vote.[4]

The following year the United States Supreme Court threw out part of the Defense of Marriage Act (DOMA), passed in 1996 to ensure that the federal government recognized only heterosexual marriage, regardless of what the states did, and while at the time they rejected on a technicality a challenge that would have required all states to recognize same-sex marriage, lower federal courts quickly seized upon the logic of Justice Kennedy's DOMA decision and struck marriage laws in numerous states—including some of the country's most conservative states.[5] While many of these decisions were stayed pending appeal, the Supreme Court's decision on October 6, 2014, not to hear appeals from federal circuit court decisions requiring same-sex marriage effectively ended the stays and allowed such marriages to proceed in numerous states. After the Sixth Circuit decision a month later upholding the law limiting marriage to a man and a woman, the Supreme Court accepted appeals from that circuit, leading to their 5–4 decision in *Obergefell v. Hodges* on June 26, 2015, denouncing such a limitation as a violation of the liberty and dignity of same-sex couples and therefore of the Equal Protection Clause. It was clear at least since 2013 that momentum had developed in the federal courts in favor of ordering same-sex marriage nationwide, but few of its advocates a decade before would have predicted the speed of the end-game.

In the paper that follows, I ask as a thought experiment what about the law and constitution of the family has to change if traditional marriage and the family that naturally results are ever to be restored in the law as the building block of social order. Suppose that same-sex marriage, even though decreed in the law and through the courts, is unsustainable as a social practice and not likely to garner much interest once it has served its revolutionary purpose. My question then is whether American democracy could recover traditional marriage as a social norm and thus make possible the restoration of a culture favorable to marriage for the generation of Americans now coming to maturity. "Does the law and the constitution of marriage have to change?" Yes, I want to suggest, not in the direction of same-sex marriage, but toward a regime of law that recognizes the natural family of man and woman and their biological children as the central case deserving of legal recognition. This requires a rethinking of family law as it is has been established, even leaving aside the same-sex question, and it means upsetting several principles and rules that are dear to pro-family lawyers and favored by good people who provide loving homes. I am only going to sketch what I have in mind, and to start, I want to say a few words about legal change.

LEGAL CHANGE

When is it legitimate, even necessary, for law to change? I don't think the answer is, whenever people *want* change. Yes, we are, or are supposed to be, a democracy, but we also know that people sometimes want something harmful or downright unjust. Law *ought* to change only when there is a good reason for change. What's a good reason?[6] First, if the lawmaker has made a mistake and discovers that a law has unintended consequences, then it makes sense to change it; people in both parties could probably give numerous, if different, examples. Secondly, if circumstances change, it makes sense to change the law to adjust to changing circumstances. For example, if a rural area gets built up and becomes congested, lower the speed limit. When new inventions such as smartphones become common, laws have to adjust, for example forbidding texting while driving or allowing text messages to validate a contract. Finally, laws might change to keep up with changes in human knowledge, either in scientific knowledge—think of DNA evidence—or perhaps even moral knowledge, for example penalizing sexual harassment. To be sure, even when change is justified, one might want to proceed cautiously: All legal change is likely to have unintended consequences; change disrupts settled expectations on the basis of which people may have risked their property or devoted their time; new laws often have to be enforced coercively, rather than relying on habit; and constant change in law calls into question the general wisdom of law and thus weakens consent. Still, laws that are just in one set of circumstances or based on the knowledge of one era may become unjust if they *don't* change to keep up.

This is certainly true of man-made laws, but even divine law (at least in the Christian tradition) is thought to change, at least in its application to human society. The chief example concerns precisely the law of marriage, which according to the Gospel has changed *twice*. Christ famously abrogates the Mosaic law of divorce, establishing that every valid marriage lasts for as long as both parties live, but he also explains that Moses permitted divorce in the first place only in response to the circumstance of a hard-hearted people, the law "from the beginning" (perhaps he means the natural law?) having forbidden it.[7] Nor is the law of divorce the only marriage law Jesus changes: Polygamy, if not adultery, was permitted to the patriarchs, perhaps by divine dispensation, but not to Christians, and we learn that the law against adultery can be broken by the eye and heart, not only by the sexual parts.

So have there been changes in circumstances or knowledge, scientific or moral, or recognition of legal mistakes and unintended consequences, that would require family law to change even without the same-sex challenge to traditional marriage? I think there have been, probably of every sort. For example, in the 1970s, every state by legislation relaxed divorce law, so that today divorce is permitted if either party requests it. This was done in part to spare children the pain of growing up in families where parents were at odds, but today it is recognized that divorce is usually more harmful to children than parental discord, at least when non-violent.[8] Likewise, contraception was declared a constitutional right for married couples and eventually expanded as an individual right regardless of marital status, with the expectation this would reduce out-of-wedlock births, but its ready availability has been accompanied by an explosion of the rate of births to unwed mothers, again to the disadvantage of children.[9] Moreover, easy divorce meant that marriage was for those who presently proclaim their love for one another, but if marriage is only about romantic love, it comes to be thought arbitrary to deny it to those romantically involved with a member of the same sex, or for that matter, to those whose romance is not dyadic. Again, these empirical and logical consequences of divorce legislation appear to have been unforeseen by those who changed the law in the 1970s. That might suggest that the legislators who passed such laws would now consider them to have been a mistake, and if so, by the principle I expounded before, they could rightfully be changed.

No one expects that, in part because social mores surrounding sex have also changed, enormously, and this should probably be considered a change in circumstance. Cause and effect are often difficult to sort out, and there are technological changes that have played a role—oral contraceptives, for example, and in vitro fertilization—breaking the natural link between sex and procreation. Perhaps premarital sex came to be tolerated by society because pregnancy could be readily prevented; the ease of divorce might also have contributed to extramarital sex, and, with remarriage, it made blended families common. Women's opportunities for higher education and work outside the home no doubt lessened their economic need to marry and perhaps added new strains to existing marriages. With many of these changes, laws changed to keep up. Prohibitions against fornication and cohabitation are gone or unenforceable; the law of alimony has changed in practice now that women are not presumed dependent on their husbands for support; the award of children in custody battles is settled by a new standard, "best interests of the child," which is probably less a legal standard than an educated (or prejudiced) guess; and much more. Of course it is a peculiarity of marriage law that its parameters are generally seen only when marriages fall apart, the family being, when functioning well, a social institution largely insulated from state regulation. But the breakup of many families inevitably places burdens on intact ones—additional rules from schools and government institutions that require both parents to give their consent for matters involving their children, for example, limiting the ability of one member of a couple to manage common property—and, more significantly, weakens social support for maintaining existing marriages. All these circumstantial changes mean not only that the law has changed to adjust, but that it would be very difficult to restore the traditional law of the family even if people decided we ought to: Repassing old law in new circumstances would in fact establish something new.

Has our scientific or moral knowledge changed in ways that merit legal change? I already suggested that social science has discovered long-term difficulties experienced by children whose parents have divorced. Another recent discovery, only in the early stages of receiving attention from social sciences, is the effect of a missing father on children conceived artificially, by sperm donation or in vitro fertilization.[10] Here what seems common is a crisis of identity, a sense of loss or absence in children who grow up ignorant of half their biological inheritance: sometimes worry about genetic risks to their health, sometimes wonder about an extended family of blood relatives they'll never know, often fear that someone to whom they are attracted might even be a biological half-sibling similarly conceived. Statistics show social risk as these children grow up, if also some tendency to form a subculture among themselves. There are poignant stories, too, for example the young boy who, unbeknownst to his mother, the only parent he knew, kept a box of little treasures under his bed to one day show the father he knew he must have but who had never been spoken of. Reading about this has persuaded me that there is a natural yearning in the child to know his biological parents, something the law has not always promoted and in the case of adoption has sometimes positively disallowed. Here, too, mores have changed. Adoptive parents more often tell their children the truth about their origin, and research shows children are better off if they know; reunions between grown children and their biological parents are now a staple of popular culture. What this discovery of the continued force of biology even in an artificial age means for the law of the family I will consider in a moment.

Has there been progress in the moral or philosophical understanding of marriage? Here, too, I think there has been. On the one hand, the philosophical basis of the traditional law of marriage, long forgotten in many quarters, has been recovered and developed under the pressure of the sexual revolution and the push for same-sex marriage. Sometimes this has involved reformulation in the language of new forms of philosophical discourse—I have in mind the work of John Finnis, Germain Grisez, Robert George, and their students[11] —while others have revived classical argumentation. In addition, there is philosophical work that has been done on moral questions made urgent in a new way by changed circumstances. Here I offer as an example a very interesting article by Oxford-trained Israeli philosopher Saul Smilansky on the question whether there is a moral obligation to have children.[12] The question is, of course, not entirely new, but ease and ready availability of reliable contraception—not to mention the "legality" of abortion—gives it an importance that used to be hidden. When philosopher Elizabeth Anscombe, mother of eight, faced the question, "why have children?" she replied, "why digest?": Children were once as much the natural consequence of sex as digestion was of eating.[13] But now people need reasons to have children—even faithful Catholics, I might add, who are permitted to use natural family planning, taking advantage of modern knowledge of the process of conception to time their marital relations for more fertile or unfertile times in the woman's cycle. Smilansky develops what reasons count, and he compiles an interesting list: (1) giving birth brings value into the world; (2) loving relationships are a major source of good, and childbearing creates these; (3) if there is a dearth of children, those without them free-ride on the others; (4) people promise each other to have children; (5) children remember parents and give their lives significance; (6) children continue a culture; (7) some traditions and talents run in families; and (8) the polity needs children, as voters and soldiers. Smilansky does not go as far as some ancient societies in recommending law or social monitoring to promote fertility, but he makes, to my mind, a cogent case to persuade couples who are able to share the gift of life—and perhaps a case sufficient to recommend changing laws that permit, not to say promote, artificial interference with the natural consequences of sex.

HUMAN NATURE

Now you may have noticed that throughout my talk thus far I have made repeated references to nature or to what is natural. To reiterate, that is indeed the central core of what I want to recommend: In rethinking marriage and family law, we need to accord particular attention to the natural reality of sex, marriage, and family. Greek philosophy began with the distinction between law and nature, between *nomos* and *physis*, and I think no small part of our difficulty is that we have allowed law to become altogether conventional or artificial. To be clear, I am not proposing the elimination of law and leaving everything about sex and procreation to ungoverned nature, but rather I think law needs to follow nature, to correct and perfect it, perhaps. In a moment I will give you an example, but I need to pause, first, and say a word about what the term "nature" in this context means.

I'm referring, of course, to human nature. One doesn't have to be a precommitted Aristotelian or Thomist to recognize that human nature entails both the biological facts of human animality and the universal experience of consciousness or rationality or intelligence. Biologically that means our bodies participate in natural processes of sex and reproduction and that we experience certain desires or urges in relation to sex, and probably reproduction, too. The biology of reproduction is in its outlines known to all, and in the past century it has come to be understood in great detail. The desires associated with sex are not as clearly understood—that's an understatement, as anyone who has ever read or written a poem surely knows—but they do have a biological component. In fact, I think that, at least when one is young and inexperienced, erotic desire is probably a first indicator to us of the power of nature itself, for it arrives at a moment in life after one has acquired self-consciousness and appears as something new and perhaps unruly. Whether as a result of the Fall, as St. Augustine thinks, or simply as a consequence of animality, sexual desire seems to arise from a source independent of the will—and therefore potentially at odds with the law. I am writing about law and the family, but it is common experience that sexual matters often seem particularly defiant of law—and that nature itself is the source of this chaos. Pleasure just is, people think, a fundamental fact. Yes, the biochemists are now beginning to explain the hormones and other substances that cause us to feel it, but how does that alter the imperative, at least in the absence of drugs?

But thus far I have been speaking of human nature while forgetting human intelligence. We are not only animals, but intelligent animals, and that means not only that we can understand our biology scientifically, but that everything we experience biologically, at least as desire, is colored by our having a mind. Consider eating, again: Digestion might be a wholly biological process, but what we eat and how is informed by our intelligence, from our diet, where the commands of health and pleasure compete for our attention, to our table manners and customs for meals and snacking, where complex practices and conscious choices inform every part of our activity of nourishing ourselves. We have to eat, by nature, but we have to learn how to eat so that food does not become a source of disorder and misery, but rather a cause of health and indeed an occasion for the distinctively human activities of conversation and companionship. Why should we expect things to be different when the issue is sex and reproduction rather than eating and digestion?

Of course intelligence has its own claims on human life, not just as designer of biological desire. With regard to sexuality and its phenomenology, I recommend the work of Roger Scruton, at least for explaining philosophically, without regard to theology, how the sexual encounter of intelligent being with intelligent being might be understood[14]—although for that matter, perhaps I should recommend the poetry of John Donne. Marriage is the institution appropriate for intelligent beings who are also animals, its pledge of fidelity and exclusivity and permanence being congruent with what it means for a person to give himself or herself wholly to another person, and also the obverse of the biological consequence of the union, for a child has naturally only one biological father and one biological mother for his entire life. In the child, the parents' love for one another is embodied and perpetuated, and the facts of heredity are such that they can usually see a mix of themselves in their child, literally in face and figure, and often in traits of character as well, for better or worse. That a child needs to be taught as he grows, over the better part of twenty (or is it now thirty?) years is another argument for stable marriages, and so are siblings, for the project of raising a family extends from the birth of the first to the graduation of the last. Did I say graduation? Perhaps I should say their marriage—for that, too, might need parental support and then grandparental support. All of this used to be so ordinary that it passed almost unnoticed, comfortable as custom, but if you think it through you can see wisdom in every step. Included are the limits of the family, too—the limits of what the family can teach an intelligent child, the need for the child to go outside the family to find his own mate, to perpetuate the family by extending it, the need ordinarily to make one's own way in a complex economy. The details of these matters change, of course, but there is, I think, an easily recognizable natural core.

One last word on the question of the natural family: I have been using the term "nature" in a way that means more than biology or physics—although it includes these—and even more than psychology or neuroscience—though these, too, cannot be ignored. I've made recourse to the classical understanding of nature as accessible to philosophy, an understanding that supposes the mind can grasp the essence of things, at least of itself, and that knowing what a thing is indicates what is good for the thing in question. Modern science usually brackets the questions of essence and good, but they creep back in: Even if biological species are more malleable than Aristotle thought, the concept of the species remains, and the substances that go into constituting every living thing are now more precisely known than ever before. As for good, it reemerges in ecology, and in the recognition that natural systems form a kind of whole. From general relativity to the "big bang," modern physics may not be said to prove being and good—these can only be grasped philosophically—but what it discovers seems consistent with them. I realize that recognizing marriage as a natural good cannot be the end of it; there are many ways our knowledge of nature allows us to manipulate nature, and it would still be a question of when and whether that is a good thing to do. But it does, I think, legitimate a political argument in favor of marriage, at least in a regime founded as ours is on the idea of natural rights.

CONSTITUTIONAL LAW

Now I've spoken about legal change and about natural marriage and the natural family as a standard to guide that change. Now let me give you a concrete example of the sort of change I see having to take place, drawing on a case from 1989 called *Michael H. v. Gerald D.*[15] The details of the case are pretty complex, but the legal question is pretty simple: Is there a constitutional right for the biological parent to establish a connection with his biological child?

Here are the facts. Carole D., an international model (I don't know her real name or face), was married to a French business executive, Gerald D., and lived in California. When he was out of the country on business she had an on-going affair with a neighbor, Michael H., and from that union a child named Victoria resulted (naturally, I'm tempted to add). Gerald was listed as the father on Victoria's birth certificate, but when he relocated to New York, Carole stayed behind in California with Victoria, finding time to visit Michael in the Virgin Islands, where he proudly showed off the baby as his own. After all, blood tests (the predecessor to DNA tests) showed Michael to be the father with 98 percent certainty. In the spring of 1982—this is all in the *United States Reports*, mind you, not in tabloids—Carole left Michael, took up with a Californian named Scott, then visited Gerald, still her husband, in New York, toured Europe with him, returned to Scott, left Scott and invited Michael to move in with Victoria and her in L.A., meanwhile filing some legal papers to ensure visitation rights, with various hearings and even four-party psychological exams. But in June 1984, Carole definitively reconciled with her husband, moved to New York, and eventually had two children with him. Michael now had to sue Gerald for visitation rights with Victoria, whom Gerald and Carole were raising as their daughter, and that is where the legal issue was joined, first in California courts. Under California law, the old common-law rule that the husband of the mother is presumed to be the father of the child was embodied in statute, and though the presumption was rebuttable, papers to do so had to be filed before the child was two, and Victoria was now three. Michael appealed to the United States Supreme Court, claiming a Due Process right as biological father, but he was rebuffed: "The presumption of legitimacy [i.e., that Gerald is the father] was a fundamental principle of the common law," wrote Justice Scalia in his plurality opinion, serving the purposes of preventing children from being disinherited and of preserving the peace and tranquility of states and families. Michael can assert no fundamental, historically grounded right that overrides the traditional presumption embodied in the law. Justice Brennan, by the way, dissented, denouncing the reliance on tradition and asserting, "We are not an assimilative, homogeneous society, but a facilitative, pluralistic one, in which we must be willing to abide someone else's unfamiliar or even repellent practice because the same tolerant impulse protects our own idiosyncrasies. Even if we can agree, therefore," he continues, "that 'family' and 'parenthood' are part of the good life, it is absurd to assume that we can agree on the content of those terms and destructive to pretend that we do. In a community such as ours, 'liberty' must include the freedom not to conform."

Being a traditionalist at heart and an admirer of the common law, I had no trouble siding with Justice Scalia when I first read this case, not only because he seemed to get the argument right, but because Justice Brennan's dissent seemed to me to express everything that was wrong with modern relativist liberalism—and wanted to attribute this error to the Constitution or to assert raw judicial power in its name. I still think Justice Brennan's statement is wrong-headed, but what I want to suggest is that we traditionalists have no choice now but to abandon Justice Scalia's former certainty and that we ought to recognize in some fashion the biological father's constitutional claim. The old law sought to correct errant nature, using positive law to reinforce the traditional family against those who would disrupt it—in this case, the adulterous neighbor, who persisted despite the reconciliation of husband and wife. But now the saga of Carole and Gerald and Michael and Scott belongs not only to what used to be called the "jet set," but to whatever is left of working class America, and of course the celebrities and pseudo-celebrities who purport to teach us all how to live. Justice Brennan's world having conquered the field for the day in American mores, the law seems crude and arbitrary in its insistence on artifice, maintaining an abandoned form against established fact. Besides, science has made the determination of paternity, once based on innuendo and the impugnment of womanly virtue, a matter amenable to scientific testing with virtual certainty. The promotion of artifice in law, meanwhile, has in my opinion migrated to the advocates of "idiosyncrasy," to use Justice Brennan's term, who insist that law can make unlike similar and similar unlike.

Actually, I think Justice Scalia has come around on this issue, too. In a case two years ago, he joined a dissenting opinion by Justice Sonia Sotomayor in the Indian Adoption Case, *Adoptive Couple v. Baby Girl*, adding his own declaration that, in reference to an unmarried biological father, "It has been the constant practice of the common law to respect the entitlement of those who bring a child into the world to raise that child."[16] The case, as defined by Justice Samuel Alito's majority opinion, involved statutory, not constitutional interpretation of the Indian Child Welfare Act of 1978, to quash the claim of a Cherokee father to custody of the child he begat outside of marriage with a non-Indian woman, who during her pregnancy broke off their engagement and arranged for adoption of the child by a married couple from South Carolina. Justice Sotomayor's dissent addressed the statutory issue, finding Alito's verbal gymnastics implausible, but behind her own reading of the law was "the principle, recognized in our cases, that the biological bond between parent and child is meaningful." It would go too far to say that, amidst social chaos, biology rules, but her recognition of its importance is something to build upon. And if the biological parent has a presumptive claim to custody of the child, doesn't a child have a claim to the care of its biological parents? If that is so, I think, the argument that same-sex marriage can be made the same as traditional marriage is undone, for in a same-sex marriage, children can be shared by the same-sex couple only if the biological tie to a natural progenitor is severed. Until children can be cloned from any mix of genes and incubated in artificial wombs, there is no getting around this fact, although Justice Kennedy's Opinion of the Court in *Obergefell* shows that it is possible to ignore it.[17] The natural origin of the human child in the union of a woman and a man is a basic fact of human existence, and in the long run, that law will succeed that recognizes rather than contravenes basic human facts.

Let me conclude with a word about adoption, for emphasis on the natural family is bound to disturb adoptive parents, who often suffer from infertility and always open up their hearts to welcome a child in need of love and care. I don't believe anything I have said diminishes their dignity or undercuts their generosity. After all, it is now the norm that adoptive parents tell their adoptive children the truth about their origin, and research shows adoptive children do better in life when they've experienced this honesty rather than the ancient artifice that hid the facts. It is only American, I think, to be willing to face the truths about our natures. I am confident that, far from working against the cause of marriage, it is the strongest card that advocates of traditional marriage hold.

NOTES

Acknowledgment: This chapter originated as a lecture prepared for a conference sponsored by the Intercollegiate Studies Institute at the University of Notre Dame in April, 2014.

1. Baehr v. Lewin, 852 P. 2d 44 (Haw. 1993).
2. *Baker v. Vermont*, 744 A. 2d 864 (Vt. 1999).
3. *Goodridge v. Massachusetts*, 798 N.E. 2d 941 (Mass. 2003), striking the restriction of marriage benefits to opposite-sex couples, followed by *Opinion of the Justices to the Senate*, 802 N.E. 2d 565 (Mass. 2004), rejecting the legislature's proposal to satisfy the *Goodridge* court through civil-unions.
4. A state-by-state review of when and how same-sex marriage was ordered or established can be found on-line at http://www.freedomtomarry.org/states (accessed August 15, 2015). See also Appendix B to the Opinion of the Court in *Obergefell v. Hodges*, 576 U.S. _____ (2015), at 34.
5. *United States v. Windsor*, 570 U.S. ___ (2013); *Hollingsworth v. Perry*. 570 U.S. ___ (2013); for a list of recent federal court actions, see the sources cited in note 4, above. The only federal court decisions upholding laws restricting marriage to a man and a woman came from district courts in Louisiana (*Robicheaux v. Caldwell*, E.Dist. La., No. 13-5090, September 3, 2014) and Puerto Rico (*Conde-Vidal v. Garcia-Padilla*, P.R.,, No. 14-1253, October 21, 2014) and from the Court of Appeals for the Sixth Circuit, *DeBoer v. Snyder*, No. 14-1341, November 6, 2014.
6. My discussion means to follow Aristotle, *Politics*, Book II, 1268b22 ff., and Thomas Aquinas, *Summa Theologica*, I-II, q. 97.
7. Matthew 19:3–12.
8. See Judith S. Wallerstein, Julia M. Lewis, and Sandra Blakeslee, *The Unexpected Legacy of Divorce* (New York: Hyperion, 2000).
9. *Griswold v. Connecticut*, 381 U.S. 479 (1965); *Eisenstadt v. Baird*, 405 U.S. 438 (1972); James Q. Wilson, *The Marriage Problem: How Our Culture Has Weakened Families* (New York: Harper Collins, 2002).
10. The principal study is Elizabeth Marquardt, Norval D. Glenn, and Karen Clark, *My Daddy's Name is Donor: A New Study of Young Adults Conceived Through Sperm Donation* (New York: Institute for American Values, 2010); available on-line at www.american values.org/search/item.php?id=25.

11. See Sherif Girgis, Ryan T. Anderson, and Robert George, *What Is Marriage? Man and Woman: A Defense* (New York: Encounter Books, 2012).

12. Saul Smilansky, "Is There a Moral Obligation to Have Children?" *Journal of Applied Philosophy*, 12 (1995): 41–53.

13. G. E. M. Anscombe, "Why Have Children?" *Proceedings of the American Catholic Philosophical Association* 63 (1990): 48–53.

14. Roger Scruton, *Sexual Desire: A Moral Philosophy of the Erotic* (New York: Free Press, 1986).

15. *Michael H. v. Gerald D.*, 491 U.S. 110 (1989).

16. *Adoptive Couple v. Baby Girl*, 570 U.S. ___ (2013).

17. Chief Justice Roberts, in dissent in *Obergefell*, does write that marriage "arose in the nature of things to meet a vital need" (slip opinion, 5). Justice Kennedy acknowledges that limiting marriage to opposite-sex couples "may long have seemed natural and just," but asserts that to some people "their immutable nature dictates that same-sex marriage is their only real path to this profound commitment."

Appendix

CITED SUPREME COURT CASES

Adoptive Couple v. Baby Girl, 570 U.S. ___ (2013).
Baldwin v. Missouri, 281 U.S. 586 (1930).
Board of Directors of Rotary International v. Rotary Club of Duarte, 481 U.S. 537 (1987).
Bowers v. Hardwick, 478 U.S. 186 (1986).
Buck v. Bell, 274 U. S. 200 (1927).
Butcher's Union Company v. Crescent City, 111 U.S. 746 (1884).
Carey v. Population Services International, 431 U.S. 678 (1977).
City of Boerne v. *Flores,* 521 U.S. 507 (1997).
Cooley v. Board of Wardens of the Port of Philadelphia, 53 U.S. 299 (1851).
Dartmouth College v. Woodward, 17 U.S. 250 (1819).
Davis v. Beason, 133 U.S. 333 (1890).
Dred Scott v. Sandford, 60 U.S. 393 (1857).
Eisenstadt v. Baird, 405 U. S. 438 (1972).
Employment Division, Oregon Department of Human Resources v. Smith, 494 U.S. 872 (1990).
Gibbons v. Ogden, 22 U.S. 1 (1824).
Gonzales v. Carhart, 550 U. S. 124 (2007).
Griswold v. Connecticut, 381 U. S. 479 (1965).
Hammer v. Dagenhart, 247 U.S. 251 (1918).
Henning Jacobson v Commonwealth of Massachusetts, 197 U.S. 11 (1905).
Hollenbaugh v. Carnegie Free Library, 439 U.S. 1052 (1978).
Hollingsworth v. Perry, 570 U.S. ___ (2013).
Lawrence v. Texas, 539 U. S. 538 (2003).
Le Grand v. Darnall, 27 U.S. 664 (1829).
Lochner v. New York, 198 U.S. 45 (1905).
Loving v. Virginia, 388 U.S. 1 (1967).
M.L.B. v. S.L.J., 519 U.S. 102, 116 (1996).
Marbury v. Madison, 5 U.S. 137 (1803).
Maynard v. Hill, 125 U.S. 190 (1888).
Meisel v. U.S. 412 U.S. 954 (1973).
Meyer v. Nebraska. 262 U.S. 390 (1923).
Michael H. v. Gerald D., 491 U.S. 110 (1989).
Minersville School District v. Gobitis, 310 U.S. 586 (1940).
Missouri v. Cummins, 71 U.S. 320 (1867).

Murphy v. Ramsey, 114 U.S. 15 (1885).
NAACP v. Alabama, 357 U.S. 449 (1958).
National Federation of Independent Business v. Sebelius, 567 U.S. ____ (2012).
National Labor Relations Board v. Jones & Laughlin Steel Corporation, 301 U.S. 1 (1937).
Olmstead v. United States, 277 U.S. 438, 478 (1928).
Obergefell v. Hodges, 576 ___ (2015).
Pierce v. Society of Sisters, 268 U.S. 510 (1925).
Planned Parenthood of Central Missouri v. Danforth, 428 U.S. 52 (1976).
Planned Parenthood of Southeastern Pennsylvania v. Casey. 505 U.S. 833 (1992).
Plessy v. Ferguson, 163 U.S. 537 (1896).
Prince v. Massachusetts, 321 U.S. 158 (1944).
Randall v. Kreiger, 90 U.S. 137 (1874)
Reynolds v. *U.S.*, 98 U.S. 145 (1878).
Roberts v. United States Jaycees, 468 U.S. 609 (1984).
Roe v. Wade, 410 U. S. 113 (1973).
Senn v. Tile Layers Protective Union, 301 U.S. 468 (1937).
Skinner v. State of Oklahoma ex rel. Williamson, 316 U.S. 535 (1942).
The Late Corporation of the Church of Jesus Christ of Latter-Day Saints v. United States, 136 U.S. 1 (1889).
Troxel v. Granville, 530 U.S. 57 (2000).
Turner v. Safley, 482 U.S. 78 (1987).
United States v. Carolene Products Co., 304 U.S. 144 (1938).
United States v. Curtiss Wright Export Corp., 299 U.S. 304 (1936).
United States v. Darby Lumber Co., 312 U.S. 100 (1941).
United States v. Lopez, 514 U.S. 549 (1995).
United States v. Morrison, 529 U.S. 598 (2000).
United States v. Windsor, 570 U.S. ___ (2013).
Washington v. Glucksberg, 521 U.S. 702 (1997).
Waugh v. Mississippi, 237 U.S. 589 (1915).
West Coast Hotel v. Parrish, 300 U.S. 379 (1937).
West Virginia State Board of Education v. Barnette, 319 U.S. 624 (1943).
Wisconsin v. Yoder, 406 U.S. 205 (1972).
Zablocki v. Redhail, 434 U.S. 374 (1978).
Zelman v. Simmons-Harris, 536 U.S. 639 (2002).

Bibliography

Alexander, Klint, and Alexander, Kern. "Vouchers and the Privatization of American Education: Justifying Racial Resegregation from Brown to Zelman." *University of Illinois Law Review* (2004): 1131–1154.

Alstyne, William Van. "The Unbearable Lightness of Marriage in the Abortion Decisions of the Supreme Court: Altered States in Constitutional Law." *William & Mary Bill of Rights Journal* 18 (2009): 9–13.

Alvare, Helene. "Same-Sex Marriage and the 'Reconceiving' of Children," 64.3 Case *Western Reserve Law Review* (2014), 831–33.

Anscombe, G.E.M. "Why Have Children?" *Proceedings of the American Catholic Philosophical Association* 63 (1990), 48–53.

Aquinas, Thomas. *Summa Theologiae.* trans. the Fathers of the English Dominican Province (New York: Benziger Brothers, 1947). Reprinted in five volumes by Christian Classics in 1981.

Aristotle, *Nicomachean Ethics*. trans. Robert C. Bartlett and Susan D. Collins (Chicago: The University of Chicago Press, 2011).

Aristotle. *Politics.* Joe Sachs, trans. (Newburyport, MA: Focus Press, 2012).

Aristotle, *Politics*, 2nd Edition, trans. Carnes Lord (Chicago: The University of Chicago Press, 2013).

Augustine, *The City of God against the Pagans*. trans. Robert Dyson (Cambridge: Cambridge University Press, 1998).

Aviv, Rachel. "Where is your mother?" *New Yorker*, December 2, 2013.

Barnette, Randy. *The Rights Retained by the People: The History and Meaning of the Ninth Amendment* (Fairfax, Virginia: George Mason University Press, 1993).

Barnette, Randy. *Restoring the Lost Constitution* (Princeton, NJ: Princeton University Press, 2004).

Bashford, Alison and Levine, Philippa. *Oxford Handbook of the History of Eugenics* (New York: Oxford University Press, 2010).

Benedict XVI. "The Regensburg Address," reprinted in Tracey Rowland, *Ratzinger's Faith: The Theology of Pope Benedict XVI* (New York: Oxford University Press, 2008).

———. *God is Love (Deus Caritas Est): Encyclical Letter.*

Bickel, Alexander. *The Least Dangerous Branch: The Supreme Court at the Bar of Politics* (Indianapolis, IN: Bobbs-Merrill, 1962).

Black, Edwin. *War Against the Weak: Eugenics and America's Campaign to Create a Master Race* (Dialog Press: 2012).

Burke, Edmund. *Reflections on the Revolution in France* (Indianapolis: Hackett, 1987).

Cherlin, Andrew. *Labor's Love Lost: The Rise and Fall of the Working-Class Family in America* (New York: Russell Sage Foundation, 2014).

Cohen-Eliya, Moshe, and Hammer, Yoau. "An Argument from Democracy against School Choice: A Critique of Zelman v. Simmons-Harris." *Loyola Law Rev* 49 (2003): 859–916.

Cooley, Thomas. *A Treatise on the Constitutional Limitations Which Rest Upon the Legislative Power of the States of the American Union* (New York: Da Capo Press, 1868/1972).

Coulanges, Fustel de. *The Ancient City* (Baltimore: The Johns Hopkins University Press, 1980).

Curtis, Benjamin R. Jr., ed. *Memoir of Benjamin Robbins Curtis, LL.D, with Some of His Professional and Miscellaneous Writings* (New York: Da Capo Press, 1879/1970).

Ely, John Hart. "The Wages of Crying Wolf: A Note on *Roe v. Wade*." *The Yale Law Journal* 82 (1973): 920–949.

Fehrenbacher, Don E. *The Dred Scott Case: Its Significance in American Law and Politics* (New York: Oxford University Press, 1978).

Garnett, Richard, W. "School Choice and the Challenges that Remain: A Comment on Richard D. Komer's 'School Choice and State Constitutions' Religion Clauses.'" *Journal of School Choice* 4 (2010): 93–99.

Gerard, Jules B. "Capacity to Govern." *Harvard Journal of Law and Social Policy* 12 (1989).

Girgis, Sherif, Ryan T. Anderson, and Robert George, *What Is Marriage? Man and Woman: A Defense* (New York: Encounter Books, 2012).

Gillette, William. "Benjamin Robbins Curtis" in Leon Friedman and Fred L. Israel, eds. *The Justices of the United States Supreme Court: 1789–1969*, vol II (New York: Chelsea House Publishers, 1979).

Glendon, Mary Ann. *The Transformation of Family Law: State, Law, and Family in the United States and Western Europe* (Chicago: The University of Chicago Press, 1989).

———. *Rights Talk* (New York: Free Press, 1993).

Grodzins, Dean. "'Slave Law' versus 'Lynch Law' in Boston: Benjamin Robbins Curtis, Theodore Parker, and the Fugitive Slave Crisis 1850-1855." *Massachusetts Historical Review* 12 (2010): 1–33.

Graber, Mark. "The Nonmajoritarian Difficulty: Legislative Deference to the Judiciary." *Studies in American Political Development* 35 (1993): 35-73.

———. "Desperately Ducking Slavery: *Dred Scott* and Contemporary Constitutional Theory." *Constitutional Commentary* 14 (1997).

———. *Dred Scott and the Problem of Constitutional Evil* (New York: Cambridge University Press, 2006).

Griswold, Robert L. "Law, Sex, Cruelty, and Divorce in Victorian America, 1840–1900," in *Family & Society in American History*, ed. Joseph M. Hawes and Elizabeth I. Nybakken (Champaign, IL: University of Illinois Press, 2001).

Green, Jamal. "Divorcing Marriage from Procreation." *The Yale Law Journal* 114 (2005).

———. "The Anticanon." 125 *Harvard Law Review* 125 (2011): 379–475.

Gutman, Amy. "Civic Education and Social Diversity." *Ethics* 105 (1995): 557–579.

Hart, David Bentley. *Atheist Delusions: The Christian Revolution and Its Fashionable Enemies* (New Haven: Yale University Press, 2009).

Harvey, Anna. "Chapter 8: Misreading the Roberts Court" in *A Mere Machine: The Supreme Court, Congress, and American Democracy* (New Haven: Yale University Press, 2013).

Hobbes, Thomas. *Leviathan* (Indianapolis: Hackett Publishing, 1994).

Hobbs, Steven H. "Love on the Oregon Trail: What the Story of *Maynard v. Hill* Teaches us about Marriage and Democratic Self-Government." *Hofstra Law Review* 32 (2003): 111–144.

Hoffheimer, Michael. *Justice Holmes and the Natural Law*. (Routledge, 2013).

Jaffa, Harry. *Crisis of the House Divided: An Interpretation of the Issues in the Lincoln-Douglas Debates* (Chicago: University of Chicago Press, 1959/1982).

John Paul II, *Man and Women and He Created Them: A Theology of the Body*, translated by Michael Waldstein (Boston: Pauline Books, 2006).

Jonas, Hans. *The Imperative of Responsibility* (Chicago: The University of Chicago Press, 1984).

Karst, Kenneth L. "The Freedom of Intimate Association," *Yale Law Journal* 89 (1980).

Klint, Alexander, and Alexander, Kern. "Vouchers and the Privatization of American Education: Justifying Racial Resegregation from Brown to Zelman." *University of Illinois Law Review* (2004): 1131–1154.
Lash, Kurt. "The Lost Jurisprudence of the Ninth Amendment." *Texas Law Review* 83 (2005): 2–33.
Last, Jonathan V. *What to Expect When No One is Expecting* (New York: Encounter Books, 2013).
Lawler, Peter Augustine. "Strauss, Straussians, and Faith-Based Students of Strauss." *The Political Science Reviewer* 36 (2007): 1–12.
Leach, Richard A. "Benjamin Robbins Curtis: Judicial Misfit." *The New England Quarterly* 25 (1952): 507–525.
Liu, Goodwin, and Taylor, William L. "School Choice to Achieve Desegregation." *Fordham Law Review* 74 (2005): 791–823.
Leuchtenburg, William. *The Supreme Court Reborn: The Constitutional Revolution in the Age of Roosevelt* (New York: Oxford University Press, 1995).
Locke, John. *Two Treatises of Government* (Cambridge: Cambridge University Press 1988).
Macedo, Stephen. *Diversity and Distrust: Civic Education in a Multicultural Democracy* (Cambridge, MA: Harvard University Press, 2000).
MacLeod, Adam J. "Birth Certificates, Fatherhood, and Same-Sex Marriage: Sotomayor v. Sotomayor." *The Public Discourse* (November 5 2015) www.thepublicdiscourse.com/2015/11/15945.
Madison, James, Hamilton, Alexander, Jay, John. *The Federalist Papers*, ed. Clinton Rossiter (New York: New American Library, 1961).
Maltz, Earl M. "The Last Angry Man: Benjamin Robbins Curtis and the *Dred Scott* Case." *Chicago-Kent Law Review* 82 (2007): 265–276.
Manent, Pierre. *Tocqueville and the Nature of Democracy*, trans. John Waggoner (Lanham, MD: Rowman & Littlefield, 1996).
Marquardt, Elizabeth. *Between Two Worlds: The Inner Lives of Children of Divorce* (New York: Three Rivers Press, 2006).
Marquardt, Elizabeth, et al. *My Daddy's Name is Donor: A New Study of Young Adults Conceived Through Sperm Donation* (New York: Institute for American Values, 2010), on-line at www.americanvalues.org/search/item.php?id=25.
Mathie, William. "God, Woman, and Morality: The Democratic Family in the New Political Science of Alexis de Tocqueville." *The Review of Politics* 57 (1995): 7–30.
Mindle, Grant B. "Liberalism, Privacy, and Autonomy." *The Journal of Politics* 51 (1989): 575–598.
Morel, Lucas E. "The *Dred Scott* Dissents: McLean, Curtis, Lincoln, and the Public Mind." *Journal of Supreme Court History* 32 (2007): 133–151.
Morgan, Patricia. *The War between the State and the Family: How Government Divides and Impoverishes* (New Brunswick: Transaction Press, 2008).
Murray, Charles. *Coming Apart* (New York: Crown Forum, 2012).
Myers, John. "A Short History of Child Protection in America." *Family Law Quarterly* 42 (2008): 449–463.
Nisbet, Robert. *The Quest for Community: A Study in the Ethics of Order and Freedom* (Wilmington, DE: ISI Books, 2010).
Okin, Susan Moller. *Justice, Gender and the Family* (New York: Basic Books, 1987).
Pearlstein, Mitch. *From Family Collapse to America's Decline* (Lanham: Rowman & Littlefield, 2011).
Pearlstein, Mitch. *Broken Bonds* (Lanham: Rowman & Littlefield, 2014).
Percy, Walker. *Lost in the Cosmos* (New York: Farrar, Straus, and Giroux, 1983).
Plato. *The Republic*. trans. Allan Bloom (New York: Basic Books, 1968).
Popenoe, David. *The War over the Family* (New Brunswick: Transaction Publishers, 2005).
Powell, H. Jefferson. "The Humanity of Law." *Villanova Law Review* 55 (2010): 1161-76.
Powell, H. Jefferson. "On Not Being 'Not An Originalist.'" *University of St. Thomas Law Journal* 7 (2010): 259–280.

Purdy, Jedediah. "The Roberts Court v. America: How the Roberts Court is using the First Amendment to Craft a Radical, Free-Market Jurisprudence." *Democracy: A Journal of Ideas* 23 (2012): 46–58.

Pybas, Kevin. "Does the Establishment Clause Require Religion To Be Confined to the Private Sphere." *Valparaiso University Law Review* 40 (2005): 71–112.

———. "Liberalism and Civic Education: Unitary versus pluralist alternatives." *Perspectives on Political Science* 33 (2004): 18–29.

Ratzinger, Joseph Cardinal. *Introduction to Christianity,* translated by J. R. Foster and Michael J. Miller (San Francisco: Ignatius Press, 2004).

———. Josef Cardinal. *Eschatology, Death, and Eternal Life* (Washington DC: Catholic University Press, 1988)

———. Josef Cardinal *Salt of the Earth,* trans. By Adrian Walker (San Francisco: Ignatius Press, 1997).

———. Josef Cardinal. *In the Beginning . . . A Catholic Understanding of Creation and the Fall* (Grand Rapids: Eerdmans, 2004).

Rawls, John. *Political Liberalism* (New York: Columbia University Press, 1993).

Regnerus, Mark. "How Different are the Adult Children of Parents who have Same-Sex Relationships? Findings from the New Family Structures Study." *Social Science Research* 41 (2012).

Rheinstein, Max. *Marriage, Stability, Divorce and the Law* (Chicago: The University of Chicago Press, 1972).

Roberts, Christopher C. *Creation and Covenant: The Significance of Sexual Difference in the Moral Theology of Marriage* (New York: T&T Clark International, 2007).

Rosenberg, Gerald. *The Hollow Hope* (Chicago: University of Chicago Press, 1991).

Ross, Jacob Joshua. *The Virtues of the Family* (New York: The Free Press, 1994).

Roth, Andrew M. "Sociological, Political, and Legal Contexts Regarding the Current Debate on Gay Marriage." *Public Affairs Quarterly* 12 (1998).

Russell, Bertrand. *Marriage and Morality* (New York: Horace Liveright, 1929).

Scruton, Roger. *Sexual Desire: A Moral Philosophy of the Erotic* (New York: Free Press, 1986).

Smilansky, Saul. "Is There a Moral Obligation to Have Children?," *Journal of Applied Philosophy,* 12 (1995): 41–53.

Strauss, David A. *The Living Constitution* (New York: Oxford University Press, 2010).

Streichler, Stuart A. "Justice Curtis's Dissent in the *Dred Scott* Case: An Interpretive Study." *Hastings Constitutional Law Quarterly* 24 (1997): 509–544.

———. *Justice Curtis in the Civil War Era: At the Crossroads of American Constitutionalism.* (Charlottesville: University of Virginia Press, 2005).

———. *The Taney Period,* vol. 5 of the *Oliver Wendell Holmes Devise* (New York: Cambridge University Press, 1974/2010).

Sussman, Marvin B., et al., eds., *Handbook of Marriage and the Family Volume I,* second edition (New York: Plenum Press, 1999).

Sutherland, George, *Constitutional Power and World Affairs* (New York: Columbia University Press, 1918).

Swisher, Carl Brent. *Roger B. Taney* (Hamden, CT: Archon Books, 1961).

Thomas, Leonard. "Eugenics and Economics in the Progressive Era." *Journal of Economic Perspectives,* 19:4 (2005).

Tocqueville, Alexis de. *Democracy in America,* trans. Harvey C. Mansfield and Delba Winthrop (Chicago: The University of Chicago, 2000).

———. *Democracy in America: Volume I,* trans. Henry Reeve (Cambridge: Sever and Francis, 1863).

Thayer, James Bradley. "The Origin and Scope of the American Doctrine of Constitutional Law." *Harvard Law Review* 7 (1893): 129–156.

———. *The Supreme Court in United States History,* vol. 2. (Boston: Little, Brown & Co., 1923).

Tushnet, Mark. "Vouchers after Zelman." *The Supreme Court Review* 2002 (2002): 1-39.

Tyler, Samuel. *Memoir of Roger Brooke Taney.* (New York: Da Capo Press, 1872/1970).

Urofsky, Melvin I. *Dissent and the Supreme Court: Its Role in the Court's History and the Nation's Constitutional Dialogue.* (Cambridge, MA: Harvard University Press, 2015).

Viteritti, Joseph P. "Reading Zelman: the triumph of pluralism and its effects on liberty, equality, and choice." *Southern California Law Review* 76 (2003): 1105-88.

Wallenstein, Peter. "The Right to Marry: Loving v. Virginia." *OAH Magazine of History* 9 (1995): 37-41.

Wallerstein, Judith, et. al. *The Unexpected Legacy of Divorce* (New York: Hyperion, 2000).

Warren, Charles. *A History of the American Bar* (Boston: Little, Brown & Co., 1911).

Wilcox, W. Bradford, et. al. *Why Marriage Matters*, 3d ed(New York: Institute for American Values, 2011).

Wilson, James Q. *The Marriage Problem: How Our Culture Has Weakened Families* (New York: Harper Collins, 2002).

Witte, John. *From Sacrament to Contract, Second Edition: Marriage, Religion, and Law in the Western Tradition*, second edition (Louisville: Westminster/John Knox, 2012).

Whittington, Keith E., "The Road Not Taken: *Dred Scott,* Judicial Authority, and Political Questions," *Journal of Politics* 63 (2001): 365–391.

Wolfe, Christopher. *The Rise of Modern Judicial Review* (New York: Basic Books, 1986).

———. *The Rise of Modern Judicial Review: From Constitutional Interpretation to Judge-Made Law* (Basic Books, 1986; revised edition, Rowman and Littlefield, 1994).

———. *Judicial Activism* (New York: Oxford University Press, 1997).

Yamin, Priscilla. *American Marriage: A Political Institution* (Philadelphia: University of Pennsylvania Press, 2012).

Yenor, Scott. *Family Politics: The Idea of Marriage in Modern Political Thought* (Waco: Baylor University Press, 2011).

———. "The True Origin of the Family: The Founders and the Family." *First Principles Series Report* 48 (2013), www.heritage.org/research/reports/2013/10/the-true-origin-of-society-the-founders-on-the-family.

Index

About the Contributors

Stephen A. Block has been a lecturer in the Department of Political Science at Baylor University since 2013, where he teaches courses in political philosophy and American constitutional law. His principal research interests are in ancient political philosophy, early modern political philosophy, American political thought, and American constitutionalism, and his publications include articles on the political thought of Aristotle and Saul Bellow. He is married to his wife, Lindsay, and they reside in Waco, TX with their son and four daughters.

Patrick N. Cain (PhD, Baylor University) is associate professor of political science at Lakehead University, where he teaches political theory and constitutional law. His publications include articles and book chapters on the political thought of Homer, Aristotle, and Pope Benedict XVI. He and his wife Courtney reside in Thunder Bay, Ontario with their seven children.

Adam M. Carrington is assistant professor of politics at hillsdale college where he teaches courses in constitutional law, the presidency, separation of powers theory, and American political thought. His writings on constitutional law have been included in such publications as *Journal of Supreme Court History, American Political Thought, Justice Systems Journal,* and *Readings in American Government* (9th ed.).

William C. Duncan is director of the Marriage Law Foundation and former research fellow at the Columbus School of Law of The Catholic University. He has previously served as a visiting professor at the J. Reuben Clark Jr.

Law School at Brigham Young University and teaches courses as an adjunct professor at Brigham Young University.

Lauren Hall is associate professor of political science at the Rochester Institute of Technology, where she teaches courses on American politics, political philosophy, and biopolitics. She is the author of *Family and the Politics of Moderation* (Baylor, 2014) and a number of chapters and articles dealing with bioethics, the family, and classical liberalism.

Terry Kleven is professor of religion at Central College, Pella, Iowa. He has published articles and book reviews in Old Testament studies, in Greek and Arabic political philosophy, in Middle Eastern studies, and in Islamic studies. His scholarship includes the codicological description and the translation of several of Alfarabi's philosophical treatises. He has taught at Memorial University of Newfoundland and Labrador, the Near Eastern School of Theology in Beirut and he currently teaches at Central College, Pella, Iowa.

Peter Augustine Lawler is Dana Professor of Government at Berry College. He is the author of a number of books, including *Allergic to Crazy: Quick Thoughts on Politics, Education and Culture Rightly Understood* (St. Augustine's Press, 2014), *Modern and American Dignity* (ISI, 2010), *Homeless and at Home in America* (St. Augustine's Press, 2007), *Stuck with Virtue: The American Individual and Our Biotechnological Future* (2005, ISI Books), *Aliens in America: The Strange Truth about Our Soul* (ISI Books, 2002), and *Postmodernism Rightly Understood* (Rowman & Littlefield, 1999). His *American Political Rhetoric*, 7th Edtion (coedited with Robert Schaefer, Rowman & Littlefield) is used in introductory American government courses at a sizeable number of colleges and universities. He was appointed to U.S. President's Council on Bioethics in 2005 and served on the Council until 2008.

Martha Rice Martini is an attorney practicing in Salem, Massachusetts. Her prior publications include the book *Marx Not Madison: The Crisis of American Legal Education* (University Press of America, 1996). She holds a PhD in political science from the University of Chicago.

Susan McWilliams is associate professor of politics at Pomona College, where she has twice won the Wig Distinguished Professor Award for excellence in teaching. She is the author of *Traveling Back: Toward a Global Political Theory* (Oxford University Press, 2014), and a co-editor of several books, most recently *The Best Kind of College: An Insiders' Guide to America's Small Liberal Arts Colleges* (co-edited with John Seery, SUNY Press, 2015). Her writing has been published widely, including in *Boston Review,*

Bust, Front Porch Republic, Perspectives on Political Science, Political Science Quarterly, The Review of Politics, and *The Star-Ledger*. McWilliams received her PhD in politics from Princeton University. In 2014 she won both the Graves Award in the Humanities and a National Endowment for the Humanities fellowship. She lives in Claremont, California, with her husband and two children.

David Ramsey is assistant professor of government and pre-law advisor at the University of West Florida, where he teaches courses in constitutional law, classical and medieval political philosophy, and American political thought. He is the author of *Antitrust and the Supreme Court* (LFB Scholarly, 2012) and has written on politics, literature, and jurisprudence.

Mark A. Scully is an assistant professor of political science at the University of the Ozarks in Clarksville, Arkansas. His research interests include Supreme Court privacy jurisprudence, American political thought, the American presidency and political parties.

James R. Stoner, Jr. (PhD, Harvard University, 1987) is Hermann Moyse Jr. Professor and director of the Eric Voegelin Institute in the Department of Political Science at Louisiana State University. He is the author of *Common-Law Liberty: Rethinking American Constitutionalism* (Kansas, 2003) and *Common Law and Liberal Theory: Coke, Hobbes, and the Origins of American Constitutionalism* (Kansas, 1992), as well as a number of articles and essays. A Senior Fellow of the Witherspoon Institute, he has co-edited three books the Institute published: *The Thriving Society: On the Social Conditions of Human Flourishing* (with Harold James, 2015), *The Social Costs of Pornography: A Collection of Papers* (with Donna M. Hughes, 2010), and *Rethinking Business Management: Examining the Foundations of Business Education* (with Samuel Gregg, 2007). In 2013 and 2014 he was Garwood Visiting Professor and visiting fellow in the James Madison Program at Princeton University.

Scott Yenor is professor of political science at Boise State University and a visiting fellow in the Heritage Foundation's B. Kenneth Simon Center for Principles and Politics during 2015 and 2016. His *Family Politics: The Idea of Marriage in Modern Political Thought* was published by Baylor University Press in 2011 and *David Hume's Humanity: The Philosophy of Common Life and its Limits* is being published in 2016 by Palgrave.

www.ingramcontent.com/pod-product-compliance
Ingram Content Group UK Ltd.
Pitfield, Milton Keynes, MK11 3LW, UK
UKHW041630031026
15587UKWH00001B/198

9 781498 528177